COMMODORE

COMMODORE

THE LIFE OF

CORNELIUS
VANDERBILT

EDWARD J. RENEHAN JR.

BASIC
BOOKS

A Member of the Perseus Books Group
New York

Books published by Basic Books are available at special discounts for bulk
purchases in the United States by corporations, institutions, and other
organizations. For more information, please contact the Special Markets
Department at the Perseus Books Group, 2300 Chestnut Street,
Suite 200, Philadelphia, PA, 19103, or call (800) 255-1514,
or email special.markets@perseusbooks.com.

Designed by Trish Wilkinson
Set in 12 point Adobe Caslon

Library of Congress Cataloging-in-Publication Data
Renehan, Edward, 1956–
    Commodore : the life of Cornelius Vanderbilt / Edward J. Renehan Jr.
       p.   cm.
    Includes bibliographical references and index.
    ISBN-13: 978-0-465-00255-9 (alk. paper)
    ISBN-10: 0-465-00255-2 (alk. paper)
       1. Vanderbilt, Cornelius, 1794–1877. 2. Businessmen—United States—
Biography. 3. Railroads—United States—History. I. Title.
CT275.V23R46 2007
385.092—dc22
[B]   2007022392

10 9 8 7 6 5 4 3 2 1

This book is warmly dedicated to
Marie Kutch, Nikki Natale and John Staudt,
who know why

CONTENTS

PREFACE

AT FORTY-SECOND STREET AND PARK AVENUE IN NEW YORK City, busy travelers rush in and out the large doors of an architectural gem: Grand Central Station, built on the site of Cornelius Vanderbilt's original Grand Central Depot of 1871. Long known as the "gateway to the nation," 1913's Beaux-Arts masterpiece—constructed by Cornelius's great-grandson William K. Vanderbilt II—is today dominated by commuters from New York's Westchester County: riders of MetroNorth, a remnant of Commodore Cornelius Vanderbilt's old New York Central. High above, at the precipice of the station's front, a massive Tiffany clock sits in the middle of a large figurative sculpture by Jules Felix Couton. Mercury, Hercules, and Minerva—the Roman gods of travel, strength, and wisdom, whom Couton assembled to sum up his assigned theme of *Transportation*—drape themselves around the timepiece. By day or by night (but especially at night, when floodlights work their magic) pedestrians strolling north along lower Park Avenue cannot help but be impressed by the enormous lounging divinities.

Several hundred feet beneath the seminude figures, close to street level, stands a barely noticeable (and thoroughly clothed) statue of the Commodore: builder of the original Second Empire–style terminal on this site. Although heroically proportioned, the bronze Vanderbilt nevertheless seems diminutive when compared to Couton's *Transportation* and the massive backdrop of the palace-like station. Barely head-and-shoulders above the rushing taxis and street grime, the bald financier, dressed in a fur-lined coat, seems somehow aware of his reduced status. He glowers grimly and stares south toward the downtown district that was once, in his day, the heart of New York. The mute Vanderbilt's left hand juts outward, the index finger extended. It's as though he has some stern injunction he'd issue, if he could, to the distracted motorists rushing over and through Pershing Square.

The statue is one of which Vanderbilt, who died in 1877 at the age of eighty-three, knew and approved. In Vanderbilt's time, the same piece began life outside yet another New York Central depot. First revealed to public view in 1871, Ernst Plassmann's version of Cornelius stood at a lofty height above the Hudson River Rail Road Freight House, known more popularly as the St. John's Park Freight House, on Hudson Street. There it formed the apex of an ambitious rooftop pediment more than a hundred feet long and thirty-one feet wide. On each side of the statue, bas-relief figures documented Vanderbilt's various triumphs on land and sea. To the Commodore's left were represented icons of his early days when he'd first earned that honorific: schooners and steamships with which he'd been associated on the Hudson River, Long Island Sound, and the Atlantic and Pacific oceans. To his right, meanwhile, lingered symbols of his later conquests: trains, tunnels, bridges. And at his feet lay a cacophony of engines, cables, anchors, and wheels.[1]

Plassmann's reputation as a sculptor has not endured. Works such as that described above, reviled in its own time, are the reason why.

Horace Greeley (a fan of the Commodore's who joined with Vanderbilt in the unpopular task of posting a bail bond for Jefferson
Davis after the end of the Civil War) used his column in the New
York *Tribune* to comment on the bronze, leaving other aspects of the
pediment undescribed. "As a likeness," wrote Greeley, "the statue
signally fails to do justice to that physiognomy, one of the finest in
America, which has never yet been rendered worthily by any photograph, bronze, or picture that we have seen." The Manhattan attorney George Templeton Strong (a trustee of Columbia University
and president of the New York Philharmonic Society) criticized the
entire installation within the privacy of his diary: "Have inspected
the grand $800,000 Vanderbilt bronze. It's a 'mixellaneous biling'
[*sic*] of cog-wheels, steamships, primeval forests, anchors, locomotives, periaugers ('pettyaugers' we called them when I was a boy),
R.R. trains, wild ducks (or possibly seagulls) & squatter shanties,
with a colossal Cornelius Vanderbilt looming up in the midst of the
chaos, & beaming benignantly down on Hudson Street, like a Pater
Patriae—draped in a dressing gown or overcoat, the folds whereof
are most wooden. As a work of art, it is bestial."[2]

A patrician from an old New York family, Strong saw Vanderbilt's
loud tribute to himself as confirmation of the Commodore's vulgarity,
self-centeredness, and lack of couth. After all, had not the installation
been partially financed, with the acquiescence of the richest man in
America, by funds raised through a public subscription? Strong also
noted Vanderbilt's recent naming of a state-of-the-art New York
Central locomotive after himself. The Commodore's painted portrait
adorned the machine's headlights: a modern, smoke-and-steel version
of worshipful stained glass. Strong found equally repugnant the
Commodore's advertised, but ultimately unrealized, plan to build a
625-foot-tall Central Park monument dedicated to celebrating the
men he considered America's two greatest native sons: George Washington and Cornelius Vanderbilt. Strong personally knew Vanderbilt

as a detestable lout who, in the lawyer's view, failed in every test of humanity other than the financial. Thus he thought Vanderbilt's comparison of himself with Washington nothing less than absurd. The Vanderbilt of Strong's acquaintance (wantonly cruel to many of those closest to him, deeply committed to his own erotic pleasures outside of marriage, proudly unschooled, utterly devoid of manners, and devoid, too, of charity) did not in any way approach the greatness of the first among the Founding Fathers.

Vanderbilt's Scrooge-like parsimoniousness was especially damning. ("Let them do what I have done," he said, with all seriousness, citing his own rise from nothing, when asked to give alms to the poor.) During 1872, Mark Twain addressed Vanderbilt directly on this topic in *Packard's Monthly:*

> All I wish to urge upon you now is that you crush out your native instincts and go and do something worthy of praise—go and do something you need not blush to see in print—do something that may rouse one solitary good example to the thousands of young men who emulate your energy and your industry; shine as one solitary grain of pure gold upon the heaped rubbish of your life. Do this, I beseech you, else through your example we shall shortly have in our midst five hundred Vanderbilts, which God Forbid. Go, oh please go, and do one worthy act. Go, boldly, grandly, nobly, and give four dollars to some great public charity. It will break your heart, no doubt; but no matter, you have but a little while to live, and it is better to die suddenly and nobly than to live a century longer the same Vanderbilt you are now.[3]

But even Twain and Strong had to afford Vanderbilt a certain grudging respect. As Strong admitted, this basest of men possessed an instinctive and furtive genius for commercial affairs. Strong, in a letter told a friend: "He is like some rudimentary but deadly and swift beast who knows not what he knows, but knows enough—through nature—to endure and thrive on the meat of lesser animals, of which the woods are full. The fumbling Commodore, that most elemental of creatures, seems capable of great intuitive leaps—resembling those of a jaguar—when it comes to enterprise. He is a breed apart: evolved for the sole purpose of money-getting. Either that or his is the dumbest of dumb luck lubricated—I should admit—by a great deal of elbow-grease. The beast is never lazy."[4] Vanderbilt, on the other hand, equated both his skills and his ambition to a mania. "I have been insane on the subject of money-making all my life," he told a reporter.[5] And money-make he did.

In other words, the pediment Strong abhorred, along with being obnoxious, was also true. By 1877, at the time of his burial on Staten Island, where his life and long hunger had begun in 1794, Vanderbilt had not only amassed a $105 million fortune but also fundamentally changed the geographical and financial face of his country. After making several small fortunes in ferrys, sailing ships, and steamboats, Vanderbilt ended his days controlling an empire in railroads. As an old man, Vanderbilt would look at the web of his numerous railroads—the New York Central, the Harlem, the Lake Shore and Michigan Southern, the Canadian Southern, and the Michigan Central—and, with characteristic bravado, sum up their combination as "the greatest creative achievement of the modern era."[6] Vanderbilt's enormous trunk line consisted of 740 miles of track connecting the Atlantic Ocean, the Great Lakes, and the nation's heartland. Four hundred and forty-five passenger cars moved 7 million paying customers every year. Four hundred and eight locomotives hauled not only passengers but also 9,026 freight cars. Everything was state-of-the-art: Westinghouse air brakes, Pullman and Wagner sleeping cars, the latest in safety couplers.

Always, Vanderbilt stayed attuned to the cutting-edge of technology, and honed it to suit his purpose. At the same time—until his last few years—he systematically deployed his capital with a relentless and incisive ruthlessness. (On one occasion, when partners conspired to steal one of his properties, he informed them coldly via the press: "Gentlemen: You have undertaken to cheat me. I won't sue you, for the law is too slow. I'll ruin you."[7] Then he proceeded to do just that.)

In the end, the Vanderbilt system of railways formed the cornerstone of the country's post–Civil War economy. At the same time, the Commodore did much to help make Wall Street the center of American finance by virtue of the simple gravitational pull of his New York–based fortune. The sheer heft of Vanderbilt's wealth staggered anyone with the wit to grasp its enormity. The Commodore's accumulated assets of $105 million would have translated in 2005 to more than $158 billion as a relative share of gross domestic product; Bill Gates's fortune was, for the same year, estimated at $51 billion by *Forbes*.[8] In leaving the bulk of his estate to just one son, William Henry Vanderbilt, the Commodore made it plain that he considered his fortune alone, by itself, his greatest personal creation: a testament to his life that rose above all other achievements, even family. "I shall leave my property . . . compact. I don't know that I am doing right, but I will not have it scattered. I will leave it as a monument to my name."[9]

Vanderbilt's great financial memorial has largely vanished. Most of the Commodore's fortune has been dissipated through numerous generations of redistribution down through William Henry's descendents. Other traces of the man have faded just as surely. Aside from the mediocre statue in front of Grand Central, few landmarks linger to summon Vanderbilt's memory in the greater Metropolitan area. On the northern end of Manhattan—in the neighborhood of upper Broadway (the street Vanderbilt knew as "Bloomingdale Road") and St. Nicholas Avenue (the strip the Commodore would have recognized as "Harlem Lane"), both unpaved in his day—one finds no hint of him, nor of the great American sport of harness racing he (along with such other wealthy contenders as Daniel Drew) helped launch here on balmy afternoons throughout the 1860s and early 1870s. (Neither is there a statue or plaque further north to commemorate Vanderbilt as one of the first incorporators of the track at Saratoga.)

On Staten Island, the mogul's boyhood home fell to the wrecking-ball decades ago, during the 1920s. Today, the only sign of the Commodore at his natal place is his ornate tomb on a private twenty acres immediately adjacent to the Moravian Cemetery in New Dorp. Elsewhere, across the water from Staten Island in Manhattan, the building that represented Vanderbilt's one semi-significant act of generosity in his home state has long gone to dust. In 1870, after Vanderbilt acquired the property for $50,000, he gave life use of the old Mercer Street Presbyterian Church to the Reverend Dr. Charles Forse Deems, who made it over into the nondenominational Church of the Strangers. Deems was at that time a close friend of Vanderbilt's newly acquired and much younger (by forty-five years) second wife, Frank Armstrong Crawford. Later on, it was at the request of Frank and the Reverend Deems that the unintellectual (in fact, anti-intellectual) Vanderbilt unenthusiastically gave a gift of $1 million, less than 1 percent of his net worth, to fund his one other notable adventure in philanthropy: the Central University of Nashville, subsequently renamed Vanderbilt University. In a recent survey, few of that school's undergraduates were able to say for sure after which of history's many Vanderbilts their school had been named.

Cornelius remains equally as obscure in literature as he is in land-scape. Although shelves of books have been written about the family as a whole (most of these dwelling on the scandals and intrigues of later generations), only three biographies to date have explicitly focused most of their attention on the fortune's creator, the one most original and interesting specimen in the clan: the bootstrapper.

The first of these, something of a hagiographic potboiler titled *The Vanderbilts and the Story of Their Fortune*, came from the pen of journalist William A. Croffut in 1884. Although rich in textual detail, Croffut's effort lacked any profound understanding of Vanderbilt's complex and often convoluted business dynamics. It also delighted too much in the rags-to-riches nature of the Commodore's saga, which Croffut cast as being entirely heroic. More than a generation later, in 1927, the journalist and novelist Arthur Douglas Howden Smith sought to revise Croffut's glowing assessment.[10] The current Cosimo Classics paperback edition of Smith's *Commodore Vanderbilt: An Epic of American Achievement* features a photograph of the Commodore's eldest son, William Henry Vanderbilt, who is misidentified as the Commodore, on the cover—a mistake for which the long-dead Smith cannot be held accountable. Smith's book suffers from the author's penchant for presenting purportedly verbatim quotes from conversations that neither he, nor anyone else living in 1927, could have been party to. The author also had an affinity for unsubstantiated gossip and folklore. However, in his portrayal of the Commodore as a native genius who was at the same time profane, self-absorbed, and devoid of ideals, Smith did correctly define the core elements of Vanderbilt's temperament: "His gift of vision was entirely selfish in its application, unconsciously so, but nonetheless selfish. He envisioned a chance, an opportunity, an invention, a trend in commerce not as it would react to the advantage of the community, but in terms of his own profit."[11]

Published fifteen years after Smith's offering, Wheaton J. Lane's *Commodore Vanderbilt: An Epic of the Steam Age* (Knopf, 1942) provided a far more thorough and informed analysis of Vanderbilt's complex business career. Lane was a distinguished Princeton historian who previously had published a respected, though dense and arcane, study of the development of steamship, railroad, and canal transportation in New Jersey from 1620 to 1860.[12] Lane's volume on Vanderbilt (published as the very first Alfred A. Knopf Fellowship Award Book in Biography) did an especially good job of revealing the Commodore's complex 1840s machinations to establish an east-to-west route across Nicaragua for Vanderbilt steamship travelers seeking the fastest possible route to the California gold rush. Generally strong on his coverage of Vanderbilt's professional exploits, Lane (perhaps because of the period in which he wrote, or else because of his own biases and pruderies) failed to scrutinize Vanderbilt's colorful private life: his numerous peccadilloes and their myriad, often profound, ramifications within the Commodore's unhappy family and upon his sometimes troubled businesses. At the time of his death in 1983, Lane was contemplating a rewrite of his Vanderbilt book based on new research which would have allowed him to expand and improve his already excellent consideration of the Nicaragua connection. In efforting the volume at hand, I have been privileged to benefit from Lane's later research, as well as his original notes and memoranda for the 1942 volume.

On other important fronts, some information Lane just did not have. Papers not available to Lane (notably those of Vanderbilt's personal physician, Jared Linsly, who treated and befriended the Commodore from the 1830s through to his death in 1877) show a man who suffered from an advanced case of syphilis at the time of his death, a fact kept from contemporary journalists and obscured to biographers ever since.

Every writer on Vanderbilt has commented on the erratic (and seemingly insane, at moments) behavior of the Commodore's latter years: unpredictable outbursts and self-destructive (therefore out-of-character) market moves interspersed between moments of suave, sharp, and confident business decisionmaking. We now have an explanation for Vanderbilt's random diminishment. Linsly's diagnosis would also go a long way towards explaining why, though married to the vivacious young Frank for the last eight years of his life, the old Commodore was noticed by servants to apparently refrain from intimacy with her, preferring instead to consort—as he always had—with more "worldly" women such as the former prostitute Tennessee Claflin. Young Tennessee was the nubile sister of women's rights advocate and spiritualist Victoria Woodhull, through whom Vanderbilt spoke regularly with his dead mother, among other worthies.

As well, Vanderbilt's sickness might well have impacted the logic (or lack thereof) of how he virtually disinherited all but one of his children. It could also explain why (erotic inspiration aside) he backed Woodhull and Claflin as Wall Street's first female stockbrokers, this despite their complete lack of financial experience. Vanderbilt gave the ladies their own firm in 1870, threw them much of his personal business, and allowed Woodhull to make investments based on advice from the dead. Signs of sporadic syphilitic dementia may also be seen in Vanderbilt's financing of a newspaper, *Woodhull & Claflin's Weekly*, which agitated for free love, muckraked stock and bond frauds, advocated spiritualism, and (ironically, given Vanderbilt's support) offered up the first American printing of Karl Marx's *Communist Manifesto*, all while never turning a dime in profit.

Another untapped collection, this comprising the papers of Webster Wagner, sheds even more light on Vanderbilt's declining mental acuity late in life. Born in 1817, Mr. Wagner invented the sleeper car, innovated the Webster Palace Car, patented the first railroad roof ventilator, and founded (with Vanderbilt) the New York Central Sleeping Car Company (later renamed the Wagner Palace Car Co.). Wagner's close business association with Vanderbilt spanned more than a decade. Detailed correspondence between the two men, as well as Wagner's diary notes of visits and chats with the Commodore, reveal much about Vanderbilt's fast mental fade from the late 1860s through to his death in 1877. (Ironically, Wagner—a New York state senator at the time—died aboard one of his own sleeping cars in 1882, the victim of a collision near Spuyten Duyvil in the Bronx, at the junction of the Harlem and Hudson rivers, both trains being owned by Cornelius's heir, William Henry.)[13]

The long interval since the 1942 publication of Lane's book means we are overdue for a modern reappraisal of Vanderbilt. On top of that, the availability of major new sources makes this endeavor all the more imperative. As was my approach in my previous biography of Vanderbilt's frequent nemesis Jay Gould, it is not my intention here to be either Vanderbilt's prosecutor or his attorney but rather to narrate his story as accurately as I possibly can and let the facts fall, like so many chips, where they may. No man influenced the development of nineteenth-century American commerce more than Vanderbilt; and few people since have loomed as large on the nation's business landscape. Vanderbilt began his career before the War of 1812 and ended it one year after the country's centennial. He was born during the administration of George Washington. He died seven years after

the founding of Standard Oil and just two months before the inaugu-
ration of Rutherford B. Hayes, the first president to use a telephone.
The Commodore's fortunes were joined completely and irrevocably,
whether he liked it or not, with those of his country. Much of the infrastructure Vanderbilt had a hand in shaping (from rail lines to navigation routes and Wall Street institutions) remains with us to this
day. Thus his story remains a vital one to know and understand.

1

MORAVIANS

THE FIRST AMERICAN VANDERBILT OF WHOM WE HAVE RECORD is one Jan Aertsen Van Der Bilt, who died in 1705.* Whether this man was the first of his line to come to the new world from Holland, or if he was native born—the son of a settler named Aert (thus Jan's middle name *Aertsen*)—is not known for certain, but the former seems likely given his early appearance in the timeline of settlement. Jan's roots in Holland could have been located either at Bildt, in the province of Utrecht, or Bilt, in the province of Friesland. No one can say for sure. Still, virtually all biographers to date have gone with the Bildt theory, despite the utter absence of documentation.

---

*Commodore Vanderbilt was to write his last name in one of two traditional manners ("Van DerBilt") popular within his clan until well into the 1820s, when at last he condensed it, going as *Vanderbilt* for his remaining fifty-odd years. Thus, in these pages, he shall always be *Vanderbilt* just as references to the family as a group shall be *Vanderbilt*. The Commodore's forebears, however, shall go under the name as they would have recognized it (most often either *Van Der Bilt* or *Van DerBilt*) whenever referenced individually.

It is also impossible to know, previous biographers' assertions notwithstanding, whether the first Vanderbilt emigrated from Holland after losing much of his assets speculating in tulip bulbs at the height of the tulipomania bubble, which peaked and crashed in 1636–1637. It should be noted, however, that of all the events that might have inspired a native to leave the Netherlands in the late 1630s, the fallout from the tulip bubble was by far the most benign. Bubonic plague ravaged Holland during the very same period. Concurrently, the Netherlands suffered severe setbacks in several key battles of the Thirty Years War. If Jan or his father emigrated at this time, any of these factors (or all of them) might have entered into the decision.

We know that Jan and his family lived in New Amsterdam during the last years of Dutch rule and thus were around to bear witness in 1664 as a grim Peter Stuyvesant, confronted by the formidable British fleet, surrendered New Netherland to the Crown. Their residency can be inferred from the 1651 Dutch Reformed Church baptismal record for Jan's son Aris, the first of four children born to Jan and his wife Dierber Cornelis, the others being Gerretje, Jacob, and Maretje.[1] Jan purchased a farm (or bowery, in the Dutch parlance) during 1667 in what is now the Flatbush section of Brooklyn. The deed still exists, along with the mortgage given to the seller, another Dutchman, Nicholas de Meyer. Jan, apparently illiterate, signed with an X above the spot where his name had been written by another. Eighteen years later, members of the Vanderbilt family still lived on the tract. Aris Jansen Van Derbilt, aged thirty-two, shows up listed along with sixteen others in the 1685 grant given by King James II's royal colonial governor, Thomas Dongan, establishing the town of Flatbush. By this time, Jan himself had moved on to another bowery near the town of Bergen, New Jersey (a part of what is today Jersey City) where he lived out the balance of his days.

Both Aris and his brother Jacob worked hard and prospered in the grim, bare-knuckles way that most early colonial farmers prospered. Each made periodic investments in Flatbush real estate, gaining more land but also more debt and more work. Annual tax assessment sheets chart the expansion of the brothers' holdings. During the late 1680s, when available plots in Flatbush became scarce, Aris began to look elsewhere for terrain suitable for investment. Eventually he acquired a large parcel of seventy-eight acres at New Dorp (*dorp* being the Dutch word for town), roughly at the center of the southern shore of Staten Island, overlooking Lower New York Bay. These acres lay just below the Dongan Hills (now Grant City and Todt Hill), named for the governor who was also a major proprietor on the island. Sixty of Aris's acres comprised a heavily forested upland that is today a part of the Moravian Cemetery, including the grounds containing the current Vanderbilt family tomb. A swampy tidal marsh and meadow approaching the water covered another eight acres: These would provide later generations of Vanderbilts with a vital supply of salt-hay for feeding their cattle during winter months. An adjacent ten acres, meanwhile, dominated the island's south shore waterfront on the western end of a stretch known as the Great Kills. *Kill* is the Dutch word for creek or stream. Great Kills is where many creeks emerge from the woods to flow into the bay.[2]

The island (named *Staaten Eylandt* in 1609 by Henry Hudson to honor the Staten-General, the Dutch parliament) lies some five miles from the southernmost tip of Manhattan. It is separated from Brooklyn by the thin tidal strait known as the Narrows, this forming the mouth of Upper New York Bay and New York Harbor, just above Lower New York Bay. During each day's brief periods of slack tide, the traverse across the Narrows between Brooklyn and the island could be made very quickly and easily by any sailing vessel adequately rigged, given the steady winds coming off the ocean. But during the long periods of sharply ebbing and flooding tides, the Narrows became treacherous, and the island relatively inaccessible. In large part because of this logistical problem, Staten Island had not, by the 1680s, attracted the same level of population as Manhattan and Long Island. Plots were thus readily available and prices attractive. Aris signed and paid a mortgage on the new acres but then left them unworked—an investment for the future. Staten Island's few settlers of the late seventeenth century, meanwhile, focused their energies not on farming but on fishing, ship-building, and oystering. (One visitor in 1671 chronicled "oysters a foot long, some containing pearls.")[3] A generation would pass before anyone thought seriously of farming there.

Aris married Hilletje Remse Vanderbeeck in 1677. The couple produced ten children, the seventh of whom was Jacob, named after Aris's brother. This man was to be Commodore Cornelius Vanderbilt's great-grandfather. Jacob's baptismal certificate gives his birth-date as January 24, 1692.[4] Twenty-three years later, in 1715, Jacob married Neltje Denyse. At approximately the same time, he struck a deal with his father to purchase the New Dorp lands for three hundred British pounds. Aris held a mortgage on the property, but Jacob was to act as proprietor, establish his home there, and make the tract pay. (Aris, meanwhile, had vacated his Flatbush farm several years earlier, dividing it among his other children. Since 1705, he and Hilletje had been living on Jan Van Der Bilt's old New Jersey bowery. Aris and Hilletje died there in 1715, not long after Jacob's marriage, thus relieving Jacob of his debt on the New Dorp lands.)

At the time Jacob and Neltje moved to Staten Island, it remained a backwater as compared to Manhattan and Brooklyn: an untamed wilderness. We can imagine the couple stowing their possessions on a boat, crossing the Narrows at slack tide, and then tacking along the island's southern coast for a few miles in Lower New York Bay until they came to the western side of the Great Kills. There they would have put in on their own land. And there they started their life. Intent on clearing the dense upland forest as his first order of business, Jacob felled enough trees to build himself a house. After that, however, he burned most of the remaining trees where they stood since lumber was in no short supply and had next to no value. Following the burning, he painstakingly grubbed out the stumps with the help of ropes, chains, and a sturdy ox. Only then, with the tedious work of clearing accomplished, could he plant grain and other staples.

The home of Jacob and Neltje—which no longer stands—was simple to the point of being Spartan. In that sense it was the same as nearly every other farmhouse on the island. A rudimentary wood-frame affair, it boasted no ornament, no luxury. Children shared not only rooms, but beds. And great economy was practiced in all things, both in the home and about the property. Wheaton Lane described the life of Jacob, Neltje, and their neighbors most eloquently:

Lime was obtained by burning shells, conveniently left in piles on the shore by countless generations of red men. The barns had low eaves but were quite capacious: another outdoor object of importance was the pigpen, the number of swine fattened annually depending upon the size of the family. In an economy that was practically self-sustaining, the women did their share. Each house had two spinning-wheels, one for wool, the other for linen; large families had looms of their own, while itinerant weavers, tailors and shoemakers made occasional visits to build up a supply of those articles that required more than common skill. Despite the proverbial large families of the Dutch, labor was ever at a premium; the more thrifty were able to meet the demand by purchasing a negro slave or two. Both slave and master worked in the fields together, apparently on terms of equality; the color line being drawn less rigidly by the Dutch than by the English.[5]

The nearly instant alleviation of Jacob's debt to his parents meant that he became fairly prosperous a bit quicker than he might have otherwise, and could afford a slave or two. (When he died in 1760, his will [dated May 10, 1759, and proved January 9, 1761] included the distribution of several slaves.)[6] He also invested in more land, purchasing some fifty acres bordering the original tract. Twelve children helped with the labor, including Jacob's and Neltje's fourth son (Jacob Van Derbilt II, born on January 6, 1723), the grandfather of the future Commodore. Jacob II and all the other children (including a brother of Jacob II named Cornelius, named after one of Jacob Sr.'s brothers) came along when their parents, previously participants in the Dutch Reformed movement, joined the Moravian Church.

Over the years, members of various oppressed sects found their way to remote Staten Island, there to practice their faiths in relative obscurity and peace. The first Dutch Walloons arrived in 1623. The French Waldenses and Huguenots came on their heels.[7] A group of German Moravians, also known as the United Brethren, settled at New Dorp in the late 1730s. The Moravians (who also had early settlements in Pennsylvania, New Jersey, and Maryland) took their inspiration from the Czech priest and martyr John Hus. A seminal figure in the Czech reformation and a forerunner of Martin Luther, Hus was burned at the stake by the Roman Catholic Church in July 6, 1415, after being convicted of heresy. The name *Moravian* derived from the fact that the sect had its origin in ancient Bohemia and Moravia, the present-day Czech Republic.

Formally organized in 1457 (some sixty years before Martin Luther began his agitation), by 1517 the Moravian Church numbered some 200,000 communicants practicing in more than four hundred parishes. This represented, perhaps, a bit too much success. In 1547, a wave of persecution caused many Moravians to depart Bohemia and Moravia for Poland. The Thirty Years War (1618–1648) brought still more attacks, including the bitter defeat of Bohemian Protestants by the combined Catholic forces of Ferdinand II, Holy Roman Emperor, and his ally Johan Tzerclaes, commander of the Catholic League, at the battle of White Mountain in 1620. Thereafter, the church subsided for several decades, and nearly died out completely, until the early eighteenth century, when Count Nicholas Ludwig von Zinzendorf, a Pietist nobleman of Saxony, adopted the faith and offered sanctuary to its devotees on his estate. Von Zinzendorf recruited numerous Germans to the religion, which eventually spread also to Holland, and encouraged Moravian emigration to America. The Count himself visited the New World in 1741 on a trip that included a stop at New Dorp.

What caused Jacob and Neltje to convert? We don't know. It may have been as simple a thing as the Moravians being their closest neighbors, and the Moravian religious services, held at first in homes, being more convenient to get to than those of more distant congregations. Or it may have been Jacob's and Neltje's personal exposure to the stirring religious rhetoric of the mesmerizing von Zinzendorf. In any event, Jacob and his sons are on record as having given significant help in the late 1740s, when the New Dorp Moravians built a large sailing ship, the *Irene,* in the Staten Island yard of shipwright John Van Deventer. The *Irene* was to make numerous trips to Europe, fetching hundreds of persecuted Moravians back to the American colonies from various points, including Amsterdam.[8]

Jacob died on December 14, 1760. Shortly thereafter, his son Cornelius (brother to Jacob II, and the second in the family to bear the name *Cornelius*) was among several signers who petitioned the

leaders of the American Moravian Church in Bethlehem, Pennsylvania, for permission to build a meeting house. Once the New
Dorp worthies received the proper authority from Bethlehem,
Cornelius, Jacob II, and many more of the by-now ubiquitous
Staten Island Vanderbilts helped construct an austere but sturdy
house of worship, which opened its doors in 1763. This building
still stands behind New Dorp's "new" Moravian Church, the latter
having been designed by the future Hudson River painter Jasper
Cropsey and dedicated in 1843 on property abutting the Moravian
Cemetery. The original church serves today as the office for the
cemetery.

Jacob II broke family precedent when, around 1740, he took a
bride who was not of Dutch descent. Mary Sprague's father, Jacob
Sprague, born in 1709, came from old New England British stock,
his father Jeremiah having been born at Hingham, Massachusetts, in
1682, and his mother, Priscilla Knight, having been born at Marble-
head in 1686. Mary's mother, Sarah Stodder, was of similar background. Mary had herself been born and raised at Hingham. We
don't know how Mary connected with Jacob Van Derbilt II of distant Staten Island, but connect she did. This couple were not only
to be grandparents to the Commodore, but also great-grandparents
to the Commodore's first wife, Sophia Johnson—the Commodore's
first cousin once removed on the Vanderbilt side.

The convoluted genealogical map is as follows: Jacob Van Derbilt II and Mary Sprague's first child, a daughter named Eleanor,
married Nathaniel Johnson. They had a son, Nathaniel Johnson II,
who married one Elizabeth Hand. Their daughter, Sophia Johnson, would be the first wife of the Commodore. To add to the already complex family tree, it must be noted that the Commodore's
father (another Cornelius, the youngest of Jacob II and Mary's
brood of seven, born in 1764) eventually married a cousin of Eliza-

beth Hand's, Phebe Hand, a native of New Jersey, who would become mother to the Commodore.[9] Thus the Commodore's first wife Sophia Johnson would not only be his first cousin, once removed on his father's side, but a second cousin on his mother's side.

The Cornelius born in 1764 was just two when his father, Jacob II, passed away, and just four when his mother, Mary Sprague Van Derbilt, died.[10] Evidently spurned by older siblings, many of whom were fully grown and embarked on families of their own, the boy wound up being raised by an uncle who treated him more as an indentured servant than a ward. But then, most Staten Island Vanderbilts of the mid-eighteenth century were living fairly close to the bone. The family acres, it seemed, could be spread out profitably among only so many descendants. As Arthur D. Howden Smith noted, in the time that had elapsed since Jacob and Neltje arrived at Staten Island, their considerable property had been much divided among the heirs of their twelve children. "Lot after lot," Smith wrote, "had been whittled away for one son or daughter or another. What had been a fine miniature estate was now a patchwork of odds and ends, no unit of it sufficient to support a family comfortably." (Two generations later, the aged, syphilitic, and at-times demented Commodore would perhaps factor the tribal memory of this diminishment into his calculations when, in making his will, he refused to divide up his $105 million fortune, instead leaving more than 95 percent of the wealth to one son, and only the sparse balance to be divided between nine other surviving children.) Smith further characterized the Staten Island Vanderbilts of the mid-eighteenth century as "a miserable set of farmers, fishermen and laborers, noses close to the grindstone and the clods never shaken off their boots—when they could afford boots."[11]

Generally, the childhood the Commodore's father suffered among these elementary people appears to have been grim. On top of their already strained circumstances, the Staten Island Vanderbilts in the

1770s and early 1780s had to deal with the added complication of British occupation throughout most of the American Revolution. The population of Staten Island was known, generally, for its Tory sympathies. (Indeed, Washington himself once labeled the islanders "our most inveterate enemies.")[12] As for the local Vanderbilts, they seem to have been generally dispassionate about the notion of the Revolution, but dispassionate too—like most of Dutch descent—about allegiance to the Crown. Thus, when it came time to choose sides between loyalty and liberty, virtually all of the Staten Island Vanderbilts came down squarely in the corner of the Staten Island Vanderbilts. For them, as for so many of the New York Dutch, the problems of the times were not political, but economic. Abstract ideas about democracy and self-governance took a distant second place to more immediate problems such as food and shelter.

The boy's uncle Cornelius owned the Rose and Crown tavern. He made the boy, whom he never sent to school, work there for long hours waiting tables, mopping floors, and hauling garbage. One island historian described the tavern, long since demolished, as "a one-story building of stone, with a hall through the middle, and rooms on either side; in front was a large elm tree."[13] Today the site, by the intersection of New Dorp Lane and Amboy Road, is marked by a plaque erected decades ago by the Richmond County chapter of the Daughters of the American Revolution. Throughout much of the Revolutionary War, the tavern served as the headquarters for British General Sir William Howe. Both the boy Cornelius, the one who would become the Commodore's father, and the boy Cornelius's uncle of the same name, doubtless waited on Howe many times and came to know him well. Prince William Henry, the third son of George III, also stayed at the Rose and Crown for an extended period during 1781. For the tavern's owner the British occupation was not an outrage but an imposition to be endured with a simple shrug and, of course, profited from to the fullest extent possible.

The future father of the Commodore emerged bitter, coarse, and humorless from the long servitude that had masqueraded as his childhood. He also emerged penniless and illiterate. Upon reaching his maturity, the young man received not even the smallest part of the once-vast Vanderbilt estate: no portion of even his own dead father's small slice of the New Dorp acres. Cornelius's disinheritance, blown in by the random winds of early misfortune, was complete and without grounds for appeal. It also seems to have been both character- and life-defining. When he was sixteen, Cornelius departed New Dorp, where his family had resided for so long. But he journeyed only as far as Port Richmond, on the north shore of the island just across the Kill Van Kull from Bayonne, New Jersey, the latter situated on the piece of land known locally as Bergen Point.

Operating out of Port Richmond, in 1780 Cornelius began work as an able-bodied sailor ferrying produce from Staten Island up the Kill Van Kull to Upper New York Bay and thence five miles up the harbor to Whitehall Landing, near the Battery on the southernmost tip of Manhattan. The vessel the boy worked was a small periauger, in the navigation of which he would have normally collaborated with just one other. Usually about thirty feet long overall, with a seven-foot beam and shallow draft, these open boats could be made to move either by the unfurling of two gaff-rigged sails or by the deployment of up to eight sweeps. (Most likely the sails were used in the open harbor, and the sweeps in the tight shoals of the Kill.) In all the world there was no simpler craft to learn to handle; and navigation on both the Kill Van Kull and the harbor was by sight. The only artful seamanship involved in Cornelius's roundabout journeys was learning the tides and winds of Upper New York Bay, especially how to time northbound and southbound voyages to dovetail with the flooding and ebbing tides, respectively. Beyond this simple knowledge, the work required only muscles, tenacity, and a tireless hunger.[14]

Exhibiting a taciturn perseverance, Cornelius worked steadily at the dull, endless round of trips between Port Richmond and Manhattan. Eventually, he saved enough to buy his own periauger, but his ambition seems to have stopped there. Contemporaries considered him something of a dullard, also something of a laggard, and not very enterprising. He later married a woman who was above him intellectually and capable of giving him more direction, but even in this he was slow. Seven years were to pass before Cornelius would meet and marry Phebe Hand, the Commodore's eventual mother. Like Cornelius's own long-dead mother, Phebe (three years younger than Cornelius, the daughter of sea captain Samuel Hand) was of old British stock. And like Cornelius himself, Phebe had been orphaned young. But unlike Cornelius, she came from people who were educated and moderately prosperous. Phebe had been adopted as a child by a family friend, a local minister, who raised her in a stable, loving home at Rahway, New Jersey.

Six sisters received placement elsewhere, as did a younger brother. "[Phebe] used to tell of the time when, as a young girl, she was walking on Broadway and saw a young stranger whose face attracted her," recalled a granddaughter, Anna Root, writing in the late 1880s or early 1890s. "Turning to look again she found him glancing back, and presently he wheeled about and coming to her asked if her name was not Phebe Hand. It was her only brother—and that accidental meeting was the first since infancy. Then he went south." According to Root, it was decades before Phebe saw her brother again.

Years afterward when she was sitting with her daughters (some of them married) in the family room of the Old Homestead, a traveler entered, and after some commonplace remark, asked if he could have lodging. My aunts did not dream of his being allowed to stay, but seeing their mother's strong look of interest and fearing that she might be persuaded, they signaled to her to refuse. Paying no attention to them, she, to their surprise, gave him permission, then he told his name and it turned out to be her own brother from Alabama. There must have been a vein of romance in this rotund relative, for he had purposely disguised himself in poor clothes to see if he would be recognized. Blood will tell, however notwithstanding the change in appearance. He had a prosperous plantation in Alabama where he had a large family, one of whom was Mrs. Robert L. Crawford, a granddaughter who was the mother of the late Commodore Vanderbilt's second wife.

Just as the brother had served at Bunker Hill, so too had other Hands been conspicuous in their loyalty to the colonial cause throughout the Revolution. Phebe's Uncle Edward Hand (destined to become adjutant general under Washington) commanded a rifle regiment at the Battle of Long Island. Phebe experienced the terror of the era at first hand when, at age sixteen, she was accosted by a Hessian mercenary who attempted to abduct her: an attack eventually repulsed by Rahway neighbors. So dedicated were the Hands to the Revolution that at one point virtually all of the family's small wealth (including a modest endowment belonging to Phebe) found its way into Continental bonds. Although this investment would eventually prove wise, once Alexander Hamilton managed to arrange the finances of the United States government so that it could make good on the bonds, Phebe was not to see a payback on her small share until 1791. Thus when Cornelius met her in 1787, the twenty-year-old was working as a caregiver/nanny in the Port Richmond household of an older sister.

They seem, in retrospect, to have been an unlikely pair. Phebe was literate, cultured, and well-mannered. She was also temperate, outgoing, and vivacious as well as frugal, shrewd, and pragmatic. All these characteristics ran directly counter to the urges of the limited and easily satisfied Cornelius, who worked out of necessity and found his only diversions in drinking grog and racing neighborhood horses. But in the end, a general scarcity of willing suitors, combined with Cornelius's good looks, seem to have combined to give him a certain appeal in Phebe's eyes. "He was a very handsome man," remembered their granddaughter Anna, who had known both of them, "and I think that with all of her strong good sense and sound judgment, she must have had some sentiment to fall in love at first sight . . . Cornelius Vanderbilt never could have done a wiser thing than when he placed his happiness in her keeping; he was naturally extravagant, but to her he owed whatever of success attended him."[15]

2

STAPLETON

The couple first rented, then in 1791 bought, a small farmhouse (no longer standing) which overlooked the Kill van Kull at Port Richmond. Given the timing, it seems likely that all or most of Phebe's small inheritance, which she received from her cashed out Continental bonds in 1791, went towards the purchase. Along with the tiny house, the property included a few acres that Cornelius tilled rather unenthusiastically to produce vegetables and grains that were mostly consumed by his own family. Meanwhile, for cash money, he continued his Manhattan runs in the periauger, charging so-much per trip to transport other men's produce and goods.

While Cornelius and Phebe lived at Port Richmond, they became parents to four children: Mary, Jacob, Charlotte, and Cornelius (the future Commodore), the last arriving May 27, 1794.[1] One year later, the Port Richmond house now being too small for the growing Vanderbilt clan, the man whom we shall from now on refer to as *Cornelius senior* or *Cornelius the elder* sold the place (preserving for himself one rocky acre that he'd never bothered to cultivate and

15

would leave fallow for at least another decade). Thereafter, Cornelius senior moved his family to a slightly larger, heavily mortgaged house confronting the Narrows in the "Edgewater" district (later known variously as "Vanderbilt's Landing" and "Quarantine") of southern Stapleton, just north of what is today Tompkinsville, on the northeastern coast of the island.[2] Here, on Bay Street (then called the Shore Road), five more children were born: Phebe, Jane, Eleanor, another Jacob (replacing the first Jacob, who died when his younger brother Cornelius was eleven), and another Phebe (replacing the first Phebe, who also died young).

In 1921, when the future Vanderbilt biographer Wheaton J. Lane was a freshman at Princeton University, he visited the dilapidated Stapleton house, which was then awaiting the wreckers. Two decades later, he described the place as it must have looked in the days of the Commodore's boyhood:

> The upper story was a loft under a steep roof pierced by dormer windows, with a chimney standing up . . . at each gable end. Downstairs there were probably no more than four rooms; the ceiling of the sitting room was of mud, so well constructed that it was to remain uncracked for over a century. The windows were high with small panes. In front of the house were some pear and cherry trees and a well-sweep which, however, did not cut off the view of the Narrows and Long Island. The house stood only about two hundred feet from the beach, and the constant stream of vessels entering or leaving the harbor provided a spectacle that never wearied. Phebe, especially, who lived until 1854, was to be an interested witness of the transition whereby steam replaced sails—a revolution in which her son was to play so important a role.[3]

This spectacle, interrupted briefly by the Jefferson embargo of 1807–1809, must have had a great influence on the future Commodore. The parade of brigantines, schooners, square-riggers, and sloops pushing through the Narrows must invariably have offered not only a pretty picture to a young man stuck in provincial Stapleton, where the local economy lurched along on a grim and tedious sustenance level, but also a vision of the vibrant work, wealth, and commerce alive and thriving in the great world beyond. The Commodore's growing fortunes would always be associated with transport. In his daily grasps for wealth, he would always look to shipping and passenger traffic rather than to coal-mining, steel-making, or garment or tool manufacture. Yes, he would carry the coal and the steel and the manufactured goods from here to there. And yes, he would purchase the coal and the steel to use in his enterprises. But his enterprises themselves (first sail boats, then steamers, then railroads) would never, ever involve anything other than the transport of passengers and freight from point A to point B. This was the only type of trade the Commodore would ever transact in a big way: the type he grew up seeing parade before him, on a daily basis, as a boy at Stapleton.

Vanderbilt family oral history, as well as urban legends still promulgated by some Staten Island historians, would have us believe that Cornelius the elder actually started the first Staten Island ferry. Relying only on folklore, Arthur D. Howden Smith credited the Commodore's father with offering "the first regular service of this kind the harbor had known."[4] But a close study of advertisements and announcements in period newspapers (both those published on Staten Island and those published in Manhattan) reveals no such regular service advertised by Van Derbilt. As well, Van Derbilt's shallow-draft periauger, which had no keel or centerboard, would have been difficult to steer to windward or against tides. Thus it would not have been the most efficient craft for navigating across the frequently swift waters of New York harbor on the type of uncompromising schedule required for a regularly operated ferry business. Additionally, from what we know about his limited imagination, the elder Van Derbilt would seem incapable of concocting such a bold and grand vision (such a genuinely *good* idea) as a regularly scheduled ferry service.

For years Van Derbilt senior and various others made frequent trips, many times a week in season, between Stapleton and Manhattan. But in no way was the senior Van Derbilt's catch-as-catch-could enterprise a formal ferry service. The business of Van Derbilt and those like him was the simple on-demand transport of small caches of produce and merchandise (and perhaps a stray human or two) between the island and the city. Not until 1816 would the Richmond Turnpike Company start running the reliably scheduled steam ferry *Nautilus* between the Battery and the island. One of the Commodore's brothers-in-law, John DeForest, would serve as the first captain of the *Nautilus*. Later on, in 1838, the Commodore would purchase control of the ferry, which he would then run exclusively (except for a brief hiatus during the 1850s) till the advent of the Civil War, at which point he was destined to sell the concern to the Staten Island Railway Company, headed by his brother Jacob.

But all of that enterprise was in the far distant future as young Cornelius, an exuberant outdoorsman, came of age at Stapleton. Recounting an episode from the family folklore that is believable because of its later authentication, Wheaton Lane tells of Cornelius as a child of six nearly foundering a horse during a frantic bare-back race along the shore, his competition being a black slave boy two years older than he. (Seventy-five years later, the former slave, now a Methodist minister, turned up on the Commodore's doorstep. The minister remembered himself to the normally forbidding, aloof, and bigoted Vanderbilt, who then mystified his servants by inviting the black man to dinner. One former retainer later speculated that the move was not meant as a kindness to a childhood friend so much as a jab at the patience of Vanderbilt's second wife, the long-suffering and thoroughly Southern Frank Crawford.)

In addition to horsemanship, the future Commodore displayed a natural talent for water-borne activities. He sailed like a master at an early age. Always large and well-muscled for his years, he was a strong rower, and he won many a local race in which he used his father's periauger—the sails down, and two sweeps out. His athleticism seems to have largely defined his youth. Throughout his life he would enjoy strenuous and direct physical competitions, carriage-racing being the favorite hobby of his last decades. He eventually came to believe that participation in such contests (as well as other pursuits like drinking and whoring) said much about one's manhood. During 1870, the Commodore would criticize the diminutive and resoundingly unathletic Jay Gould (who so regularly beat him in Wall Street's more abstract competitions) by characterizing Gould as an effeminate man who lacked physical courage. Vanderbilt sneered at Gould's bookish habits, his fondness for parlors and gardening, and his faithfulness to his wife. Gould liked his family and library and flowers. The rough-hewn Vanderbilt preferred other pastimes, many of them born of the waterfront, and was never ashamed to say so. Even his worst critics admitted that he never made any pretense to being a gentleman.

Gould could have his damn books. The barely literate Vanderbilt, who was always destined to stay so, appears to have been taken from school at age eleven, upon the death of his older brother Jacob, the dead Jacob soon to be memorialized in the naming of the next born male child. Thereafter, instead of focusing on the schoolwork he'd long despised, young Cornelius found himself, as the oldest boy, impressed to the service of the father and working, for the most part, on the water. And he rather liked the water. Early on, he learned the names of the various brigantines and square-riggers that passed through the harbor, all bound from or to distant lands. He also became acquainted with the many sloops and schooners which made the local waters home. Some plied the Jersey and Staten Island coastlines. Others carried trade and passengers up the Hudson (still known to many of Dutch descent as the North River) as far as Albany, or into Long Island Sound to reach points along the Connecticut and northern Long Island coasts.

The first vessel young Cornelius worked was the periauger owned by the father. He and another boy, a neighbor, frequently made runs to the Battery for pennies. The father also employed the son on other missions, such as when the child found himself drafted to help salvage the goods of brigs and square-riggers run aground at treacherous Sandy Hook: the barrier beach which defined the southern mouth of Lower New York Bay. Sandy Hook was a notoriously treacherous strip of real estate on which many vessels foundered, this despite the presence of a five-hundred-foot-tall lighthouse built in 1764. Groundings were so common that many New Jerseyans and Staten Islanders—the senior Van Derbilt among them—enjoyed busy ancillary careers as "wreckers" looting the cargoes of errant vessels, which by law became the property of anyone willing to do the work of salvage.

Of course, all of the Sandy Hook catastrophes occurred on the ocean side of the "Hook," where smaller craft dared not go lest they be run aground themselves. Thus the process of wrecking involved bringing smaller boats to the bay side of the Hook, and carting salvaged property overland from the ocean beach to the awaiting bayside vessels. On such occasions, young Cornelius's job was to bring horses and a wagon via ferry from Staten Island across the Arthur Kill to South Amboy, thence drive the team south along the Jersey coast to the Hook, where the same were used to cart goods from the ocean side of the Hook to Cornelius Senior's waiting vessel on the bay side. Finally, after a long day, once all that work of carting was through, the boy would drive the wagon and team back north along the Jersey coast, recross to Staten Island on the Amboy ferry, and drive home to Stapleton.

At home, Cornelius and the other children helped their mother Phebe tend several small garden plots of vegetables, some of which were consumed by the family, others of which were sent to market. The cultivation accomplished on the Vanderbilt's small Stapleton plot appears to have been Phebe's initiative, her husband having little interest in farm work and little inclination toward laboring longer or harder than mere survival demanded. Phebe was economical and ambitious, but her husband was content to live life on one basic level: hauling and salvaging freight, and moving the occasional passenger from here to there, to the end of his days. He did not dream of riches. In fact, he did not aspire to wealth any more than he aspired to sainthood. And he aspired to sainthood not at all: not for himself, not for his family.

Bowing to tradition, the elder Cornelius registered the births of his children in the old Moravian church of his forebears. However, his interest in things religious seems not to have gone beyond this ritual. Thus, what little Godly instruction the children received came from Phebe. As an old man, the Commodore—who during the bulk of his life displayed no more piety than had his father before him—recalled his mother teaching the children hymns and instructing them in lessons from the Bible. He also remembered the Bible as being the one book he was made to practice reading in school, this being just one more despised element of a generally despised education. Unlike so many other Vanderbilt households on the island, this one was primarily Episcopal in flavor, Phebe's family tradition being confined to the Anglican communion. Since there was no Episcopal Church (save for a Methodist denomination) on the island during young Cornelius's youth, his and his siblings' participation in religious services would have been restricted to infrequent visits by roving Episcopal clerics. For the most part, then, what religious devotion existed in the Commodore's childhood was home-made and (at least as Cornelius and his father viewed it) probably inconvenient. As an adult, the son was to go decades without stepping into a church for anything other than baptisms or funerals.

Beyond all this, what was the world young Vanderbilt grew up in? The boy was nine years old when New York's Robert R. Livingston—President Thomas Jefferson's minister to France—negotiated the Louisiana Purchase, and ten in July 1804, when Vice President Aaron Burr fatally shot Alexander Hamilton in a duel on the banks of the Hudson at Weehawken, just a few miles to the north of Staten Island. Some months later, black slaves at work enlarging the Brooklyn Navy Yard accidentally unearthed the remains of hundreds of American patriots, all of them having been starved to death on the prison ship *Jersey* in New York Harbor during the American War of Independence and secretly buried by the British. A group known as the Columbian Order, or Tammany Society, which none other than Burr himself had recently molded into a formidable local political machine, collected the sacred bones and transferred them to a temporary wooden tomb, actually more like a warehouse, nearby. In November that same year eleven gentlemen of Manhattan (among them Mayor DeWitt Clinton) formed the New York Historical Society.

Three years later, Robert Fulton (born in 1765) launched one of the first successful steam-driven boats. Fulton took his vessel, known simply as the *North River Steamboat*, onto the East River from lower Manhattan. From there he steered her around the tip of the Battery and then pointed her north up the Hudson. Twenty-four hours and 110 miles later, Fulton pulled in at Clermont, the Germantown manor estate of his benefactor, the same Robert Livingston who had acquired the Louisiana territory not long before. Despite the initial success of Fulton's experiment, steam would not become a dominant force in maritime commerce for several more decades. Meanwhile, there were no railroads anywhere on the continent, nor was there a direct interior water route from the northeastern seaboard to the nation's interior. (The Erie Canal, linking the Hudson River near Troy, New York, with Lake Erie, and thereby connecting via water the harbor of New York with the country's interior as far west as Detroit, would not be completed until 1825.)

The largely agrarian economy of the country in which the Commodore grew up reflected these limitations. The economists Louis D. Johnston and Samuel H. Williamson estimate the gross domestic product of the United States in 1794—the year of the Commodore's birth—at $309,960,000, or $70 nominal GDP per capita for a population of 4,428,000. The same economists estimate the gross domestic product of the United States for 1877—the year of the Commodore's death—at $8,249,675,000 (or $175 nominal GDP per capita for 47,141,000 inhabitants).[5] In other words, Vanderbilt was to see the net worth of the United States grow more than 26.6 times in his lifetime, while the U.S. population would only grow 10.6 times in the same period. As young Vanderbilt set out upon the voyage of life, the society through which he navigated was nothing more than a puddle, commercially speaking.

It was also a nation that lingered quite close to its roots: some of them being healthy, some not. The state of New York would not finally eradicate all slavery within its borders until July 4, 1827, even though various laws calling for the "gradual emancipation" of all New York blacks had been on the books since 1799. Additionally, virtually all of New York, including the larger share of Manhattan Island itself, remained essentially rural and agrarian, the latter being but a shadow of the mercantile and banking center it was to become. A small formal New York market for stocks and bonds, with just twenty-four members, had been launched in 1792. But the exchange (named the New York Stock Exchange Board in 1817, shortened to the New York Stock Exchange in 1863) was destined to remain subservient to the Philadelphia Exchange until the Pennsylvania market collapsed during the Panic of 1837.

New York banking was also in its infancy. For fifteen years, the Federalist-dominated Bank of New York, founded by Alexander Hamilton and chartered in 1784, enjoyed a virtual monopoly in the city. Not until 1799, when Aaron Burr maneuvered the New York State Legislature into approving a broadly-phrased charter for the Manhattan Company (a firm originally intended to run fresh water into Manhattan) did another bank emerge: one established by the Manhattan Company utilizing charter language which allowed it to deal in financial instruments. In a short time, the Bank of Manhattan rivaled the size of the Bank of New York. Just as the Bank of New York had once used its resources to aid Federalist merchants, farmers, and candidates, the Bank of Manhattan now arranged its affairs to be of maximum aid to the friends of Tammany. The bank eventually played an important role in Thomas Jefferson's 1800 election to the presidency, thus breaking the back of Federalist domination in New York's commercial and financial institutions.[6]

On his death bed, Cornelius Vanderbilt would tell one of his doctors that ever since he'd been young he'd been "insane" on the subject of "money-making."[7] The promising but as-yet largely virgin financial landscape that confronted Vanderbilt in youth was to prove ideal terrain for one possessing his mania, his hunger, and his energy.

3

PROFITABLE WAR

PER THE LAWS OF THE DAY, YOUNG CORNELIUS WAS NOT FREE to embark upon his own enterprises until he was twenty-one. In the absence of that majority, he was little more than his father's property—the elder Cornelius's chattel. But in his sixteenth year, growing weary of not being his own master, young Vanderbilt seems to have come to two fundamental realizations that would serve him well all his life. First: The complexion of any set of facts could always be altered by the addition of new facts. Second: Everything was negotiable. *Everything. Always.*

To the grim prospect of feudal servitude to the elder Cornelius for the next five years, the sixteen-year-old now added an additional wrinkle. The boy voiced his desire to go to sea. More important, he expressed his willingness to run away to the South Street piers on the lower east side of Manhattan, which, now that Jefferson's embargo had finally ended, once again played host to scores of brigs and square-riggers from around the globe, on any one of which he could sign-on and be gone out of United States territorial waters before any given nightfall. Where would the father's legal rights be then? What profit would be left for the elder Cornelius to make? And what long nights of worry would lay ahead for Phebe, contemplating the dangers likely confronting her boy on the far shores of distant continents, thousands of miles from home, in the midst of the bloody Napoleonic Wars which had been ongoing since 1803?

After dangling that dire possibility, young Cornelius offered his parents a comparatively attractive compromise. If they would lend him $100, he could buy his own periauger, one that he'd seen for sale at Port Richmond, and pay them back in due course while also remaining safely and profitably at home as their tenant. According to Vanderbiltian folklore, the parents agreed to the loan, and Cornelius worked so hard at running his small craft as a business that he was soon able to repay them every dime as well as a portion of his profits. But Vanderbilt's testimony late in life reveals a different story. The discussion evidently took place in the early spring of 1810, right before the planting season, just as young Cornelius was approaching his sixteenth birthday. The parents still owned one acre of rocky, uncleared soil at Port Richmond, and had long cherished the idea of making it tillable and planting something there.[1] Now they offered to pay Cornelius outright $100 if he would move the rocks and trees and stumps off the acre and plant it with corn before it got too late in the season.

To this young Cornelius readily agreed. It appears he spent the better part of the month before his birthday clearing and planting. Then, with the land-grubbing work finished, he delightedly took to the water. As an old man he recalled, nostalgically and probably not completely truthfully: "I didn't feel as much real satisfaction when I made [millions in the corner of the New York & Harlem River Railroad] as I did on that bright May morning sixty years before when I stepped into my own periauger, hoisted my own sail, and put my hands on my own tiller."[2]

Wheaton Lane, Arthur D. Howden Smith, and William Croffut have all pictured young Cornelius (just as so many others have pictured Cornelius's father) using his periauger to conduct a ferry trade. Lane says that at Whitehall Landing, near the Battery, Cornelius "landed the passengers he picked up at Stapleton every morning, bringing them back at night."[3] But this was 1810, well before the age of daily commuters to and from Manhattan. Most of New York City's 96,000 souls worked near where they lived in town, and most were simple merchants, farmers, and laborers. Farms dominated the landscape of Manhattan from Canal Street as far north as the rocky heights on the opposite end of the island, and shops and homes dominated to the south in the blocks immediately above the Battery. The heights of the skyline downtown were defined entirely by spires, including those of St. Paul's Chapel and the second Trinity Church. And the waterfront itself was dominated by the constant flow of inbound and outbound ships and the frantic activity associated with that commerce. Every day a thousand or more rough longshoremen loaded freight on and off the vessels, while rowdy seamen drank their pay, tore up pubs, and carried on with whores in flophouses and alleys.

If young Cornelius did indeed conduct a regularly scheduled ferry business, it went unadvertised. More likely, he picked up what freight work he could on a spot-job basis during the early summer of 1810, and also conveyed locals on demand to the city, there to make purchases and enjoy professional services such as were not available on Staten Island. Lawyers were abundant in Manhattan; so too were leather merchants, dressmakers, booksellers, and physicians. Islanders had long considered it a "given" that they needed to go "to town" for certain errands. Such shoppers as these—together with the odd young man leaving Staten Island forever to make his way in the world—comprised the bulk of Cornelius's human cargo. As for freight, he carried produce as well as other products from the island (among them rope).

Anecdotal evidence suggests that he much preferred rope to humans. Even Vanderbilt's first admiring biographer, William Croffut, had to admit the reality of numerous first-person accounts swearing to the young boatman's lack of social graces. Wheaton Lane echoes Croffut's impression: "Tradition records that [Cornelius] was unnecessarily curt and rude with his passengers and merchant customers. His language was rough and he cared little what people thought about him."[4] The young man was selling transport, not conversation. He was also passionate about commanding his craft efficiently and maximizing its profitability, often at the expense of politeness and passenger comfort. Gruff, severe, and sure of himself as a youth, Vanderbilt was to remain so all his life: never suffering fools gladly, always going his own way, and always looking out for himself first. After Vanderbilt's death, his friend and physician, Jared Linsly, who'd known him for decades, would recall the Commodore as being "less influenced by the men around him than any man I ever knew. He had a peculiarity, if interrupted while telling anything, of stopping right there and never resuming. This peculiarity stuck to him all his life. He never would take a suggestion from anybody—that is, not directly."[5]

Whatever he lacked in manners, Vanderbilt made up for in his tenacity as a businessman and his diligence in leveraging every opportunity for profit. In this spirit, unlike most of his less hungry competitors, he would dare the foulest of weather, going out on the most tempestuous waters, winter or summer, for a price. Vanderbilt also gained a reputation for ruthlessly undercutting his competition: breaking ranks with his peers, doing whatever it took to discount his services low enough to assure that his daily schedule and the hull of his little boat remained packed. This too would become a trademark: the conduct of price wars and the sacrifice of margin in return for full loads and the impoverishment of those who would dare go against him.

Meanwhile, Vanderbilt's boat did not remain little for long. In short order, the young man deduced what his father had not had the wit to realize over the course of many years: that the shallow-draft periauger was the least likely vessel for navigation across the complicated waters of New York Harbor. Soon Cornelius adopted a wide-beamed centerboard sloop as his craft of choice for the Staten Island/Manhattan run. The sloop, sixty-five feet in length overall, allowed him to sail on days when periaguers could not, to go where periaugers dared not, and to take on considerably more in the way of freight and passengers than the average periauger could ever hold. At the same time, the sloop's dropped centerboard gave Vanderbilt stability with which to ply the waters of the harbor in all directions at any time of day, regardless of wind and tide.

Vanderbilt's vessel resembled the classic New York Harbor and river sloops described so eloquently after the turn of the century by Hudson rivermen and historians William Verplanck and Moses Collyer. "The mast was placed well forward," they wrote, "thus giving the boat a large mainsail, and small jib. A topsail too was generally carried, but not set like the club topsail of the modem yacht."[6] Unlike his periauger, however, Vanderbilt's sloop *Swiftsure* (brazenly named after a British warship that had distinguished itself at the Battle of Trafalgar) was so large that it could not be sailed single-handedly. Thus Vanderbilt must have taken on at least two deck-hands to help him.[7] Vanderbilt commissioned the building of the *Swiftsure* in 1813, when he was nineteen, in the midst of the war of 1812. The sloop was launched from Belleville, on the Passaic River in New Jersey, that summer.

The War of 1812 affected harbor trade significantly. In fact, those waters became complicated even before the start of the declared hostilities between the United States and Britain. As of 1803, and the commencement of the Napoleonic wars, the influence of patrolling British vessels in and around Lower New York Bay had been profound.

Near the end of April 1806, the British frigate *Leander* became notorious in the city. The *Leander* fired a shot across the bow of the American schooner *Richard,* as the latter sailed near Sandy Hook, bound to New York from Philadelphia. In response, the officers and men of the *Richard* instantly hove to and awaited boarding by the British, who, desperate for Navy personnel in the midst of their war with France, had lately outraged the public of the neutral United States by seizing crewmen from American vessels and "pressing" them into service on Royal Navy ships. But even after the *Richard* hove to, another cannon-ball whizzed close, then one more (possibly a miss-aimed shot across the bow of another vessel moving nearby), which decapitated the *Richard*'s helmsman, John Pierce. A few days later, Pierce's headless body went on display in New York before burial at public expense. Furious, Mayor DeWitt Clinton, joined by other leading Manhattan citizens, demanded loudly that something be done to build-up the defenses of New York Harbor.

At the time, these defenses were woefully inadequate. As Edwin G. Burrows and Mike Wallace have written: "The invasions of 1664, 1673, and 1776 left no doubts as to Manhattan's vulnerability to attack by sea, but only star-shaped Fort Jay on the northern end of Governors Island—thrown up during the war scare of 1794 and rebuilt as Fort Columbus in 1806—afforded the city any protection from enemy warships. Over the spring and summer of 1807, therefore, teams of military engineers got to work on a system of forts and batteries for the Upper Bay that would take four years to complete."[8] The four new forts included the West Battery, located on a rocky outcropping near the southern tip of Manhattan; Castle Williams, on the southern end of Governors Island; the North Battery (located on Manhattan farther up the Hudson shore from the West Battery); and Fort Gansevoort, even farther north on the same shore. Castle Williams could crossfire with Fort Columbus and the West Battery, and the North Battery could crossfire with the West Battery and Fort Gansevoort. Local authorities constructed additional small forts and batteries on Bedloe's Island, Staten Island, and the Brooklyn shore. Once completed, the combined installations would be able to train more than three hundred cannon and mortars on any ship entering the harbor. (In the end the Brits would not mount even one successful incursion.)

The West Battery featured eight-foot walls and seats for twenty-eight cannon. Castle Williams stood three stories tall and housed a hundred guns. The North Battery and Fort Gansevoort (sometimes referred to as the White Fort because it had whitewashed walls) were just as formidable—all of them massive construction projects. For several months throughout the autumn of 1810, Cornelius devoted his boat and all his energies to servicing lucrative government contracts transporting brick, sand, workers, supplies, and soldiers between the various sites—the continuing transport of the last two items being work that allowed Cornelius to prosper even after the British blockade of 1813 effectively closed the port. During the spring of 1814, he serviced a three-month contract making weekly deliveries of supplies to six batteries at Fort Richmond, Bedloe's Island, Governors Island, Hell Gate, Ward's Island, and Harlem.[9]

The narratives of Croffut, Smith, and Lane are alive with anecdotes about young Vanderbilt's exploits in New York Harbor during the hostilities with Britain. Not one can be verified. They are folklore, but like much folklore, the tales must be rooted in at least some fact. At the very least, they seem in synch with the well-documented attitude, tone, and demeanor that characterized Vanderbilt later in life. On one occasion, amid a gale, Cornelius reportedly proved to be the lone boatman willing to transport officers and reinforcements between Whitehall Landing and the garrison at Sandy Hook. (When asked whether he could move the men, he reportedly replied: "Yes, but I shall have to carry them under water part of the way.") On another occasion, for fear of being cheated out of receipts for the transport of a small cadre of soldiers, Vanderbilt flatly refused an order from an officer that he transship his passengers mid-voyage to one of his competitor's vessels. When the officer subsequently leapt the gunwale of Cornelius's boat with sword drawn, the young man reportedly beat him with his fist before tossing him back into the other boat.[10] Whether or not these tales are true in essence, one senses their visceral truth in spirit.

Tall, lean, and muscled, young Vanderbilt was as tough as any creature of the waterfront: a rambunctious place where the strong endured and the weak were quickly trod over. Like other men of that milieu, he worked hard. We may also surmise, given his habits later in life, that he played hard. And the New York waterfront was rife with opportunities for hard play. Bars and whores abounded. While men of means usually enjoyed the favors of courtesans working in whore houses on Chatham Row, off upper-Broadway, working-class seaman of Vanderbilt's variety patronized women of a lower order who plied their trade in the bars and streets around Catherine Slip, confronting the East River near South Street. Years later, when wealthy and old, Vanderbilt would still, on occasion, come here for at least some of his sexual diversions, preferring the rancid and rough women of the docks to the more elegant whores available in cushioned bordellos uptown. In fact, his affinity for such women, in the form of the syphilis he'd pick up along the way from one of them, would ultimately kill him.

Despite his strength and his height—more than six feet—the robust Vanderbilt seems to have had no interest in military service. The concept of abstract duty to country, of citizenship generally, appears to have been completely foreign to him. Smith (so frequently wrong on factual details about Vanderbilt, but so frequently on target when intuiting the Commodore's motivations and outlook) wrote that Vanderbilt "never knew the meaning of the word *ideal*. Life, to him, was simply a question of battling for what you desired, regardless of whom you trampled on. The country, the state, the city, were abstract words; they had no concrete significance—no more significance than politics, except as he happened to discover that some politician or party principle impinged upon his affairs. . . . [Vanderbilt] simply had no conception of life, save as an egocentric proposition." During his latter decades, wrote Smith, the Commodore "would have mocked at anyone who claimed that he worked for the public good. Consciously, he did nothing of the sort. He worked for the hand of Cornelius Vanderbilt. Happily, what was good for Cornelius Vanderbilt was good for America."[11] (This same attitude was to endure into the next generation of the family, with the Commodore's son William Henry Vanderbilt being the one to utter this particularly infamous phrase: "The public be damned.")[12]

No, Cornelius Vanderbilt was not going to surrender to military discipline for mere pennies, not when there was serious money to be made by an enterprising workaholic commanding a good boat in troubled waters. Add to this young Vanderbilt's already demonstrated aversion to taking orders from anyone, anywhere, at any time. One guesses he might have known himself well enough to realize that a stint in the military would invariably lead to insubordination on his part. And insubordination, in the end, would not have been profitable at all.

While Vanderbilt worked and wenched, and the war waged, wheels turned that were destined to shape the geographical, financial, and cultural map through which he'd move in future. In 1810, the same year young Cornelius bought his first boat, DeWitt Clinton joined with other Federalists, including Gouveneur Morris, Philip Schuyler, and Jonas Platt, in calling for what was to become the Erie Canal. That summer, Clinton himself accompanied engineers on a journey to chart the course of the future waterway. In their subsequent report, Clinton and the other men appointed by the New York Legislature as a Board of Canal Commissioners, called the proposed project a great "national work" that would prove key to "the commerce of the western world."[13]

In Manhattan during the spring of 1811, another legislature-appointed commission, the Streets Commission, published a grid-like vision for the future of the island: twelve avenues running north/south, up and down, these bisected every two hundred feet by east-west streets, each of the streets running from the East River waterfront to the Hudson. Elsewhere in the city, a young writer with Federalist sympathies, Washington Irving, basked in the celebrity he'd achieved two years before with the publication, under the nom-de-plume Diedrich Knickerbocker, of *A History of New-York from the Beginning of the World to the End of the Dutch Dynasty*. Like virtually every other book issued in his lifetime, this was one Vanderbilt would never read. In true Federalist fashion, Irving's Knickerbocker took time out from his writing of history to ridicule the political pretensions of the working class, that "swinish multitude," the "enlightened mob" who sought increasingly to "meddle in things above their comprehensions."[14]

Eleven years Vanderbilt's senior, Irving, via the pen-name he applied to the spectral author Knickerbocker, unwittingly created a moniker that would henceforth be applied to an entire class of educated and moneyed New Yorkers of Dutch descent. Irving himself eventually became close with John Jacob Astor, thirty-one years Vanderbilt's senior and twenty years Irving's senior: America's first true millionaire. Irving went on to write the official history of the Astor-financed 1810–1812 expedition to the Pacific Northwest and the rise and fall of Astoria, Astor's fur-trading outpost on the Oregon coast. In addition to commissioning work from Irving, Astor also helped out Edgar Allen Poe on occasion, remembered the poet Fitz-Greene Halleck in his will, and provided generous support for various early and important American artists, among them Audubon. In this the fur and real estate baron, destined to die in 1848, left an example of philanthropy that was not to be followed by the richest man of the succeeding American generation.

4

MARRIAGE

Cornelius's numerous dalliances with easy women of the New York waterfront did not stop him from wanting to marry. The girl he eventually courted and won was, as previously mentioned, a first cousin once-removed on Cornelius's father's side, and a second cousin on Cornelius's mother's side. Just as Cornelius was a grandson of Jacob Vanderbilt II, Sophia Johnson was a great-granddaughter of the same man. Sophia's grandmother was an Eleanor Vanderbilt, the daughter of Jacob Vanderbilt II, who married a Nathaniel Johnson. That couple's son, Nathaniel Johnson II, in turn married one Elizabeth Hand (a cousin to the Commodore's mother, Phebe Hand). That couple, living at Port Richmond, became parents to Sophia in 1795.[1]

Like Cornelius, Sophia was raised barefoot on the waterfront. Like Cornelius, she was one of a large brood. Also like him, she was healthy and handsome when they began casting glances at each other during the summer of 1813: the year he turned nineteen and she eighteen. He'd known her since they were children, though now she possessed a sultry beauty containing within it a distinct resemblance to Cornelius's mother, Phebe. Despite her beauty and intelligence, the girl seems to have been quiet and deferential: attributes that must have appealed to Cornelius. Lane refers to Sophia as a "willing, good-natured worker who cheerfully looked forward to a lifetime of monotonous toil and child-bearing."[2] (Indeed, it seems Sophia was trained for her perceived future by her parents, who let her out to serve as a scullery maid in affluent households of Port Richmond.) In future, she would nearly always defer to Cornelius, even though she was better educated than he. She gave birth to thirteen of his children (twelve of whom survived into adulthood), all the while enduring in silence his insults and infidelities (as well as his nearly constant verbal abuse of their offspring). Eventually he would give her syphilis and have her committed to an asylum for a period during the 1840s, when she went through menopause. Near the end of her days in the 1860s, she would live alone in a large mansion built by the Commodore on Staten Island while he spent his nights, not always alone, in a Greenwich Village townhouse.[3]

Croffut says that Vanderbilt's mother at first objected to the match because of Cornelius and Sophia's "consanguinity."[4] Smith makes much the same assertion, as does Lane, who states things more bluntly. According to Lane, Phebe's arguments against the marriage were based on her "elementary knowledge of eugenics."[5] Frankly, however, even the most rudimentary understanding of eugenics would have been a revelation in the year 1813, for the British mathematician Sir Francis Galton was not to define the new science, and give it a name, until 1883. In any event, whatever risk there was attached to the cousins creating off-spring, it seems to have manifested itself in only one out of the thirteen. Cornelius Jeremiah Vanderbilt, the ninth child born in 1830, struggled all his life with epilepsy and a propensity for manic depression. Each of these maladies earned him more then his share of paternal rebuke and, in time, caused him to take his own life.

According to published sources, Cornelius and Sophia took their vows on December 19, 1813. No record of this appears in the annals of the Moravian Church at New Dorp, nor in the records of the Dutch Reformed Church of Port Richmond. One assumes the couple may have been wed by an Episcopal cleric, both households being more in step with that branch of Protestantism than any other. But this is an assumption. After the service and a modest gathering that was probably part celebration, part family reunion, Cornelius brought his bride to a small rented house at Stapleton. The next morning, he went to work on his sloop and she set about making a household. Sophia was soon pregnant with the couple's first child, Phebe Jane, who'd be born during the summer of 1814.

The rest of the children arrived in fairly rapid succession during the next twenty-five years: Ethelinda (1817), Eliza (1819), William Henry (or Billy) 1821, Emily Almira (1823), Sophia Johnson (1825), Maria Louisa (1827), Frances Lavinia (1828), Cornelius Jeremiah (1830), Mary Alicia (1834), Catherine Juliette (1836), and George Washington (1839). (Within this mix another child, a daughter named Francis, lived briefly and died sometime before 1828, at which point her replacement took her name.) Cornelius was, through the years, to loudly and regularly take umbrage at the high percentage of females in the mix of his offspring. He was also to complain nearly just as loudly about the overall quality of the mere three boys. To the troubled Cornelius he would never give any quarter or any charity. And Billy would be merely tolerated until the day his fortunes reversed: the day his brother George, the father's pronounced and undisputed favorite, died of consumption contracted at the Battle of Shiloh during the Civil War.

∞

But all of that contempt and meanness was in the future as Cornelius and Sophia set about making a home, and Cornelius continued to build his business interests. In his pursuit of the latter, he was often gone from the home sixteen hours or more every day, and Sophia left to tend the household. There, one imagines, she soon settled into a daily round of cleaning, cooking, and minding to the nursery needs of one, then another small child. Her in-laws did not live far away, and were most likely a significant presence in Sophia's household. This was evidently especially the case with regards to Phebe, the one member of the family to whom her son always deferred, and with whom he regularly consulted.

Indeed, it has been said that Phebe was the only person in the world whose opinion Vanderbilt genuinely valued. This may be overstating. But nevertheless, it appears to have been true that Phebe's advice loomed large in Cornelius's business decisions during the early phase of his career, and also in the running of his household. In short, Sophia had little say in anything, not even domestic matters. Lane paints Sophia's grim situation with chilly clarity:

> Sophia kept the household expenses at a minimum in an attempt to keep pace with her husband's thriftiness. When he came in wet and sullen, as he often did, there was always hot food on the stove to restore him to good humor. The strain of overwork and continuous child-bearing soon made Sophia a middle-aged woman and laid the seeds of a tragic illness. Yet Sophia, with all her self-sacrifice and readiness to meet her husband's demands, never won his complete confidence. That was reserved for his mother. When Cornele, in one of his rare moods when he had to talk of his plans and ambitions, confided in anyone, it was Phebe Hand to whom he turned. Sophia, like everyone else, had enormous respect for her mother-in-law, yet, docile as she was, she

must have been hurt that decisions affecting her life and family were made without taking her into consideration.[6]

Cornelius's austerity stemmed from his growing insistence that every spare dime be invested in more and better sailing vessels, and men to skipper them. His deference to his mother stemmed in part from the same insistence. From the outset, Vanderbilt involved his parents as partners and investors in many of his initial endeavors, sometimes even including their names on the customs certificates of enrollment denoting the owners and co-owners of various craft. Thus the senior Cornelius held a title interest in the *Swiftsure*, just as he would in several other vessels.

During the first year of Cornelius and Sophia's marriage, as the War of 1812 began to wind down in anticipation of the Treaty of Ghent (signed in December 1814), Cornelius moved in a significant manner to expand his presence in the newly reopening coastal trade. That March, Vanderbilt invested several thousand dollars for the building of a new sloop (the *Governor Wolcott*) and two schooners (the *Dread* and the *General Armstrong*). Each of these centerboard craft was constructed and launched by the master ship-builder James Day of Norwich, Connecticut, with whom Vanderbilt seems to have had a cordial association. Throughout the spring of 1814, Vanderbilt made several trips to Norwich. He usually traveled there on the *Swiftsure*, sailing the sloop up the East River, through Hell Gate, and thence into Long Island Sound. In summer, when the new craft were ready for launch, Vanderbilt himself took command of the *Dread*, and hired crews for the other new vessels along with the *Swiftsure*. All three of the new vessels took up residence on the Hudson River, where they embarked on runs between Albany and Manhattan.[7] (Croffut mentions that the *Dread* also did some duty coasting about Long Island Sound and New Jersey, "wherever a paying cargo could be found."[8] But the bulk of the *Dread*'s operations seems to have been on the Hudson, including making numerous excursions up the tributary Croton River to deliver raw grain and pick up ground flour from the Underhill Mill in Crotonville.)

One year later, in 1815, Cornelius invested in another vessel: a schooner especially designed for the coasting trade which he co-owned with her master, Captain John DeForest. Several years older than Cornelius, DeForest had extensive experience navigating between New York and various southern ports such as Charleston and Savannah. The schooner Vanderbilt and DeForest partnered on, the *Charlotte*, was named after one of Vanderbilt's sisters who also happened to be DeForest's wife. (Decades later, Cornelius was destined to beat Charlotte to the grave by just one day.) During an extensive voyage down the coast to Savannah and back during the autumn of 1815, DeForest taught Cornelius virtually everything he'd ever know about ocean navigation and sailing—the open sea posing far more complex problems than the relatively simple waters of the closed harbor, the Hudson River, or the Long Island Sound.[9]

Lane claims that Vanderbilt and DeForest made their first shared 1815 voyage to the South in a "flat bottomed schooner" (in other words, a scow utilizing a schooner rig on a blunt-ended hull) left over from the war effort. Lane says further that Vanderbilt acquired the scow from the United States Navy for $1,500.[10] But records show no such transaction, and Lane cites no reference. Also, it is unlikely that Vanderbilt and DeForest would embark upon such a significant voyage in a cheaply made craft when the new *Charlotte* lay ready. As a centerboard craft, the *Charlotte* (just like the rest of Vanderbilt's fleet save for the ancient periaguer) provided him and DeForest with the best of both worlds when it came to operation. With her board down, the *Charlotte* offered great stability while under sail. With her board up, she could go confidently into the same shallow water otherwise dominated by scows and periaugers.

Vanderbilt and DeForest most certainly had the board up that autumn when, on their way back from dropping freight at Savannah and Charleston, they stopped in the Virginia tidewater shallows of the Chesapeake Bay to fill the *Charlotte*'s hull with oysters. Five days later, they sold the oysters in New York at a smart profit: the entire trip netting $1,500 for ten days of voyaging. On the heels of this trip (this "shake-down cruise") Vanderbilt left the captaining of the *Charlotte* to DeForest, putting his partner in charge of the coastal run back and forth, down and up the coast, to and from southern ports. As for himself, he jumped between his other vessels but most often took the helm of the *Dread,* whether on the Hudson, the Sound, or the Jersey shore.

The days in his work week numbered seven. And the vessels in his fleet numbered five: the schooner *Charlotte* commanded by DeForest, the schooner *Dread* commanded most often by Vanderbilt himself, the schooner *General Armstrong* skippered by a paid captain out of Albany, the sloop *Governor Wolcott* commanded by a paid captain out of Manhattan, and the original little unnamed periauger still doing runs on demand between Stapleton and Whitehall Landing, sometimes with Vanderbilt's father at the helm, sometimes with a cousin doing the work.

Through 1815, Vanderbilt worked aggressively to build his business on all fronts. Personally, he became omnipresent throughout the waters around Manhattan, and especially on the Hudson River, where he gained fame (and the nickname *Commodore*) for making superb times between Albany and Manhattan's west side North River piers. Hudson River sailing was then, as now, a sometimes daunting and frustrating task: especially in the summer, when winds could be scarce. (Indeed, legend has it that Alexander Hamilton wrote an entire chapter of *The Federalist* while sitting on the deck of a Hudson River sloop loitering "in irons" near West Point, waiting for the wind.) The flushing, tidal nature of the Hudson (which in many ways is more a fjord and estuary, and an arm of the ocean, than a river) also complicated things. As the modern Hudson River historian Robert H. Boyle has observed of nineteenth-century sail commerce on the river:

> The duration of a trip depended upon a combination of winds and tide. The sloop *Caroline* once sailed the sixty miles from Manhattan to Fishkill in five hours. Then again, the same trip sometimes took four or five days. When wind and tide were unfavorable, there was nothing to do but drop anchor. The tide in the Hudson has its vagaries. In some places, the flood tide will "make" almost an hour earlier on one shore than the other, and in certain parts the ebb will "hang" longer. The winds offered a problem, particularly the northwest wind that roars through "Mother Cronk's Cove," the gap between Storm King and Crow's Nest mountains at the north gate of the Highlands. There, in 1824, the sloop *Neptune* capsized and thirty-five persons drowned.[11]

In response to the Hudson's vagaries, Vanderbilt seems to have quickly become a master of timing things well. When there was no wind, he waited for the tide that would take him the direction he desired. In the presence of any winds at all, even the most unfavorable, he tacked if necessary in order to make even the slowest progress against contrary breezes. The voyages he made up and down the river numbered in the hundreds, his hull filled variously with flagstone from quarries at Kingston and Saugerties, leather from Catskills tanneries, and produce from such ports as Albany and Newburgh. In many ways, Vanderbilt's schooners were better suited for the river trade than the sloop he also ran on these waters. "The schooners were not as good in windward work as the sloop, but with a fair or beam wind they were faster," noted Verplanck and Collyer. "The rig, however, soon commended itself, for the sloop with her long boom, tall mast, and heavy mainsail was difficult to handle at all times and especially in a blow and required a crew of six men to the schooner's four."[12]

One wonders exactly how many times Vanderbilt ran the *Dread* past a key site on the eastern river shore: a beautiful spot ninety miles north of Manhattan at Hyde Park, just above Krum Elbow and just below Bard Rock, where his grandson Frederick W. Vanderbilt would, in 1899, build a fifty-four-room Italianate-style mansion that still stands. One also wonders whether, as he cruised those same waters north or south, he imagined the Hudson River Railroad, which others would build in 1851 and he would eventually acquire, running down the eastern shore from Albany all the way to New York.

One thing he could not have missed in 1815, however, were the few stray steamboats, just about three among hundreds of sloops and schooners, but nevertheless loudly present. Each one of the steamers were either owned or controlled by the inventor Robert Fulton and his benefactor Robert R. Livingston, to whom the New York Legislature had granted the exclusive license for "navigating all boats that might be propelled by steam, on all waters within the territory or jurisdiction of the State." Though they did not rely on the wind for propulsion, the vessels were still nevertheless greatly influenced by the directions of wind and tide to the extent that their schedules (though more predictable than those of the sail vessels) were hardly fixed. The earliest steamboats, which most sailors dismissed as outlandish and unruly contraptions, were not designed to carry freight and so posed no immediate threat to the sloop and schooner trade.

Belching flames and smoke, those first steamers—boats such as the *Car of Neptune* (1809) and the *Paragon* (1810), both of them roughly 160 feet long and 50 feet wide amidships, with capacity for about a hundred paying passengers—did look and sound ridiculous. By day, their coarse mechanical clanking could be heard echoing through the normally tranquil Hudson Highlands long before they were sighted rounding river bends. By night, still just as loud, they looked like nautical hobgoblins lighted by their own vomit of live cinders as they pushed across dark waters. The first steamers were fueled with dry pine wood; this burned fast and hot and produced a furious combustion, the flames accompanied by sparks shooting considerably higher than the limits of the engine's short smoke pipe. The fires licked out of the little chimneys as the boats journeyed onward. Male passengers complained about the noise. Female passengers complained about the soot. And Hudson River sailors, in the moments when wind and tide combined to allow them to dash past the clamoring steamers, waved their hats in condescension. They sometimes also turned their backs, bent down, and revealed their bare rear ends to the dignified ladies and gentleman who had paid lofty prices to flirt with the future.

Cornelius sometimes made such a salute. Nevertheless, he was glad about the steamers because he was delighted to be rid of the ticket-buying public's petty requests and complaints. He was also happy to spend most of his time with his favorite companions: silent and profitable produce and merchandise.

5

ECONOMIC MAN

IN 1817, VANDERBILT WAS TWENTY-THREE, AND, ALTHOUGH NOT rich, he was more prosperous than most of his generation. Despite this, he was already a purely economic man of the type Charles Dickens would draw in the character of Ebenezer Scrooge some twenty-seven years later. No cult of idealism claimed him, as is often the case with energetic, up-and-coming youths. Like many other young entrepreneurs then and now, he worked conspicuously and diligently for his own personal profit, but never, so far as existing records and contemporary accounts show, for any greater good. Vanderbilt gave no alms to the poor, subscribed not a penny for the support of hospitals or foundling homes, and gave not a nickel to such organizations as the New York Humane Society (which at that time existed to serve the needs of destitute humans, rather than stray dogs and cats).

Vanderbilt was not, and never would be, one to need any confirmation of his own behavior by others. Sadly, however, in his fundamental lack of charity, young Vanderbilt was not unlike the bulk of the successful, middle-class businessmen of his day. In point of fact, the first few decades of the nineteenth century were a largely cynical and callous time in American history—a period of institutionalized harshness. It was in 1817 that a group of prominent New York merchants and professionals (many once having been the principal supports of such institutions as the New York Hospital and other worthy causes) officially and publicly began to rethink their charitable habits. Such previously generous philanthropists as DeWitt Clinton (now governor of the state), Thomas Eddy, and John Griscom took their cue in this from British reformers. In so doing, they succumbed to the rhetoric of several hard-nosed British social thinkers, most notably Thomas Robert Malthus, Jeremy Bentham, and the Scottish conservative Patrick Colquhoun.

Twenty years earlier, all three of those gentleman had been instrumental in the founding of the London Society for Bettering the Condition and Increasing the Comforts of the Poor. Despite the burden of its long-winded name, the London Society did not distribute charity but specialized in cutting off funds for social welfare. Malthus, Bentham, and Colquhoun believed that a distinct line must be drawn between the "deserving poor" (those facing hard times as a result of unfortunate histories) and "undeserving paupers," namely, the drunk, the lazy, and the whorish members of society for whom aid was considered a reprehensible act of facilitation. Another key underpinning the London Society's logic was the *presumption* (for lack of a more accurate term) that paupers outnumbered the deserving poor by a factor of about nine to one. In reform meetings and from church pulpits, politicians and clerics repeatedly cited this astonishing though unverifiable statistic, which soon became accepted as fact. In time, the public mind became convinced that a mere 10 percent of London's poor were the crippled and the orphaned, while 90 percent were degenerates. For every one person in London's slums who genuinely needed aid, popular wisdom said there were nine who required something else entirely: intolerance, punishment, and correction. As a corollary to this line of thinking, logic dictated that 90 percent of the charitable aid previously offered was superfluous. In turn, wallets closed.

For decades the London Society remained influential in the development and spread of such institutions as workhouses and debtors prisons. It was also influential, through its example, in New York and other American cities. By the end of 1817, Clinton, Eddy, and Griscom, joined by hundreds of other New Yorkers, had formed a clone organization on the banks of the Hudson: the Society for the Prevention of Pauperism (SPP).

Several months before the founding of the SPP, New York's Humane Society forlornly announced the startling result of recent research: no less than 15,000 men, women, and children—the equivalent of one-seventh of the city's population—had been "supported by public or private bounty and munificence" the previous winter.[1] Historians Edwin Burrows and Mike Wallace have eloquently described the SPP's point of view, expressed in response to the above data. In the London Society's grand tradition, the SPP said it believed that "willy-nilly benevolence" only made things worse. "Giving alms to the undeserving poor not only undermined their independence but also drove up taxes and sapped the prosperity of the entire community." Thus, "for their good as well as everyone else's . . . the SPP recommended that all paupers in the city be cut off from all public assistance forthwith."[2] Soon the Humane Society itself announced its intention to disband in the wake of its realization that the very act of giving charity had "a direct tendency to beget, among [the citizenry] habits of imprudence, indolence, dissipation and consequent pauperism."[3]

"Tough love" was in. Cruelty equaled kindness. Frugality equaled generosity. And all three were not only cheap, but easy. A few ministers sang out against the SPP's reverse logic, but most praised the organization. God himself, it seemed, was on the side of self-reliance. A generation later, Social Darwinists would express a similar viewpoint: The strong must be allowed to flourish and not be hamstrung by the needs of the clawing weak. Charles Darwin's *The Origin of Species* would not be published until 1859. Indeed, Darwin was but eight years old in 1817; he would not depart on the voyage of HMS *Beagle* until 1831. Nevertheless, the seeds of what was to become the Social Darwinism of Herbert Spencer (born in 1820), not to mention the nearly identical philosophy of the twentieth century's objectivist saint of selfishness, Ayn Rand, were evident in the grand pronouncements of the London Society and its New York equivalent, the SPP.

Even before the advent of the SPP, Cornelius Vanderbilt had not been a member of the Humane Society, nor was he on record as helping any other noble initiative on either Manhattan Island or Staten Island. A few notable men of the city, such as the venerable John Jacob Astor and the young Peter Cooper (an entrepreneur three years older than Vanderbilt and of equivalent wealth to him in 1817), repudiated the SPP, ignored the trend toward avarice, and continued their charitable giving, even expanding it in many areas to make up for some of their contemporaries' rapacity. But Vanderbilt did not; nor did he join the SPP. And a few years later, when the social wind changed and charity again became fashionable, he would steadfastly refuse to alter his course. On the sea of life, as on the Hudson River, the Jersey coast, or Long Island Sound, Vanderbilt was completely capable of sailing either with or against whatever breezes or tides prevailed. And the star by which he would continually steer was named Cornelius.

Had Vanderbilt harbored half an interest in cultivating social relationships with other rising entrepreneurs of his generation, he might have joined the SPP or the various other fraternal and trade organizations such as existed at the time. But he did not. Nor did he give any contributions whatsoever to such high-profile (and therefore prestige-enhancing) religious outreach organizations as were prevalent in Manhattan: the New York Mission Society (founded in 1812), the New York Marine Mission Society (founded in 1817), or the Port of New York Society for Promoting the Gospel Among Seamen (founded in 1818). Had Vanderbilt desired respectability and recognition as a gentleman slowly rising in the ranks of New York's waterfront entrepreneurs, he most certainly would have been conspicuous in his support of religious outreach along the waterfront no matter how cynical that support might have been. Not a few other owners of sloops, schooners, and ferries were themselves, like Vanderbilt, active participants in those waterfront vices which the New York Marine Mission Society and Port of New York Society for Promoting the Gospel Among Seamen sought to reform. However, that small fact did not stop the vessel owners from at least making a show of being on the side of the angels.

Young Vanderbilt, whatever else one might say about him, was not a hypocrite. He made no pretense at good works; and never pretended to be anything other than what he was: a sharp and versatile player in the harbor and coastal waters, a cut-throat competitor, a tireless worker, a reliable contractor, and a prodigiously promiscuous adulterer. As Vanderbilt himself clearly understood, what made his fortunes rise was not a reputation as a good man and a worthy citizen. No, his escalating income derived from a reputation as someone who could be counted upon for timely deliveries of freight at bargain prices. The farmers, quarrymen, tanners, and others who trusted him with their cargoes cared not a whit about Vanderbilt's personal habits, the extent of his philanthropy, or the condition of his soul. They cared only that he promised and delivered steady service at steep discounts. Although his reputation for driving hard bargains was undeniable, so too was his reputation for standing by his word, honoring his agreements, and doing everything he had promised.

Thus, Vanderbilt's boats were always full and busy, and his books always in the black. On the rare occasions when freight contracts became scarce, he improvised. Whenever a more profitable opportunity than the simple moving of freight appeared, he seized it. For several weeks each spring, Vanderbilt hired several New Jersey men to fish for shad during the annual spawning run up the Hudson River. During those weeks, he would use the *Dread* to make regular trips to downtown dockside fish markets to unload, then rush back to his nets on poles across from Washington Heights, off the coast of Edgewater, New Jersey, to resupply. More nets and men, allied with the *Charlotte,* provided shad for the Philadelphia market through a similarly brisk business on the lower Delaware River. Vanderbilt and DeForest also occasionally used the *Charlotte* to service their own interests as sporadic wholesalers of farm produce. During early summer, they'd purchase early cash crops of corn, melons, and apples in the south and bring them to the New York market for sale to wholesalers at attractive prices, well before northeastern crops were ready for harvest. Additionally, Vanderbilt frequently deployed his old original periauger as a lorry delivering rum, beer, and other desirables for sale to the crews of newly arrived packet ships at anchor in New York Harbor. The same periauger ferried men from ships' crews to the wharf, from there to access the saloons and brothels of downtown.

The further the United States moved away from the diminishment caused by the War of 1812, the faster the wheels of the

American economy turned and the better the coasting and river trade became. By 1817, the name Vanderbilt was known in ports up and down the northeastern coast from Providence all the way to Savannah. Anyone standing back and considering the young man's prospects would have thought it likely that he would either continue to expand his interests in coastal and river sail commerce or commence investing in larger sailing vessels capable of ocean passages. Either or both of these tacks would have made great sense, and would have led to continued success for some time to come. Although steamboats would increasingly make inroads, sloops and schooners were (thanks to a rapidly expanding economy) to be quite profitably deployed on northeastern rivers and coastal waters for the next sixty years: the duration of Vanderbilt's lifetime. Much the same can be said with regard to transatlantic travel.

As early as 1819, the packet *Savanah* would be outfitted with a small auxiliary steam engine. But there would be no major ocean-going steamships until the simultaneous maiden voyages of the relatively inefficient side-wheelers *Great Eastern* and *Sirius* in 1838. Following this, the first steam-screw vessel (the *Great Britain*) would not be launched until 1845. And not until the advent of steam turbine engines at the turn of the twentieth century would steam ships totally and irrevocably replace sailing vessels on the high seas. Looking forward from 1817, new transcontinental square riggers and brigantines would continue to be built and launched well into the 1880s, several years after the Commodore breathed his last. If Cornelius had decided to take himself and his family into the ocean-going sail trade, the Vanderbilts' financial fate would have resembled that of such prosperous New York clans as the Aspinwalls, Howlands, Bayards, Griswolds, and Delanos—all of whom made fortunes in the China trade during the next generation. Thus, either by staying coastal or going global, Vanderbilt could have built considerable wealth in sailing ships, and he might have been thinking about doing so until mid-1817, when a move by his brother-in-law, DeForest, gave him cause to reconsider.

In the spring of that year DeForest asked Vanderbilt to buy his interest in the *Charlotte*. DeForest told Cornelius he'd made a decision to accept an offer from the recently retired New York governor Daniel Tompkins—the Federalist founder of Tompkinsville on Staten Island, immediately to the north of Stapleton, and the country's newly sworn vice president under James Monroe. Tompkins had asked DeForest to sign on as the first skipper of Tompkins's *Nautilus,* a steam ferry running between Whitehall Landing and the Staten Island ports of Tompkinsville, Stapleton, and Clifton. As chairman of a firm called the Richmond Turnpike Authority, Tompkins had recently negotiated a license from Livingston and Fulton to operate the *Nautilus* in New York Harbor. As DeForest explained to Vanderbilt, the money Tompkins had offered DeForest to make a few easy daily runs across the harbor in the *Nautilus* was nearly double what DeForest had been making as a partner captaining the far-flung, highly speculative, and often grueling voyages of the *Charlotte*.

Vanderbilt could not argue with his brother-in-law's logic. He agreed to purchase DeForest's half interest in the *Charlotte* for approximately $700. Thereafter, he hired a captain who, like DeForest, had experience in coastal sailing as far south as Georgia. Throughout the balance of 1817, advertisements in various newspapers and maritime trade publications across the eastern seaboard continued to promote the *Charlotte*'s availability as well as that of Vanderbilt's other vessels for loads large and small. Vanderbilt continued to captain the *Dread,* at the same time overseeing the books and schedules of the other vessels. Concurrently, however, he appears to have been weighing the value of continuing to run things as they were, without the benefit of having DeForest as a capable and trusted second manager on whom he could depend, or closing out his interests, liquidating, and setting off in a new professional direction.

Analyzing Vanderbilt's position in late 1817, the biographers Croffut, Smith, and Lane have all speculated about the impact of the *Nautilus* on Cornelius's own ferry business between Staten Island and Manhattan. As Lane wrote: "Revenue from Cornele's periaugers took a sickening drop, the trend of the times was clear. B'ilers, as Cornele always called them, were proving more powerful than wind."[4] But, as previously mentioned, Vanderbilt never ran a scheduled ferry service between the island and the city prior to Tompkins's venture. Further, by 1817, the few runs that Cornelius's old periauger still made along that route represented only the smallest sliver of his overall trade. Add to this the fact that steamer travel remained, at this time, a luxury for the wealthy. Add also the fact that virtually no freight was carried on the steamers, so much of their space being reserved for their pine wood fuel. Thus it seems unlikely that the *Nautilus* put much of a dent into Cornelius's bottom line, just as it was not so that other steamers on other waters were affecting him.

Nevertheless, Vanderbilt did, evidently, take stock of the slowly increasing number of steam vessels along his various routes. As well, he appears to have pondered (as amazing as this might sound, and despite his later claims of having always been a maniac on the subject of moneymaking) the extent of his own ambition. As the end of 1817 approached, Cornelius had some $9,000 in ready cash on hand. He also held another $7,000 in the value of his vessels. Keeping tabs on the various boats, captains, and crews, and keeping those captains and crews honest, appears to have been a logistical problem in the absence of DeForest, who had previously shared duty with Cornelius in doing diligence on the combined Vanderbilt operations. Vanderbilt could be in only so many places at once. With schooners and sloops afloat from New England to the southern coasts and as far north inland as Albany, he seems to have been suddenly and quite uncharacteristically overwhelmed by management logistics, unsure of whether he should grow or maintain his present operation.

In addition to the logistical burden, Cornelius was apparently unsure of the weight of the threat posed by the steamboats. As he reportedly told DeForest, he had no firm grip on just how fast steam would emerge as serious competition. The wild card was technology, and how quickly it might improve to Vanderbilt's disadvantage. Should steam develop and sail rapidly become obsolete, Vanderbilt did not want to be left holding a large interest in antiquated and relatively valueless boats. On the other hand, steamboating was not necessarily a business on which he personally wanted to embark. Cornelius's own personal knowledge of steamboating was limited to having ridden as a passenger on a single Livingston/Fulton boat, round trip, between Manhattan and Albany. As well, he considered the hefty commissions (such as those which Tompkins had been forced to pay as a licensing fee to Livingston and Fulton) as barriers to entry for mere mortals such as himself. Additionally, he did not like the limits placed on those expensive Livingston licenses. God save Tompkins if the *Nautilus* ever strayed anywhere but Staten Island and Whitehall.[5]

Vanderbilt pondered all these things as 1817 wound down and Christmas approached. What he told Sophia of these meditations, we do not know.

6

MR. OGDEN AND MR. GIBBONS

Robert Fulton and his benefactor Livingston had by no means been the first innovators to succeed in creating a steam-powered vessel. As early as 1787, John Fitch (born in 1743) ran a simple steamer on the Delaware River near Philadelphia, launching her before an audience that included George Washington and other delegates to the Constitutional Convention. A year later, Fitch launched the first paddle-wheel steamer—a sixty-foot vessel capable of carrying thirty passengers. He later put this to successful commercial use as a ferry between Philadelphia and Burlington, New Jersey. In time, Fitch became so respected for his invention that the New York State Legislature granted him an exclusive license to run steamboats on New York waters. This license was repealed in March 1798, when the same legislature transferred the privilege to one of its own: the well-connected Robert Livingston, then busily funding Fulton's work.

Another American inventor, James Rumsey (born in 1743), also fabricated a fairly elementary steamer, one of even less sophisticated design than Fitch's simple first boat, which he launched on the Potomac in 1787 but never used commercially. A little later, in 1804, New Jersey's John Stevens (born in 1749) built a small prototype steamboat equipped with twin screw propellers which he named *Little Juliana* (after a daughter) and operated on the Hudson River, with limited success, before her boiler joints began blowing out. Five years later, Stevens launched the *Phoenix,* a paddle-wheel steamboat he deployed on a voyage from New York City to Philadelphia, the first ocean trip ever made by a steamboat, before using her as a ferry between Manhattan and Hoboken.

An attorney as well as an engineer, Stevens had long lobbied Congress to establish standard patent law for the United States. This he succeeded in getting on the books in 1790. Subsequently, after protracted wrangling and charges and countercharges between the three inventors, Fitch, Rumsey, and Stevens each received precisely stated patents for their own unique vessels; thus, no one owned a broad monopoly patent on the concept of steam navigation. Later on, when Fulton had his boat, he and Livingston were granted a similarly singular patent on Fulton's unique design, but not a monopoly patent.

But Livingston's and Fulton's monopoly had nothing to do with patents, at least not when it came to the lucrative waters of New York. "On April 6, 1808," writes Livingston biographer George Dangerfield, "the New York legislature extended [Livingston's and Fulton's] privilege up to a limit of thirty years and imposed thumping penalties on anyone who dared, without a license from the monopoly, to navigate by steam upon any of the waters of New York. . . . [Then] on April 9, 1811, the New York legislature passed a monopoly act even more stringent in its penalties than the one enacted in 1808. And in April, 1811, the legislature of the Territory of Orleans conferred upon Livingston and Fulton privileges fully as extensive as those granted by New York. Thus they controlled two of the greatest commercial waterways in the United States." Elsewhere, the states of Connecticut, Ohio, Massachusetts, Georgia, New Hampshire, Vermont, and Pennsylvania followed the example of New York, passing laws that conferred Livingston-like steamboat exclusivity upon their own favored sons.

At the same time, the state of New York announced that it claimed control of all water to the low-water mark of the Jersey side of the Lower New York Bay, effectively extending Fulton's and Livingston's domain all the way to Sandy Hook and virtually closing the western Jersey shore to steam navigation not approved by the Livingston cabal. In 1809, John Stevens had already found himself banished from his New York/Hoboken run. Unwilling to fight the Fulton-Livingston monopoly, and unwilling to pay a hefty licensing fee, Stevens instead retreated from New York waters, to return only after others had broken Livingston's iron grasp. (Stevens subsequently ran the *Phoenix* on the Delaware between Philadelphia and Trenton; he also experimented with America's first railroad in New Jersey, obtaining the first U.S. railroad charter in 1815.)

Others, however, chose to fight the monopoly head on. As Dangerfield writes:

> The litigation reached its climax in 1811, when twenty-one enterprising gentlemen of Albany started a rival steamboat, the *Hope*, upon the Albany–New York run, and threatened to follow her up with a sister ship, not inaptly to be called the *Perseverance*. The monopolists, of course, fought back in the courts, and in March, 1812, New York's [Chancery Court] Chief Justice James

Kent issued a permanent injunction against the *Hope*. Kent's very learned opinion may be reduced to this simple proposition: either the New York steamboat acts violated the federal Constitution or they did not. A stern supporter of states' rights, Kent ruled that they did not. Obviously, he said, where a national and a state law are aimed against each other, the state law must yield. But this was not the case here, since all commerce within a state was exclusively within the power of that state. Supported by Kent, one of the most respected jurists in the nation, the monopoly had certainly become respectable.[1]

Amid all this, the New Jersey/New York steamboat trade quickly became quite complicated, Byzantine, and tempestuous—all because of the New York monopoly. During 1812, the New Jersey Legislature (impatient with the idea of the Fulton-Livingston monopoly's inhibiting water commerce along the eastern New Jersey coast) authorized any citizen of New Jersey whose steamboat might be seized in New York to fight back by confiscating any New York steamer found in New Jersey waters. A year later, the New Jersey Legislature went a step further by granting outgoing governor Aaron Ogden (born in 1756) an exclusive license to operate in New Jersey waters: this license being a virtual clone of the exclusive right the New York Legislature had voted Livingston and Fulton in the adjacent state.[2] Subsequently, Livingston's *Raritan* ceased its daily runs between Manhattan and New Brunswick on the Raritan River. In turn, Ogden's *Sea Horse*, which he operated in partnership with one Daniel Dod, tempted fate with incursions into New York Harbor just as far as Bedloe's Island, where Ogden transshipped his passengers to a periauger for the quick hop across the water to Whitehall Landing.

Ogden was a colorful and controversial character. Born in what is now Elizabeth, New Jersey, he graduated from the College of

New Jersey (now Princeton University) in 1773. Thereafter, he was variously a soldier in the colonial army (including service at Yorktown), an attorney, an active Federalist who eventually served as a clerk of Essex County, a United States senator, and a governor. Headstrong and pompous, Ogden made his share of enemies in public life: a habit that came back to haunt him. Lane writes: "As Governor, Ogden had made himself obnoxious to his political opponents, and the latter were willing to swallow their state pride in order to secure personal revenge. In 1815 the New Jersey Legislature repealed the monopoly granted to Ogden, pressure being used upon recalcitrant Republicans, one of whom was dragged by force into the chamber to vote."[3]

Not to be outflanked or ruffled, Ogden, his own short-lived New Jersey monopoly in tatters, retaliated by going to Albany to take on the Fulton-Livingston monopoly in the New York Legislature. Perhaps it was because of the death of Robert Livingston in 1813 and the subsequent demise of Robert Fulton in 1815 that Ogden was able to pose a formidable threat to their interests. Although Ogden did not succeed in overturning the legislation enabling the exclusive rights enjoyed by the Fulton-Livingston heirs, he did surprise his antagonists by getting his question on the docket and by coming within one vote of achieving victory. Afraid that Ogden might try again, and next time do better, Robert Livingston's brother John now decided to do business with Ogden and to grant him, at a low price, an exclusive license to operate the *Sea Horse* between Elizabeth, on Newark Bay, and Whitehall Landing, via the Kill van Kull and Upper New York Bay. Thus Livingston diffused Ogden's threat while securing for himself a staunch ally. (John had in 1808 purchased from his brother and Fulton, for one-sixth his gross receipts, the exclusive right to navigate steamboats from lower Manhattan to Staten Island.)

What would make things complicated for John Livingston, as well as for the other heirs of Robert Livingston and Robert Fulton (indeed for all who sought to benefit from state-granted exclusive rights to local waters) was Aaron Ogden's complex and tumultuous partnership with another steamboater, one Thomas Gibbons.

Born in 1757, Thomas Gibbons came from old southern planter stock. Thomas's father, Joseph, and Joseph's brother, William, were two scions of a rice-planter who owned a large plantation in South Carolina. Thomas's mother shared a similar pedigree. During the decade commencing 1752, Joseph Gibbons acquired (through purchase and royal grant) a large rice plantation, Mulberry Hill, consisting of several thousand acres in the tidal range between the Ogeechee and Savannah rivers in coastal Georgia. It was here that Thomas, the fifth youngest of six children, was born and raised. When the father died in 1769, he left a prosperous operation worked by 108 slaves. Gibbons was eighteen, finished with private school at Charleston, and deep into the study of law under a Savannah barrister when the American Revolution erupted.[4]

Unlike the majority of his family who fervently and boldly supported the colonial cause, Thomas and one of his brothers-in-law remained Tories throughout the hostilities, and even went so far as to sign formal oaths of allegiance to King George III in 1779. (More than one historian has speculated that the Toryism of Thomas and his brother-in-law, Nathaniel Hall, paired with the outspoken revolutionary politics of so many other Gibbonses, represented a contrivance to assure stability for the considerable property of the Gibbons clan, no matter which side, the loyalists or the revolutionaries, proved victorious in the end. If so, the scheme did not work.)

After the surrender of the British in 1782, Thomas Gibbons, Nathaniel Hall, and several other Savannah worthies found themselves arrested by Colonel James Jackson who, though born in Great Britain in 1757, was an avowed patriot. Jackson, in turn, handed his prisoners over to the authorities, who put them on trial for treason. Eventually the accused were duly convicted and their estates confiscated. Magistrate court records indicate that on January 11, 1783, supported by siblings who had been conspicuous patriots, Thomas petitioned the Georgia House of Assembly with a request that he be readmitted to citizenship and that his name be removed from the list of those whose property would be taken. Six months later, the House of Assembly approved this request, with the stipulation that the mansion and lands at Mulberry Hill were still to be confiscated, and that for fourteen years Thomas could not vote, hold office, or practice law. Evidently a diligent negotiator, Thomas in short order whittled the fourteen-year prohibition down to four. By 1787, he'd been elected mayor of Savannah. He would be elected three more times (1791–1792, 1794–1795, and 1799–1801), and assemble a new rice plantation which he shared with his older brother, William. Whitehall, as it was called, consisted of 10,640 acres on the banks of the Savannah River and on Argyle Island, in the middle of the river.[5] Perhaps as a sign of his wealth, Gibbons became rotund: more than three hundred pounds by some accounts.

Meanwhile, the house at Mulberry Hill had been given to Colonial General Anthony Wayne ("Mad" Anthony Wayne). Born in 1745, Wayne was a Pennsylvanian who, after distinguishing himself in the upper New York theater during the Revolutionary War, had been instrumental in breaking up the British alliance with Georgia's Native American population. Mulberry Hill was his reward. Of course, Thomas Gibbons naturally harbored a dislike for Wayne, but a man he disliked even more was his fellow Savannah attorney, Colonel Jackson, who'd arrested him and put him on trial. Thus, when Wayne chose to oppose Jackson in the latter's bid for reelection to the House of Representatives in the autumn of 1791, Gibbons not only backed Wayne but ran his campaign.

Wayne won election to the House of Representatives, and Jackson, who had also been running both for re-election as national delegate and for election to the Georgia State Legislature's lower house, won the latter vote. A few hours after the winners were announced, Jackson challenged the results of his contest against Wayne, implied voter fraud orchestrated by Gibbons, and produced verifiable evidence of same. Shortly, he served on an investigating committee in the Georgia House of Representatives which served articles of impeachment against Superior Court Judge Henry Osborne, a Gibbons crony who evidently had facilitated and tolerated fraud in several districts. The Georgia Senate quickly convicted Osborne: He was stripped of his title and his position as a local magistrate, forbidden to hold public office for a period of thirty years, fined $600, and disbarred.

Jackson, meanwhile, proceeded to the nation's capital, where he presented the results of the Georgia deliberations and made an impassioned speech before the bar of the House of Representatives, asking them to abjure Wayne's credentials. During his remarks, Jackson minced no words in describing Gibbons as a person "whose soul is faction, whose life has been a scene of political corruption, who never could be easy under Government."[6] In the end, the House of Representatives resolved that Wayne was not a duly elected member; however, a second vote that would have seated Jackson failed by one vote. Although not backed up by newspaper reporting or other contemporary accounts, oft-repeated folklore has it that after Jackson's return to Savannah in April 1792, Gibbons cited the colonel's words on the House floor and challenged him to a duel. According to legend, the two men met with seconds on a barren strip of land. Shots were fired, none hitting. If the story is true, one wonders about Jackson's eyesight, given Gibbons's heft. Six months after the duel, Gibbons again faced charges of voter fraud following his election (over a Jackson ally) to represent Chatham County in the Georgia State Senate. Gibbons was eventually ousted from the seat by a vote of the Senate on account of those charges. Jackson, meanwhile, went on to become governor of the state.

Through the following nine years, Gibbons continued to practice law and run his various plantations. These eventually grew to include the large rice farms Rosedew and Long Payment in Chatham County and Tusculum in Scriben County, as well as an inherited rice plantation in South Carolina and Schooley's Mountain in Georgia's Morris County. Gibbons also invested in real estate in the city of Savannah, and with his wife, Ann, raised their children. Amid all this, much intramural political skirmishing continued to mark his life. Finally, in 1801, perhaps as an effort to escape the malaria that plagued the Georgia tidewater region during the summers (a disease that had taken several of his children), Gibbons followed the example of numerous other planters by establishing a summer-home in New Jersey, at Elizabeth. Here he and his wife along with his surviving daughter and two sons (Ann, Thomas Heyward, and William) could enjoy the season with minimal risk of disease. In time, Gibbons began spending more of his year in New Jersey, leaving the tending of his Georgia properties to relatives (and perhaps hoping to leave his contentious reputation behind him in the South).

Gibbons's considerable estate on Newark Bay at Elizabeth was called Rose Hill. He also invested in lands in and about Amboy, and in other nearby towns and villages. Eventually he owned three additional New Jersey farms, these named Wheat Patch Farm, Rising Sun Farm, and Howard's Farm, along with numerous lots and houses in New Brunswick and elsewhere. Gibbons also owned the Union Hotel in Elizabeth, an old tavern-inn on the Raritan River at New Brunswick, and stagecoach businesses and turnpikes, such as the Morris Union Turnpike, connecting New Brunswick with Trenton on the Delaware River.[7] Through the first decade or so of the nineteenth century, Gibbons made enormous profits from his southern operations that needed reinvesting. Indeed, this alone might have explained his move to New Jersey since he already owned so much of his native Chatham County in Georgia.

During the early teens, he became involved in the rising new steamboat trade. Initially, he did so in partnership with Aaron Ogden—the former New Jersey governor who, after much agitation, had been granted exclusive license by John Livingston to operate his steamboat *Sea Horse* between Elizabeth and Whitehall Landing. Initially, Gibbons's arrangement with Ogden called for the former to supply steamboat service between Brunswick and Gibbons's Rose Hill Point on the waterfront at Elizabeth, where passengers traveling to or from Manhattan would be transshipped between Gibbons's steamer and the *Sea Horse*. In this way, Gibbons and Ogden together took up the business formerly possessed by Livingston's *Raritan*, which had been absent from New Jersey waters since 1813.

As has been described, both Gibbons and Ogden were strong personalities: men possessed of massive egos backed up by a very large measure of worldly success. Each not only had a reputation for over-achieving but also for truculence and not playing nicely with others. Tensions over schedules, shares in profits, basic house-keeping matters of passenger comfort, and, ultimately, control, erupted early in their relationship. Each man was a natural leader, neither a natural follower. Both men were accustomed to giving orders rather than taking them. As well, with one having been a noted Tory and the other a noted fighter for the Revolution, they could not even claim a shared history of national loyalty.

The natural tension between the two was exacerbated when Ogden found himself drawn into a family feud. During the early years of Gibbons's partnership with Ogden, he made himself notorious with local worthies (as well as his wife and other family members) when he set himself up with a bachelor apartment near Rose Hill and there began entertaining young women. Gibbons's new hobby eventually led not only to a paternity suit but also to nasty squabbling within his own clan. In time, Gibbons's son-in-law, one John Trumbull, sought to intercede with Gibbons and force him to end his philandering. For this, Trumbull found himself disinherited along with his wife. Thereafter, Trumbull (wisely or not) hired none other than Ogden as attorney to represent their interests and force Gibbons to change his will.

The decision proved disastrous for the Trumbulls, who remained disinherited, for Ogden, who thereafter found himself in perpetual (and losing) warfare with his former partner, and ultimately for state-sanctioned steamboat monopoly as a concept. In the short term, Gibbons printed a handbill denouncing Ogden and Trumbull both as having spread slanders about him. Going to Ogden's house, Gibbons nailed one of the handbills to his door along with a note: "I hope you are prepared to explain yourself of your wanton interference in a case so delicate. If you stand mute I shall judge you as pleading guilty, and treat you as a convict." The note went on to challenge Ogden to a duel. Ogden's response was to sue Gibbons as a trespasser, and to win a state indictment of him for proposing the duel, the practice of dueling having been outlawed in New Jersey several years before. (According to Lane, Ogden also had Gibbons arrested and briefly incarcerated on a technicality arising from a protested note of tiny indebtedness, with which Gibbons's only connection was through third-party endorsement. The arrest was meant as an annoying jab on the part of Ogden, but more than annoying Gibbons, it infuriated him.)

In the long term, Gibbons's major response to all this was far more damaging and complex than merely disinheriting a daughter and son-in-law, printing a pamphlet about Ogden, or proposing guns at sundown. No, what Gibbons decided to do in late 1817 was go into direct competition with Ogden, running his own steamboat from Elizabeth to New York. Towards this end, immediately after the New Year in 1818, Gibbons approached John Livingston about acquiring a license for such an operation, only to be informed that Livingston's agreement with Ogden guaranteed Ogden's exclusivity in the waters between Elizabeth and Manhattan. After chewing on this for a month or two, Gibbons decided that he would go head-to-head with Ogden and Livingston by operating a competing steamboat service; he claimed his right to do so under the Commerce Clause of the United States Constitution, which gave the federal (rather than state) government authority to regulate interstate commerce.

Given the fierceness with which the Livingston-Fulton interests had gone after other would-be challengers to their franchise, and given Gibbons's knowledge of Ogden's temperament, he must have known that he was in for a major battle. But Gibbons, whatever his other shortcomings, had never been one to flinch in the face of a fight. That spring, he slowly set about preparing his little side-wheeler *Stoudinger* (named after the prominent steamboat designer and boatwright Charles Stoudinger, who had died in 1816, but far more familiarly known as *Mouse* or *Mouse of the Mountain* due to its diminutive size) for its first Manhattan run. At the same time, he began searching for a captain who was just as pugnacious and tenacious as he: a man well versed in the waters of New York Harbor, un-intimidated by the power of the Livingston-Fulton forces, and willing to make a bet on an uncertain future.

7

MOUSE AND *BELLONA*

ONE WONDERS WHETHER OR NOT GIBBONS OBSERVED TWO
items that made headlines in February 1818 just as he was contemplating whom he could get who might have both the maritime skills
and the personal tenacity to join him in opposing the monopoly. The
first item, which appeared in the New York *Evening Post* of February
12, noted the heroics of a young man named Vanderbilt one day earlier, in Upper New York Bay. It appeared that the *York,* a Livingston
steamer servicing Jersey City from Manhattan, had gotten trapped
in a vicious northeaster. She wound up unable to achieve the Jersey
City pier and, worse, being swept toward the Narrows by the wash of
tide and wind. According to the *Post,* "waves beat knee deep over the
vessel" and the passengers found themselves in grave danger. "During the most violent part of the gale, and while the steamboat was
drifting between Bedloe's Island and Robins' Reef, at the mercy of
the seas, Mr. Vanderbilt's packet ferry boat *Dread* went off to her assistance, and succeeded, at great risk, in taking from her 12 passengers, and landing them at Whitehall."[1]

Less than a week later, the *Post* chronicled what happened when the brig *Neptune,* returning from Jamaica with a cargo that included more than $400,000 in currency, ran aground at Sandy Hook: "Much credit is due to Mr. C. Vanderbilt, of the packet ferry-boat *Dread,* for his exertions in getting the specie from on board the ship *Neptune* (ashore at the Hook) which he accomplished yesterday afternoon, at great hazard. Notwithstanding there had been two other boats there during the afternoon, nothing effectual was done until Mr. Vanderbilt ran alongside the ship, and took out of her $406,000 in boxes which he afterwards put safely on board [a federal revenue cutter]."[2]

Within days of the second article, Vanderbilt received a summons to come and see Gibbons at his Elizabeth estate. Although he did not know Gibbons personally, young Vanderbilt (nearing twenty-four) almost surely knew of Gibbons by reputation. Everyone did. After all, Gibbons was one of the richest and most prominent men on the East Coast—indeed, one of the richest in the country. Normally unimpressed by anyone, Vanderbilt appears to have been duly and totally impressed with Gibbons. "I think he [Gibbons] was one of the strongest minded men I ever was acquainted with," Vanderbilt told a reporter years after Gibbons was dead. Then he added, as if describing himself: "I never knew any man that had any control over him."[3]

Indeed, Vanderbilt must have seen something truly remarkable in Gibbons, for after just one meeting he agreed to come into the employ of Gibbons's firm, the Union Line of steamboats, for a pittance of what he'd been making on his own as a proprietor of sloops and schooners. As has been indicated, Vanderbilt had been toying with the idea of divesting his sail fleet since late 1817. Once he signed on with Gibbons, he promptly made good on that notion. Liquidating his sloop and schooner collection, he realized some $7,000, which he tucked away with his $9,000 in savings.

Vanderbilt kept only one old periauger, which either he, his father, or his brother Jacob ran sporadically between Staten Island and Manhattan. At the same time, Vanderbilt swapped an estimated $3,000 in gross profit per year for terms from Gibbons that, on their face, seemed far less attractive.

According to an agreement drawn up between Gibbons and Vanderbilt on June 26, 1818, Gibbons was to pay Vanderbilt $60 per month along with half the net proceeds from the bar aboard the *Mouse*. Gibbons was to provide the bar furniture, and Vanderbilt was to preserve the furniture and make the whole good at the end of the season. Vanderbilt was to perform all duties required of him as commander of the craft.[4] The steamer was to make stops at two New Jersey points of departure (New Brunswick and Gibbons's Rising Sun landing at Elizabeth), thence running from Elizabeth to Whitehall Landing, above the Battery, and back. At New Brunswick and Elizabeth, the steamer would connect with stagecoach operations in which Gibbons had an interest, the New Brunswick coach connecting through to Trenton, which in turn gave access to ferries going to Philadelphia.

As another part of the deal, Vanderbilt and his family moved from their apartment on the second floor of an unlovely house on Renwik Street, Stapleton, to a rundown riverfront tavern-inn, known as Halfway House, which Gibbons owned at New Brunswick. Here they could not only live rent-free but also make extra money. Gibbons's charge to Cornelius and Sophia was that they should improve the dingy place and make it back into a going-concern, managing it themselves and giving him 20 percent of the net receipts. Arthur D. Howden Smith, who had spoken to some of Sophia's daughters about their mother's recollection of the tavern, said that when Sophia first inspected the property she found it to be "a mess of filth and vermin."

According to Smith, Sophia (undaunted) "cleaned and fumi-gated the tavern from cellar to attic" and got it into shape in short order.[5] In doing so, she seems to have set a trend. Going forward, Sophia did most all of the work of the tavern: cleaning, cooking, and serving. She also seems to have been the one who would, through the coming years, actually run the business of the place (including purchasing food and liquor wholesale, and keeping all the books) while Cornelius was busy with boats. In time, Sophia renamed the tavern-inn Bellona Hall, and established it as a most profitable appendage to Gibbons's Union Line. Several of the older Vanderbilt children were eventually pressed into service at Bellona Hall, and a few others were born on the premises. Pregnant most of the time, Sophia nevertheless managed to hold both Bellona Hall, and her family, together.

Cornelius began his regular runs on the *Mouse* in July 1818. As has been previously mentioned, the *Stoudinger*'s nicknames of *Mouse* or *Mouse of the Mountain* derived from her modest size: a mere 25 tons. Other steam craft operating in and around New York averaged five times that tonnage. The latest, most state-of-the-art steamboats weighed even more. In addition to being small, the *Mouse* was rick-ety and unsophisticated. On the other hand, Vanderbilt was able to run the *Mouse* with just one deckhand, whereas seven or eight were required for larger boats. As well, the *Mouse* used a smaller boiler, and thus demanded less fuel than did her larger competitors. How-ever, when patrons complained of crowded conditions as compared to those on the comparatively luxurious Ogden boats, Vanderbilt had to speak to Gibbons about reducing prices. In short order, the discounts that became necessary to lure passengers onto the clanky and puny *Mouse* completely eliminated the healthy margin previ-ously afforded by the crew and fuel economies. Therefore, within weeks of his taking over the helm of the *Mouse*, Vanderbilt convinced Gibbons of the need for investment in a larger, more comfortable, and more competitive steamer.

Built on a fast schedule and launched in the early autumn of 1818, the *Bellona* was everything the *Mouse* was not. Vanderbilt designed her himself with the help of a naval architect and a mechanical engineer commissioned by Gibbons, all three men keeping in mind passenger comfort and efficient operation. Large and impressive, the *Bellona* weighed in at 142 tons. Her engine, all copper, had been built at New York's Allaire Works under the direct supervision of James P. Allaire, a prominent New York City brass founder and an early protégé of Robert Fulton who was widely considered one of the best mechanical engineers at work in American steamboating. While the engine was being built, Vanderbilt made regular trips to Allaire's factory at 466 Cherry Street for consultations. In this way, a long partnership was begun. Until his retirement in 1850, Allaire would supply engines for numerous Vanderbilt-commissioned vessels.

The *Bellona*'s hull was constructed by Jacob Bell of the firm Brown & Bell, in New York. Vanderbilt made frequent visits to the Brown & Bell shipyard, on the East River at the foot of Stanton Street, to scrutinize and consult on the progress of the work. Again, a long-term partnership formed. Brown & Bell would create the hulls for many, but by no means all, Vanderbilt steamers through the coming decades. It says something about the lingering dominance of sail over steam, however, that large clipper ships would comprise the bulk of the Brown & Bell's work for the next sixty years, steam craft remaining a modest sideline for the firm.

As soon as the *Bellona* hit the water, Vanderbilt took the helm and left the *Mouse* in the command of a subordinate. Both boats made alternating runs between New Brunswick and Manhattan with stops at Elizabeth in between. Several times a day, Cornelius cruised past his Stapleton birthplace as he ran up and down the

Kill van Kull between Newark Bay and Upper New York Bay. Proceeding outbound from Elizabeth on Newark Bay via the Arthur Kill to Amboy, he'd pass the little ferry where, as a boy, he'd moved carts and horses from Staten Island to the Jersey mainland for his father during their old salvaging days. From that point, he'd head north up the Raritan River to New Brunswick, there to deposit and collect passengers, and then turn round for the inbound journey back to Elizabeth and Manhattan.

Early on, in the course of Cornelius's and Sophia's intermingled responsibilities (his as steamboat captain, hers as proprietress of Bellona Hall) there appears to have been some tension between Cornelius and a man who worked Gibbons's stage route, one Letson. Evidently working on commission, Letson took to offering potential hotel guests late-night carriage service to Jersey City, and thus to another Manhattan ferry, as an alternative to an overnight's stay at the hotel; thus Sophia was deprived of her own commission. In his pitch to seduce travelers, Letson implied deceit on the part of Vanderbilt: a precocious timing of steamboat trips to force some travelers to stay the night in New Brunswick. In the face of both Letson's rhetoric and the competitive drive that lay behind it, Cornelius rebelled. His letter of complaint to Gibbons is useful not only in elucidating the episode but also in depicting Vanderbilt's pathetic grasp of spelling and grammar: "Last evening New Brunswick wais in an uproar. Letson toald the passengers that retaining them their was all my fait that all I did it for was to get their supper and lodging from them he offered to take 7 of them for 3 dollars each in one of the Line Stages the bargain wais maid and upon reflection Letson flew. Cannot you stop Letsons mouth?"[6]

Gibbons proved either unable or unwilling to stop Letson's mouth. Perhaps he liked having a bit of creative tension between his various revenue streams. Whether a passenger spent time in the carriage or in the hotel and on the steamboat, Gibbons made his money. A week or so after the note, when Vanderbilt observed no change in Letson's behavior, he reportedly dragged him behind the hotel and resorted to fists, in the way of the waterfront. Thereafter, Letson's business practices moderated.

Other conflicts were not so easily resolved. By mid autumn of 1818, no less than four steamboats plied the waters between New Brunswick and Manhattan: Gibbons's *Mouse* and *Bellona*, Ogden's *Atalanta* (a larger, recently built boat replacing the *Sea Horse*, the latter having been relegated to less important waters), and the somewhat-ironically named *Olive Branch*, a 115-foot vessel launched 1816 which, by 1818, John Livingston and Ogden were running together along the same route expressly for the purpose of trying to drive Gibbons out of business.

The chess pieces were so arranged when, that autumn, Ogden brought suit in the New York Court of Chancery against Gibbons, claiming his violation of rights granted exclusively to Livingston by New York State, and exclusively to Ogden by Livingston, to operate between low water on the Jersey shore of Upper New York Bay and Manhattan. That winter, the Court of Chancery granted Ogden's petition. And so, once the spring thaw opened up the Arthur Kill, Vanderbilt found himself unhappily ferrying passengers between New Brunswick and Elizabeth, or sometimes as far as Jersey City on New York Harbor with Ogden's permission, the *Bellona* serving as little more than a feeder for the *Atalanta*, which it met at both places. Meanwhile, Gibbons contemplated his next move.

However forced the brief remarriage of Ogden and Gibbons may have been, it evidently proved an economical and profitable combination, for the two were able to lower rates to a point where they seized virtually all business away from Livingston's *Olive Branch*, with which Ogden was no longer allied, still endeavoring to make runs between New Brunswick and New York. For this reason, as Lane tells us: "[Livingston] twice approached Gibbons with the purpose of effecting a connection between the *Olive Branch* and the *Bellona*. When Gibbons rejected the proposal, Livingston asked Chancellor [Judge] Kent [of the New York Court of Chancery] for an injunction against the combination of the *Atalanta* and *Bellona*, claiming that Ogden was illegally enlarging the scope of his license."[7] Livingston also argued, successfully, that the *Bellona* was operating illegally whenever it entered Upper New York Bay, as it had to do to reach Jersey City. In the end, Kent disallowed the *Bellona*'s Ogden-sanctioned runs to Jersey City, but otherwise he took no action, leaving the Gibbons-Ogden combination free to operate so long as passengers were exchanged at Elizabeth. The situation did not change until October 1818, when Livingston and Ogden came together and, partnering on terms more favorable to Ogden than Gibbons had been offering, allied their boats once more, and so froze Gibbons out of all New York through-traffic.

The only other player on the scene beyond Gibbons, Ogden, and Livingston was Vice President Daniel Tompkins. As previously mentioned, under the authority of a license from the Livingston interests, Tompkins's Richmond Turnpike Company operated the steam ferry *Nautilus* (under the command of Vanderbilt's brother-in-law DeForest) between Tompkinsville and lower Manhattan. In December 1818, following the move by Ogden and Livingston to sever Gibbons's operations from a through-connection to Manhattan, Gibbons purchased a subsidiary license from the Richmond Turnpike Company to operate his vessels as far as Tompkinsville on Staten Island, there to make a connection with the Richmond Turnpike's *Nautilus,* the proceeds from through passengers to be split between the two entities. Once again, Gibbons's partnership proved profitable for all concerned, and one assumes that Vanderbilt enjoyed working with DeForest again, even if they did no more than swap customers several times a day.

That winter, as business slowed for the season, Gibbons set Vanderbilt to the task of enlarging the *Bellona*, getting her ready for the next season. A surviving letter from Vanderbilt to Gibbons displays Vanderbilt's thoroughness, but also, once again, his problems with the rudiments of spelling and grammar:

Mr. Gibbons–Sir:

. . . I have aplide to Lawrance & Sneeden and another Ship carpenter of New York to no the Lowest price they would hall up the Bellona and make hir 12 feet Longer. Lawrance & Sneeden is the Lowest that offered and their price is $1000 and they find the meateareals which is Lower than any other in New York. Sir the reason of my writing you of this business now is that I have sean Lawrance & Co. and if the boat is to be dun this winter they must no as quick as possible so that they may repair Stuff in time. You will reccolect the bellona must be halled up weather you have hir 12 feet Longer or no in order to repair hir bottom that is if you do hir Justice I understood . . . that She would be halled up at al events if you was willing. Sir you will considder that if you have hir Lengthinged it will give us a good forward Cabban and will make the boat Draw 6 inches Less water which will inable us to go to the dock at all times . . .

. . . Sir I hope you not considder that I feel anxious to have this dun ofor it is a matter of indifference to me any other way than the presirvation of the boat. Sir She now Leaks considerable. . . .

Your obl. Ser.

C. Vanderbilt[8]

On the home front that winter, the pregnant Sophia perhaps enjoyed the off-season at Bellona Hall, which she would have been spending, for the most part, in the company of four-year-old Phebe Jane and one-year-old Ethelinda. Ice had closed much of the shoreline. The *Bellona* had been hauled out for work, and travelers using the inn became scarce. Scarce also, however, was Sophia's husband. In addition to overseeing the work on the *Bellona* at the New York yard of Lawrence & Sneeden, Cornelius sought additional income by making runs with his periauger between New York and Staten Island. Frequently, that winter, he was home only a day or two each week, then off again to run his little boat, monitor the *Bellona*'s progress, and (of course) enjoy the various temptations available to a healthy young man in the neighborhood of Whitehall Landing.

8

PROUD FUGITIVE

W HEN THE WATERS OPENED UP THAT SPRING OF 1819, VANDERBILT
on the *Bellona* (and another captain, reporting to Vanderbilt, at the
helm of Gibbons's *Mouse*) continued to make runs from New Brunswick to Elizabeth and Staten Island. At Staten Island, the boats exchanged passengers with Tompkins's *Nautilus*, under the command
of DeForest. During the same period, with Gibbons's permission,
Vanderbilt began making occasional runs on the *Bellona* all the way
to Whitehall Landing—brazenly defying the monopoly, and Tompkins as well, by discharging and taking on passengers in Manhattan.
(Virtually no travelers coming from New Brunswick or Elizabeth
had Staten Island as a destination, but rather New York. Thus the
stops at Tompkinsville, Stapleton, and Clifton on Staten Island
could be easily bypassed without inconveniencing passengers.)

Letters in the Special Collections Library at Drew University
show that Vanderbilt, on more than one occasion, urged this action
upon Gibbons. Vanderbilt argued that the monopoly was unpopular
with the general public, and that any rebellion against it was bound

to be greeted with general approval. So, the idea of frequent but randomly scheduled runs into Whitehall seems to have germinated with Cornelius, although Gibbons had no short history of rebellion himself. After having received Gibbons's go-ahead, Vanderbilt had Sophia sew a large flag inscribed with the motto "New Jersey Must Be Free!" The flag, with its message of states' rights, was one he displayed at the *Bellona*'s bow on those days when he intended not to stop at Staten Island but rather make a direct voyage to Whitehall.

At first, the Livingston-Ogden cabal clearly did not know how to deal with the *Bellona*'s unsanctioned incursions to New York. Given Chancellor Kent's previous orders, they might easily have asked for a writ by which the New York sheriffs might impound the *Bellona* at the dock in Manhattan. However, Livingston and Ogden wisely hesitated to do this, on the grounds that such an action might cause Gibbons to seek redress in the New Jersey courts, and one of their boats in Jersey waters wind up being impounded. Instead, as Vanderbilt, the defiant young steamboat captain, gained more and more notoriety, and became something of a Robin Hood–like hero in the folklore of New York harbor, they contrived to have him arrested.

This approach backfired, however, and served to only expand Vanderbilt's growing legend. For two months that spring, Vanderbilt made nearly daily runs into Whitehall, and each time he eluded his would-be captors. At first this was easy. Dressed as a common seaman, Vanderbilt waited until the unwitting constable had boarded the boat in lower Manhattan; then he disembarked, not to return until it was time for the *Bellona* to slip her mooring lines and depart. On those occasions when the constable, spying Vanderbilt, would hop aboard the outbound vessel, Cornelius would mockingly inform the officer of the court that he had ten seconds to get off the boat, after which time he'd be committed to a New Jersey voyage and subject to the fare for same. Later in the season, when more than one constable started showing up, Vanderbilt simply hid in a specially designed secret compartment behind a panel in the *Bellona*'s hold.

By summer, the Livingston-Ogden forces had thought of a new strategy. Rather than ferret out the hard-to-find Vanderbilt, they'd simply go after the crew, all of them operating in contempt of the New York Chancery Court. The constables, meanwhile, devised a strategy for catching the perpetrators "in the act" in the middle of the harbor, where there would be no avenue for either crew or captain to escape or retreat. This was a wonderful plan that would have worked nicely, one supposes, had Cornelius not received advance word of the intervention. On the day the constables stopped the *Bellona* and boarded her, they found not one crew member in attendance. A prim and smartly attired young lady—Cornelius's sister Charlotte, though she did not divulge her identity to the marshals—stood at the wheel. Everyone else on board appeared to be passengers: smirking, jeering passengers. An inspection below decks revealed no one in residence. Nevertheless, once the constables debarked, the *Bellona*'s steam engine miraculously started up after the young lady stamped her foot loudly on the deck. Perhaps a ghost had begun the contraption; either that or Vanderbilt himself had emerged from his hiding place below and started her up.

Vanderbilt's skills at rebuffing and deceiving the constables became so widely discussed that in late summer, when he appeared to allow himself to be captured, many suspected a put-up job. It did, indeed, seem a bit too easy when the marshals found themselves suddenly confronted with their quarry standing, as if waiting, on the docks just below Whitehall. Smith tells the tale smartly:

Another jape of Corneel's was to allow himself to be captured in broad daylight, on the Battery wharf. His enemies were delighted. At last this obnoxious fellow was to be punished for his innumerable insults and impertinences; and they promptly shipped him off to Albany to answer before Chancellor Kent for contempt of court. A rigorously legalistic gentleman, the Chancellor, conservative in his views and impressed with the necessity of maintaining the dignity of courts. He could be depended upon to put this insolent young ruffian in his place. But Corneel was strangely unperturbed; and when he was arraigned for trial he completely flabbergasted the court by producing papers to prove that for the day of his arrest, and for that day only, a Sunday, on which the Gibbons line did not run, he had hired himself out to D. D. Tompkins, who held a license from the monopoly. Perforce, he was released, with a deal more bad language, and scorching comments from the Chancellor upon the unwary attorneys who had suffered themselves to wander into his trap. The waterfront roared its approval.[1]

The event, clearly contrived by Vanderbilt, was not random. It also had a far greater purpose than to simply humiliate the monopoly, insult the constables, and gain press. After Cornelius's arrest and transport to stand before the chancery court in Albany, Gibbons used the episode to persuade the New Jersey Legislature to pass a new law that he thought would be useful, at least to himself and Vanderbilt. Fired by outrage over Vanderbilt's detention, the legislature in Trenton quickly passed Gibbons's proposed measure: a retaliatory law stipulating imprisonment for any New York officer of the court who dared arrest a citizen of New Jersey for operating a steamboat in New York waters. Implicit in this legislation, as in the previous retaliatory act passed by the New Jersey Legislature, was the idea that the government of the State of New Jersey (which was no longer granting an exclusive license in its own waters to Ogden or to any other player) refused to recognize the power of any state to grant such a monopoly in so far as that monopoly would interdict or interfere with commerce overlapping state borders.

At about this same time, Gibbons filed a suit in the New York Court of Chancery—the same one at which Vanderbilt had just appeared—for the lifting of Ogden's injunction forbidding the operation of Gibbons's boats between points in Upper New York Bay. Trained as an attorney himself, Gibbons had his counsel at Albany present a carefully framed challenge to the New York State–sanctioned Livingston-Fulton monopoly. Citing Gibbons's possession of a federal coasting license, counsel argued that this alone gave Gibbons leave to enter New York waters, and all other waters within the domain of the United States, at will. To back this up, counsel further insisted, first, that the state law granting the monopoly conflicted with the commerce clause of the United States Constitution, and, second, that the federal law should be regarded as superseding the state legislation.

Gibbons fully expected Chancellor Kent to rule in favor of the monopoly, just as he had in all previous related decisions. In this, Gibbons was not disappointed. As well, he fully expected a similar result when he appealed to the New York Court of Errors that December. In this too he would not be let down—and he knew as much. Indeed, he appears to have hoped for it. At the very least, he was planning for such a result and for the opportunity to appeal the case to the highest court outside of New York jurisdiction: the Supreme Court of the United States. Along with his friend and ally, Attorney General William Wirt (recently appointed by the Federalist president, James Madison), Gibbons was sure the Court would want to take up the question of the constitutionality of the New York statute. It says much that the Court of Errors had not yet even rendered its judgment when Gibbons moved to retain one of the finest constitutional lawyers in the land to represent his challenge before the Supreme Court. The date on Gibbons's letter to Daniel Webster—the Federalist Whig politician—is December 13:

> Sir—
>
> I have a case before the Court of Errors of New York of Aaron Ogden vs. Thomas Gibbons on the constitutionality of the Laws of the State of New York granting an exclusive right to Messrs. Livingston and Fulton to navigate the waters of the state of New York with steamboats—this case has been argued and is now under consideration in the Court of Errors. If that Court should decide against me and in favour of the law I shall carry it before the Supreme Court of the United States at Washington where I shall wish your services associated with Mr. Wirt the Attorney General.
>
> I will thank you to inform me by Mail whether you are at liberty to act on such case and whether I can have the benefit of your services therein—please to direct to me Thomas Gibbons Elizabeth town New Jersey.
>
> Th. Gibbons[2]

Gibbons had reason to expect his chances for success to be good in the Supreme Court, and reasons also for expressly wanting Webster to lead his representation there. John Marshall, the court's fourth chief justice, had been in place since 1801. As an ardent Federalist, Marshall believed firmly in a strong central government and was highly dubious of states' rights as a principle. In fact, he had repeatedly already shown a decided preference for the primacy of Federal law over state law. Further, he believed in a very broad reading of the "enumerated powers" granted by the Constitution to the United States Congress. As Gibbons well knew, the sixty-four-year-old Marshall—a native of Virginia—was an ally in waiting.[3]

So were the majority of the remaining justices on the Court, so many of them being Federalists. As for the thirty-seven-year-old Webster, the former two-term congressman from Massachusetts was known to be a favorite of Marshall's.

During 1819, shortly before his solicitation by Gibbons, Webster had won a landmark case before the Supreme Court which went to the heart of many of the issues underpinning the arguments in *Gibbons vs. Ogden*. In the matter of *McCullough vs. Maryland*, the state of Maryland had endeavored to unduly regulate the business of an out-of-state bank, the federally chartered Second Bank of the United States, which operated a branch office in Baltimore headed by cashier James McCullough. Maryland attempted its regulation by levying a special tax aimed only at notes issued by banks not chartered by Maryland. In deciding for McCullough, the Supreme Court established two fundamental principles which would guide it in virtually all related matters going forward. First, the Court determined that the Constitution grants to Congress certain implied powers for implementing the express powers enunciated in the Constitution, in order to create a viably functioning national government. Second, the Court determined that state action or legislation may never supersede or inhibit the exercise of Constitutional power by the Federal government. The second point, in particular, was to have ramifications in *Gibbons vs. Ogden*.

As all this was going on, the monopoly tried and failed to buy Vanderbilt for their own side. During the autumn of 1819, Ogden (after consultations with John Livingston) approached Cornelius with an attractive offer: $5,000 per year if Vanderbilt would throw over Gibbons, come to work for Ogden, and take command of Ogden's large

Atalanta. By this time, Gibbons had raised Vanderbilt's salary to $2,000 per year, with perhaps another $2,000 coming in annually as Sophia and Cornelius's share of the receipts from Bellona Hall. One assumes, therefore, that the Ogden offer must have been more than tempting. It appears, however, that Gibbons made no move to match it. Nevertheless, Vanderbilt turned down Ogden's offer. Why? After all, Vanderbilt was never altruistic, despite the quote attributed to him at this time: "I don't care half so much about making money as I do about making my point, and coming out ahead."[4]

At least the last four words were true. By what was to transpire in the next few years, we can reasonably assume Gibbons and Vanderbilt had an understanding that at a particular point in the future, Vanderbilt was going to be permitted to purchase some, if not all, of Gibbons's interests in New Brunswick to New York steamboating—an offer Ogden could not or at least did not make. Thus Vanderbilt decided to remain loyal to Gibbons, telling the New York *Evening Post:* "I shall stick to Gibbons. He has always treated me square, and been as good as his word."[5] As well, Gibbons held the promise of breaking the monopoly, whereas Ogden did not. And Cornelius was smart enough to realize that no steamboat franchise doing trade in New York—or in any other of the corridors of the country where individual steamboat fiefdoms had been awarded by state governments—would be worth building until such legislative monopolies were done away with. (It could always quite honestly be said of Vanderbilt that he staunchly opposed any monopoly he himself did not personally control.)

Beyond that, Vanderbilt genuinely liked Gibbons, or at least the archetype he represented. Indeed, there is reason to believe that, through later years, he used Gibbons as something of a role model. Fabulously wealthy and a brilliant business strategist, Gibbons was nevertheless uncouth, quite common in his manners, and base in his desires. He was likewise abrupt and abrasive in his dealings with family, subordinates, and citizens, and he generally made no attempt at being a gentleman. He did not pretend to like books, nor did he appreciate art. He did not give alms to worthy public appeals. He neither visited nor endowed museums. When he sought amusement, he found it either in the arms of a young woman, in a tankard of rum, or both. His only other hobbies were betting on horse races and on fist-fights, his stable-boys being paid, on occasion, to orchestrate both. There was also his long-cherished hobby of hating, the most recent target of that penchant being Ogden, and the most recent beneficiary being Vanderbilt, who smartly sowed the seeds of his fortune with Gibbons's venom. In sum, Vanderbilt appears to have applauded Gibbons's simple, animal tastes and his rudimentary honesty about himself: his desires, his ambitions, and his motivations. Gibbons's style—if we can call it that—was something Vanderbilt would emulate with alarming transparency to the end of his days.

This is not to say that the two were friends. Hardly. From the formality of their correspondence, it seems clear that Gibbons and Vanderbilt were strictly business associates, employer and employee, with Vanderbilt always in the subservient role. Thus it was Cornelius who was dispatched as a messenger to Washington that January of 1820, there to finalize arrangements with Webster, after Webster answered in the affirmative to Gibbons's letter of inquiry. Vanderbilt carried with him two checks from Gibbons for $500—one for Webster, another for Attorney General Wirt, who had agreed to serve as Webster's co-counsel, with Webster to take the lead in all arguments.

Twelve years Vanderbilt's senior, Webster seems to have made quite an impression on Cornelius. In subsequent years, Vanderbilt would support Webster in politics, and would even name a steamboat after him. Both men came from humble backgrounds. Webster had been born on a poor farm in Salisbury, New Hampshire. Unlike Vanderbilt, however, Webster had, through the exertions of his hard-working father, received a fine education at Phillips Exeter Academy and Dartmouth, graduating Phi Beta Kappa from the latter institution in 1801. Also unlike Vanderbilt, Webster was urbane and eloquent: one of the most gifted orators the United States had ever, or would ever, produce. Nevertheless, Webster appears to have come away from his meeting with Vanderbilt nursing a certain respect for the burly steamboat man in so far as he wrote to Gibbons to compliment him on his choice of a "trusted agent" to hammer out the details of their agreement.[6]

Upon his return to New York after the meeting with Webster, Vanderbilt became the hero of another episode in New York Harbor unrelated to the debate over steamboat monopoly. In the frigid temperatures of that harsh winter, even the brackish waters around Manhattan froze, trapping ships at their docks. One of the afflicted vessels was the packet *Elizabeth*, commissioned by the American Colonization Society to convey eighty-eight former slaves to Liberia, the West African colony founded by the society in 1817. (In fact, the blacks aboard the *Elizabeth* were the first such group of refugees to depart for the colony.) Ready to set sail that January, the *Elizabeth* sat trapped at her wharf at the foot of Rector Street. For days on end, the crew of the ship, joined by others, worked feverishly to chop away the ice that held the packet, and open a channel for her to escape, only to see the water freeze again every night. Meanwhile, the black passengers suffered mightily from the cold. When Vanderbilt told agents of the American Colonization Society that he could get the *Elizabeth* free in less than twenty-four hours for a fee of $100, they fairly leaped at his offer.

Lane describes what happened next:

[That evening Vanderbilt] appeared with five men, three long pine boards, and a small anchor with rope. The principal difficulty was that between the ship and the channel lay a belt of ice, two hundred yards wide, that was too thin to bear a man's weight. Cornele put the anchor on one of the boards and pushed it out on the ice; he then crawled out on another board and pushed the first forward; he repeated the process by using the third board. The anchor, tipped over on the thin ice far from shore, broke through and took bottom. He then had a small boat hauled out by the anchor rope, and his men, working their way in from the channel in the boat, were soon able to chop a path for the *Elizabeth*, which left the next morning.[7]

9

GIBBONS VS. OGDEN

THE PRO-MONOPOLY STALWARTS SITTING ON NEW YORK'S COURT of Errors, as well as the agents and attorneys acting on behalf of the Fulton-Livingston monopoly, could read the United States Supreme Court just as easily as had Gibbons. Neither John Livingston, Aaron Ogden, Chancellor Kent, or anyone else on the other side of the debate had any doubt that, given reason, the Supreme Court would agree to hear an appeal of any decision that went against Gibbons, and would most likely overturn any such decision. Thus, the tactic on the other side became one of delay. Gibbons could not appeal a ruling that had not yet been made. For this reason, the Court of Appeals was not to rule against Gibbons for another three years.

Such was the backdrop as the spring season of 1820 opened. That May, to add a bit more vindictiveness to an already tense atmosphere on the Jersey and Staten Island shoreline, Gibbons arranged for the New Jersey State Legislature to pass yet another retaliatory measure: the third. The new law in Jersey stipulated that anyone taking action in the New York Chancery Court against a New Jersey–based steamboat operator might be in turn assessed threefold damages by the New Jersey Court of Chancery, these damages to be forwarded to the injured Jerseyan. Specifically, the writ provided that should any citizen of New Jersey be "enjoined or restrained by any writ of injunction, or order by the Court of Chancery of the State of New York, by virtue, or under color of any act of the Legislature of that State, from navigating any boat or vessel moved by steam or fire, belonging in part, or in whole, to him, on the waters between the ancient shores of the State of New Jersey and New York, the plaintiff or plaintiffs in such writ or order shall be liable to the person or persons aggrieved for all damages, expenses and charges occasioned thereby, to be recovered with triple costs . . . "[1]

Meanwhile, with the *Olive Branch* effectively banned from the Raritan River, the Livingston-Fulton cabal continued to be hurt by constraints on their navigation in New Jersey waters. Livingston's passengers from Perth Amboy complained bitterly about having to travel on a scow for long, uncomfortable connecting with the *Olive Branch* at Staten Island. Aaron Ogden, equally hampered and seeing his business shrink, sought to populate the *Atalanta*'s decks by negotiating a peace with Gibbons, but found himself rebuffed. As for the *Bellona* under the command of Vanderbilt, she—like the *Mouse*—continued her regular runs along the New Brunswick, Elizabeth, and Staten Island route, rendezvousing with Tompkins's *Nautilus* at Tompkinsville most of the time. Vanderbilt continued, however, to make oddly timed scattershot runs at Manhattan whenever the whim hit him, or whenever the time seemed opportune.

Friends and associates on the New York waterfront kept Vanderbilt abreast of the marshals' comings and goings. Public speculation on when next the daring Vanderbilt would challenge and triumph over the monopoly with a sudden visit to Manhattan became a popular hobby. In some quarters, the gossip became the object of gambling pools. Passengers, as well, entered into the game—and did not seem to mind sometimes being left off at oddly configured places on the New York waterfront, well away from the main Whitehall Landing dock, perhaps on the East River at South Street or a bit further north of Whitehall along the Hudson. The game was entertaining: an adventure. Newspaper reporters delighted in regaling their readers with tales of the incursions of the Commodore, as he was now more frequently called: a title that indicated his general mastery not only of things nautical but also of those who would wish to subdue him.

The only man who ever succeeded in taking the *Bellona* was Jacob Hays who—as High Constable of New York and Sergeant at Arms to the New York Board of Aldermen—was literally the living embodiment of law-enforcement in Manhattan during the early 1820s. Born to Jewish parents at Bedford, New York, in 1772, Hays had been bonded out when he was twelve to Presbyterian farmers in New York's Orange County. The Stitt family, in turn, seem to have imbued Hays with some stern Presbyterian (or simply Old Testament?) traits. In any event, he emerged from his service to the Stitts as a stark, brooding, forbidding, and formidable man. In sum, Hays possessed the ideal, incorruptible temperament for an enforcer of the law. He also possessed the right physique: tall and generally massive. Mayor Varick appointed Hays New York marshal in 1798. Subsequently, in 1803, Mayor Edward Livingston—of the same ubiquitous Livingston clan that eventually came to dominate New York steamboating—appointed Hays High Constable. Hays was to maintain that title for nearly fifty years, until his death in 1849, at which point the position would be retired. By all accounts, Hays was quite a daunting and imposing figure—as he must have been for Vanderbilt to yield.

Late in life, Vanderbilt himself told of Hays coming upon him just as he'd docked the *Bellona* in Manhattan. "I was mad enough to defy the whole Livingston tribe, old Hays included, but when I caught a glimpse of his calm and smiling face and a twinkle in his eye, which, singularly enough, said as plainly as words could express it: 'If you don't obey the order of the court, and that damn soon, I'll make you do it, by God,' I concluded to surrender. I didn't want to back down, however, too hurriedly, and I said that if they wanted to arrest me, they should carry me off the boat, and don't you know, old Hays took me at my word, and landed me on the dock with a suddenness that took away my breath."[2] The tool used was most likely the long gold-tipped staff that Hays famously carried with him, and routinely used to clobber wrong-doers. (Years later, in the 1830s, Hays and Vanderbilt would find themselves allies in Whig politics. Thus, on Wall Street, when Vanderbilt eventually encountered Hays's son, William H. Hays—a moderately successful broker and for a time president of the Eighth Avenue Railway Company—he'd show no signs of holding a grudge, and would refrain from crushing him.)

Neither Vanderbilt nor the *Bellona* spent much time in custody. Thomas Gibbons went to the Federal Circuit Court and got a writ of *replevin*. The writ of *replevin* was a writ remanding illegally or wrongfully withheld property to the custody of U.S. marshals, or the custody of another designated official (in this case, Gibbons) under order and supervision of the federal court. Vanderbilt, the possession of whom was not the object or desire of the monopoly, got out just as quickly. Such games as these were to continue, however, throughout the next three years, with Vanderbilt often spending a few odd hours in jail, and just as often harassing the masters and crews of the Livingston-Fulton and Ogden boats, while the main contenders lingered in legal limbo, waiting for *Gibbons vs. Ogden* to be settled.

Letters from Vanderbilt to Gibbons tell the tale. "I could not leave the Boat," he noted on one occasion, with his usual lack of spelling and grammar prowess, "as [Livingston] would take all the men if I am not their. I now keep all my men out of the way so that they cannot take them and wile I am agoing in & out to the dock in NY I work the boat myself and let them take me but I will not let them take them as it is intended with some difficulty to get bail for the men."

On another occasion: "I have this day impoyed a lawer here to Bring an action againts all the men of the Olive Branch to take them 6 miles in the woods from [New Brunswick] before a magistrate and make them give bail. I no we cannot recevir but it will give them troble it will give them more trouble than I have in N.Y. This day [Livingston] brought a sute againts all my men even the kook but caught no boddy but me. If you like these proceedings or not please to let me no by to days mail. We had hav this moment arrived town. I have not sean him [Hays]—these little sutes will cost nothing much."[3]

While such games as these were played, the face and texture of the northeast (indeed, the entire map of American commerce) was changing in significant, though sometimes subtle, ways. As both Vanderbilt and Gibbons knew, ever since 1815 John Stevens had possessed a charter empowering a firm he called the New Jersey Railroad Company to build a railroad from near Trenton on the Delaware River to New Brunswick. However, the project had not yet and would not in the near future come to fruition due to Stevens's troubles in acquiring financing. But by 1825 Stevens had devised a fully functional steam locomotive capable of pulling several passenger cars on a working prototype railway draped about his estate near Hoboken. Much farther to the north, engineers and laborers of the Niagara Canal Company worked to complete what would come to be called the Erie Canal, connecting the Hudson (and therefore New York Harbor) to the Great Lakes. Work had commenced on July 4th, 1817. The first section of the canal had opened in 1819. And the entire project (including eighty-three locks enabling the rise of some 568 feet from the Hudson to Lake Erie) was destined to sit finished by the end of October 1825.

Once the Erie Canal opened, the entire logic of trade into, out of, and through the port of New York would be changed forever. As Roy Finch of the New York State Engineer and Surveyor Bureau observed on the occasion of the hundredth anniversary of the canal's opening: "After the building of the original canal the city of New York grew by leaps and bounds. Before the canal was built Philadelphia had been the nation's chief seaport, but New York soon took the lead and too late Philadelphia made heroic but futile efforts to regain its supremacy." Finch added that Massachusetts "had been another rival, having been about on a par with New York State in exports." Nevertheless, a mere sixteen years after the opening of the canal, Boston's exports were only one-third those moving through New York. "In that period, too, the value of real estate in New York increased more rapidly than the population, while personal property was nearly four times its former value, and manufacturing three times as great. There were then five times as many people following commercial pursuits in New York as there were before the completion of the Erie Canal."[4]

Men of vision saw this boom coming. Indeed, the boom was being counted upon to help pay off the massive $7 million investment it had taken to accomplish the terrific feat of engineering. Almost more important than the straightforward logistical advantage of the Erie Canal, however, was the sheer heft and grandeur of the project, which captured the imaginations of average Americans and made them feel inspired. Great things were possible; terrific accomplishment was, indeed, achievable—especially in the United

States, a country with a brief past and a wide-open future. Not until the late 1860s would another such project, the Transcontinental Railroad, seize the public mind so totally and offer a similar promise for changing the economic map. Then again, in the late 1870s, as Cornelius Vanderbilt lay on his death bed, observers would note the same phenomena (the same public awe and pride, the same marvel at the majesty of American innovation and drive) with the building of the necessary and massive, but also sublimely beautiful, Brooklyn Bridge.

The New York Court of Appeals finally ruled against Gibbons in mid-1823. At that point, Gibbons began to strenuously lobby Webster and Wirt to move promptly and get the United States Supreme Court to agree to hear an appeal based on Gibbons's previously stated argument of the Constitution's Commerce Clause superseding and having force over any state or other local legislation. A letter to Wirt highlights the very personal aspect of the case for Gibbons, who was intent on seeing his nemesis Ogden repudiated. "I entreat you to press on the trial, or death will take from me the pleasure of rejoicing with you on the event." Gibbons did not merely want to win; he wanted to see Ogden lose. Sixty-six years of age, and not in the best of health, Gibbons knew that his time was ticking away. But, Gibbons was not the only one who was anxious. A large collection of would-be steamboat entrepreneurs from all over the United States, wherever a state-sanctioned monopoly stifled competition, impatiently awaited the arrival of a free market. Thus Gibbons spoke for an entire class of businessmen when he told Webster to "hasten the cause [because] this section of the Union is extremely agitated from the imposition & the actions of that proud state, New York."[5]

The Court heard arguments during the winter of 1824.

Counsel for Ogden was Thomas Jackson Oakley. Born near Poughkeepsie, New York, in 1783, Oakley had graduated from Yale. Somewhat ironically, he was a Federalist by party affiliation, but not in philosophy when it came to the potential primacy of federal statute over New York statute with reference to steam navigation on New York waterways. Oakley had served in the New York State Assembly, and as well had been Attorney General for the State of New York, serving from 1818 to 1820. Counsel for the Livingston-Fulton interests was Thomas Addis Emmet, previously the attorney for Robert Fulton. Born 1764 in County Cork, Emmet was an older brother to the famed Irish nationalist (and martyr) Robert Emmet. (Their father, another Robert Emmet, had at one time served as personal physician to the Lord Lieutenant of Ireland.) One of the first cases Thomas Emmet ever tried in the Irish courts, long before coming to America, had been the defense of the Irish patriot leader James Napper Tandy. Emmet wound up arrested by the British himself in 1798 for his involvement with the Society of the United Irishman, and was held at Fort George in Scotland until 1802. Upon his release, he traveled to Paris. From there, in 1803 (following the failure of his brother's uprising in Ireland and his brother's gruesome execution by being hanged, drawn, and quartered) Thomas Emmet went to New York, where he began the practice of law. By the time of the Supreme Court arguments in *Gibbons vs. Ogden*, the 60-year-old Emmet had become one of state's most prominent and respected attorneys, having served as Attorney General from 1812 to 1813.

With Wirt and Emmet serving as backup, Webster led the rhetorical fight for the Gibbons side, and Oakley the charge for Ogden. Eloquently, and at great length, the brilliant and mesmerizing Webster surveyed the whole history of the dispute and explained in a carefully crafted argument how the legislature of New York had acted illegally in establishing the Livingston-Fulton monopoly. That action, said Webster, ran counter to the language of the U.S. Constitution's Commerce Clause, which said: "Congress shall have power to regulate commerce with foreign nations, and among the several States and with the Indian tribes." Webster argued that New York State had attempted to usurp the specially delegated powers given to the Congress by the Constitution: that navigation was commerce, and that Federal regulations must govern.

In responding, Oakley abandoned his Federalist ethic to argue for states' rights and the limitation of federal power. Oakley said that the authority given to Congress "by the sovereign State of New York" was limited in that all rights not delegated were reserved. Oakley argued further that restraints imposed by the laws of New York on the navigation of the state's waters were merely internal regulations of the right to move from one port of the state to another. Oakley also insisted that any and all state laws regulating commerce within a given state remained valid and demanding of respect at the federal level, even if they might "incidentally" impact "intercourse between the States."

The majority of the Court, via a decision written by Chief Justice Marshall himself and announced on March 2nd, roundly rejected the idea of the primacy of any New York law which hindered out-of-state commercial steamboats from doing business in New York. Marshall's opinion closely mimicked the arguments made by Webster, while elaborating those arguments in more magisterial and less grandiose language than Webster himself had adopted before the Court. Marshall said that Congress, having been given the power to regulate commerce by the Constitution, had also been given the implied power to regulate navigation. Marshall added that, as phrased in the Constitution, Congress's "power to regulate commerce" bore no hint of a limit as regards technology.

[S]teamboats may be enrolled and licensed in common with vessels using sails. They are, of course, entitled to the same privileges and can no more be restrained from navigating waters and
entering ports, which are free to such vessels, than if they were
wafted on their voyage by the winds instead of being propelled
by the agency of fire. The one element may be as legitimately
used as the other, for every commercial purpose authorized by
the laws of the river, and the act of a State inhibiting the use of
either to any vessel, having a license under the act of Congress,
comes, we think, in direct collision with that act. The acts of the
Legislature of the State of New York, granting to Robert R. Livingston and Robert Fulton the exclusive navigation of all the waters within the jurisdiction of that State, with boats moved by
fire or steam, for a term of years, are repugnant to that clause of
the constitution of the United States, which authorizes Congress
to regulate commerce, so far as the said acts prohibit vessels licensed, according to the laws of the United States, for carrying
on the coasting trade, from navigating the said waters by means
of fire or steam.[6]

In this way the Livingston-Fulton steamboat monopoly in New
York, as well as every other such fiefdom granted by local commissars
in various states, was struck down, opening the way for enterprise
across state lines. So far as the vindictive Gibbons was concerned,
however, the most important result of the decision was the ruination
of his old enemy Ogden, over the fate of whom he now had the privilege of gloating. The case bankrupted the former New Jersey governor. Ogden had spent virtually all his ready cash on representation.
As well, the struggle to maintain his steamboat business as a going-
concern in the face of Gibbons's and Vanderbilt's cut-throat pricing
(together with their numerous incursions to Manhattan with the *Bel-*

Iona, despite court orders to the contrary) had proved costly. Now, with not even the courts standing in the way of the serious competition offered by Vanderbilt and Gibbons, Ogden was ruined. So ruined, in fact, that he soon gave up his steamboat assets and wound up imprisoned in New York for not paying his debts.

Ogden would not emerge from jail until 1829, after Aaron Burr (both a boyhood friend and a Princeton classmate) pushed through a statute prohibiting the jailing of Revolutionary War veterans for indebtedness. No longer a force in commerce, the broken Ogden eventually returned to the simple practice of law in Jersey City, where in 1830 he was made collector of customs. He was still in that position nine years later, at the time of his death. Gibbons, meanwhile, was to go to his grave on May 16, 1826, content with the thought of Ogden languishing behind bars.

In the immediate aftermath of the decision in *Gibbons vs. Ogden*, the first area of waterborne commerce most immediately impacted was the traffic between Philadelphia and Manhattan. Gibbons had long enjoyed a close business relationship with John Stevens, the latter controlling a fleet of several steamers on the Delaware River. Passengers traveling west to east used Stevens's steamers, operating on the Delaware with stops at Philadelphia, Bordentown, and Trenton, to start. They then boarded stagecoaches (some owned by Gibbons, some by Stevens) running on alternating schedules between Trenton and New Brunswick before embarking on Gibbons's steamers to either Jersey City or Manhattan. Travelers going from New York to Philadelphia did the same thing in reverse. Philadelphia/New York through-traffic had been growing exponentially in recent years. In fact, the through-traffic was so great by 1824 that Stevens adopted the name of Gibbons's "Union Line" for his own operation so that passengers would feel they were traveling on a truly unified route for all of their journey between city and city. The Stevens and Gibbons entities, seamlessly integrated, were run cooperatively, but with revenues accruing to two separate profit centers. Thus, up to 1824, the Philadelphia/New York business had gone on unhindered and without much in the way of competition. But that changed quickly following the Supreme Court decision.

Not long after the decision, in the spring of 1824, Gibbons launched a new steamer which had been largely designed by Vanderbilt. The *Thistle,* considerably larger than the *Bellona* at 200 tons, would now be the Union Line's lead boat on the New Brunswick to New York run, with the *Bellona* taking up the slack and the *Mouse* relegated to runs between Stapleton and Manhattan, competing with Tompkins. In short order following the launch of the *Thistle,* however, Gibbons and Stevens found themselves confronting their first serious challenge for Philadelphia/New York traffic in the form of no less than three rival concerns.

The new Citizen's Line was a start-up that had taken over Ogden's boats, including the grand *Atalanta.* Meanwhile, the Columbian Line of steamboats and stages directly paralleled the operations of the Union Line, as did the third entrant, the Exchange Line. Each competed on three different levels—luxury, speed, and price— with the Exchange Line proving the most formidable opponent. The Exchange Line's *Legislator,* which began service between New Brunswick and New York during the spring of 1824, was advertised as an elaborate, luxurious, floating hotel. Built by the prominent New York engineer and shipwright Noah Brown, the *Legislator* ran considerably faster than the *Bellona,* against which she was matched, both of those boats being on schedules that had them leaving New Brunswick for New York at the stroke of noon every day. (The

Thistle, equally as luxurious as the *Legislator* and now under the personal command of Vanderbilt, departed New Brunswick early in the morning. A scarcity of morning trade, combined with the *Legislator*'s obvious advantages over the *Bellon*a, led the *Legislator*'s owners to opt for the later departure, the richer traffic, and the easier direct competition offered by a noon launch.)

Both the *Thistle* and the *Legislator* were built to state-of-the-art standards. Comfortable saloons provided cushioned seats and tables served by uniformed attendants. Fresh food was prepared on board, and the bars never closed. Each boat featured three levels. The topmost deck provided a terrace from which, in fair weather, one could take in the scenery, enjoy the sun, or study the stars. Below this, another deck provided the comfort of a roof, but was otherwise open, thus allowing travelers to enjoy the fresh air without being exposed to sun or rain. Each of the upper decks provided a plentiful supply of comfortable seats and tables. The lowest level, completely enclosed, housed the main saloon, where food and beverages were served, and where passengers gathered during inclement weather. Equal in comfort, the *Thistle* and the *Legislator* were also equal in speed, each being capable of a whopping fifteen miles per hour. Quite soon, when the *Thistle* and the *Legislator* started competing with each other directly, speed was to become a major (and deadly) issue.

10

UNION LINE MAN

IN THE FACE OF THE NEW COMPETITION, VANDERBILT STUCK loyally with the Union Line interests of Gibbons. In addition to commanding the *Thistle*, he had the captains of the *Bellona* and *Mouse* reporting to him. It was Vanderbilt who set the schedules and fares for all the boats, administered the budgets, managed the food and drink service on the various boats, and made sure the craft were maintained properly. Vanderbilt also hired and fired crewmembers, negotiated the purchase of wood for fuel, and arranged advertising in New York and New Jersey newspapers.

Sophia, meanwhile, continued to oversee the doings at Bellona Hall. In addition to running the tavern and inn, during 1824 she oversaw a significant expansion of the small enterprise. Early that spring, while *Gibbons vs. Ogden* was being hashed out down in Washington, Sophia negotiated a contract for a local contractor to build an extension "to be attached to the house now occupied by C. Vanderbilt, 40 feet in front and 32 feet deep, with three rooms on the first floor and ten rooms on the second, one room in the third."[1] The fee for the work—which also included enlarging the hotel's piazza overlooking the river and converting a hallway into an expansion of the bar—was $2,850 payable by Thomas Gibbons. (While seeing to all of this, Sophia at the same time tended to her growing brood. In addition to Phebe Jane, Ethelinda, and Eliza, she now was also taking care of William Henry, known as Billy, born in 1821, and Emily Almira, born in 1823. Maria Louisa would emerge in 1827, and Frances Lavinia in 1828, with four more still to come after Frances. The boy Billy had been named for William Henry Harrison, the hero of the 1811 battle of Tippecanoe, fought against Tecumseh's native confederacy in what is today Indiana during the siege known as Tecumseh's War.)

Gibbons appears to have been more than willing to invest the nearly $3,000 required for the enlargement of the hotel. The northern end of the Union Line from New Brunswick to New York, which Gibbons controlled exclusively, was yielding approximately $40,000 per year in net profits, with ridership steadily on the increase. These profits accrued despite the discounting and advertising costs necessitated by increased competition. At the same time, Gibbons was getting his management for a small price. After a couple of raises, Cornelius's annual salary was now $3,000 a year; beyond this, Sophia mined whatever profits she could from the hotel, paying Gibbons his percentage. So, all in all, Gibbons was enjoying a bargain in what he paid for oversight of his operations—one that most certainly could only have been obtained with the promise of large and quite significant rewards still to come.

Competition continued fast and furious in 1825. At the opening of the spring season, the owners of the Exchange Line put their state-of-the-art flagship *Legislator* on morning runs out of New Brunswick and afternoon runs out of New York. This schedule put her in direct competition with the Union Line's *Thistle*, Vanderbilt at the helm. The reason for the change in the *Legislator*'s schedule was simple: The proprietors of the Exchange Line had no other choice. Throughout the previous year, when the *Legislator* had been running against the *Bellona*, Vanderbilt had adopted a strategy of starving out the *Legislator*. Since the *Bellona* was a slower and generally less palatial craft than the *Legislator*, Vanderbilt had competed on price, launching a rate war. Both vessels began the season of 1824 with a price of seventy-five cents for one-way passage between New Brunswick and Manhattan. Soon, however, Vanderbilt dropped the *Bellona*'s ticket to a mere twelve and a half cents. Then, when the proprietors of the Exchange Line dropped the *Legislator*'s price to match that, Vanderbilt dropped the *Bellona*'s price yet again: to nothing. In addition to offering free rides between New Brunswick, Elizabeth, and Manhattan, Vanderbilt threw in free food.

The *Bellona* was paid for. Smaller than the new *Legislator*, which had been built entirely with leveraged money, she demanded considerably less in the way of overhead for fuel and crew, and no overhead for principal/interest payments. In sum, it cost the Union Line considerably less per passenger to offer free rides and free food on the *Bellona* than it did for the Exchange Line to run a largely empty boat at twelve and a half cents per head and to charge for food. The managers of the Exchange Line simply could not afford to offer free rides, but neither could they afford to keep running empty. Thus, at the start of 1825, the Exchange Line proprietors made a calculation that if they positioned the *Legislator* to run against the equally expensive to maintain *Thistle*, the price war would cease.

In this they were wrong. Although Vanderbilt and Gibbons did not wind up offering passage on the *Thistle* gratis, they cut the price significantly. At the most ruthless moment of the price war, the Union Line fee was thirty cents between New York and New Brunswick, with a complete through-fare between New York and Philadelphia being available on the Union Line for a mere $2, when normally prices for the same package ranged as high as $5. The Exchange Line scrambled and operated at a loss just to match the Union Line's price between New Brunswick and New York, and they offered no through-service from New Brunswick to Philadelphia. Thus the bulk of the business to be had (the through-traffic between Philadelphia and New York) naturally continued to migrate to the integrated Union Line. Amid all this, while the Exchange Line bled precious cash in order to appear competitive between New York and New Brunswick, the well-financed Union Line simply took some planned temporary losses, marking them down for what they were: an investment in future profits.

Unable to compete effectively on price over a long period of time, the management of the Exchange Line initially sought to compete on speed: pushing their *Legislator* to outpace the equally fast *Thistle*. Just ahead of one such exercise on June 2, 1825, an engineer aboard the *Legislator* fastened down a safety valve on the ship's boiler, thus to keep steam from escaping, and so ramp up the rpm of the steam-engine's fly-wheel. The boat was still tied up at the foot of Rector Street in Manhattan when her boiler exploded. Four members of the crew were scalded to death, three more injured. A short while later, the repaired *Legislator* returned to the water, offering nervous passengers transport on a "safety barge" towed behind the main craft, such safety to be had for a moderate step-up fare. This offer, like the boiler with the closed valve, soon went bust, as even more passengers migrated to the Union Line, from which it appeared all the safety and efficiency in the world could be had for pennies.

The Exchange Line would eventually collapse and surrender. However, the war was still ongoing on May 16, 1826, when Thomas

Gibbons died. Keeping his old promise to disinherit his daughter and her husband (the despised John Trumbull), Gibbons left his entire fortune and all his real property to his sole surviving son William Gibbons, who had long been absent from New Jersey overseeing his father's properties in Georgia.[2] "To my son William Gibbons, of Savannah, I give . . . my plantation Rosedew in Chatham County [GA], and Tusculum in Scriben County [GA], with all my negro slaves in the states of Georgia and South Carolina . . . all my lots of ground in the city of Savannah . . . And in New Jersey, my Rose-hill farm, my Wheat-patch farm, a house and lot on the turnpike road, my two farms, Rising Sun and Howard's Farm, and the three lots in New Brunswick . . . and in Elizabethtown, the Union hotel, with all the houses, lots and premises thereto belonging . . . I also give, devise and bequeath to my said son William Gibbons my swamp plantation in South Carolina, my plantation in Chatham County called Long Payment, and the lot in Morris County called the Mountain Lot . . . also all my bank stock in New York, New Jersey, and Georgia, and all money in any bank in either of the states, and also all my steamboats and sailboats and all money due to me, and all my plate, household furniture, and stock of liquors, in Georgia or elsewhere."[3] Vanderbilt received no bounty from Gibbons's estate, but there is no indication that he was expecting any. What he most likely did expect, however, was an opportunity to buy out Gibbons's northern end of the Union Line on favorable terms when the time was right. Therefore he kept on administering the line between New Brunswick and New York for the distant William.

Within days of Thomas Gibbons's burial, the Union Line launched a new steamer. Like the *Thistle*, the side-wheel *Emerald* had been largely designed by Cornelius himself. With many amenities built in and an extra large boiler for maximum swiftness, the *Emerald* was the most expensive steamer yet built. She'd been constructed by the New

York shipwrights and engineers Smith & Dimon for roughly $75,000. Vanderbilt took the helm, bequeathing the *Thistle* to a newly hired captain, and he ran the *Emerald* between New Brunswick and Manhattan with great success—watching the Exchange Line sink before his very eyes. On July 11, Vanderbilt transported the president of the United States, John Quincy Adams, from New Brunswick to Manhattan on the morning run. Adams had evidently enjoyed his stay at Bellona Hall, and the hospitality of Mrs. Vanderbilt, but the voyage to New York did not go smoothly. Adams noted in his journal that he and his party embarked "at Brunswick in the steamboat *Emerald* at five in the morning, an hour earlier than we had been told last night, whereby several passengers narrowly missed losing their passage. The boat grounded three times, and we were detained nearly two hours. We reached New York at half-past eleven."[4]

Normally the *Emerald*'s voyages were less eventful, swifter, and far more pleasant. The ship received rave reviews from most passengers. Nevertheless, her career was to be brief. One night in November as Vanderbilt, his family, and guests snoozed at Bellona Hall, the *Emerald* caught afire at the New Brunswick pier on the Raritan, right in front of the hotel. Summoned from his bed, Vanderbilt ran to the water in his nightclothes. By the time he reached his boat, however, she was "one enormous sheet of flame."[5] The fire was too far gone to be fought. All Vanderbilt could do was loosen the *Emerald*'s forward lines and thus allow her to swing round with the current, in this way moving her away from a sloop which, being moored near the *Emerald*'s fiery bow, would otherwise have been at risk. The crew escaped with their lives, but the *Emerald*, which was uninsured, stood a total loss. One week later what remained of her barely floating hull wound up being sunk not far away as a breakwater. Thereafter, the *Bellona* and *Thistle* filled in with extra duty on the New Brunswick/New York run while Vanderbilt awaited the construction of yet another, even more elaborate boat: the *Swan,* launched early in 1827.

A passenger from the *Swan,* William Gorgas, described in a journal entry his passage from New Brunswick to New York. His impressions are worth quoting, for they accurately paint the land and seascape which dominated Vanderbilt's life during these early steamboat years:

All along the Raritan River, is an uninterrupted plane [*sic*] called the salt meadow I suppose several thousands of acres of no manner of use excepting for pasture, the banks are quite low—About 13 miles below N. Brunswick is Pert Amboy a small place situated on the bank—to the right of which is Staten Island, a large and elevated tract of land but is said to have but few inhabitants for its size. To the left before as you enter N. York bay can be seen at a distance the Jersey City. On entering New York Bay, Fort Lafayette is seen in the narrows, between Staten and Long Island which is the passage to the sea. The City presents a close mass of houses with Castle Williams on Governor's Island, seen near it on the right, and Ellis and Bedloe's Island on the left with their fortifications. On approaching, the prominent objects are the tall pyramidal steeple of Trinity Church, the more ornamental one of St. Paul's and the distant top of the Catholic Cathedral & The cluster of trees observed on the shore in front of the City are on the Battery place once fortified, but now the principal public square; and Castle Clinton just west of it, is a place of amusement. We landed just above the Battery ground at about 6 of the clock and were almost like lost sheep, but steered our course for Broadway.[6]

These were the sites with which Vanderbilt had been surrounded, day after day in season, for years: ten years, in fact, as of

1828. These shores and waters (the stretch between New Brunswick on the Raritan River, then the Arthur Kill, the town of Elizabeth on Newark Bay, and the Kill van Kull flowing out past the northeastern tip of Staten Island into New York Harbor) had comprised the lion's share of Cornelius's world ever since he first joined with Thomas Gibbons in 1818. One wonders whether he ever contemplated leaving this geography before the necessity to leave was thrust upon him. After all, his family was well ensconced and happy in the now-comfortable Bellona Hall, and he and Sophia between them were making more than a good income. If there was to be any change at all, he probably assumed it would simply be in his position: a gradual shift from mere management to ownership, while William Gibbons (as Thomas Gibbons had long promised) allowed him to buy out the Gibbons piece of the Union Line on liberal terms.

Years later, Vanderbilt would tell an associate that he'd learned a profound and invaluable lesson when William Gibbons, without warning and without consultation, put the Gibbons interest in the Union Line up for sale on the common market. That happened early in 1828. Gibbons's asking price was $400,000 cash. By his own account, Vanderbilt's life savings at the time amounted to approximately $30,000. Of course, he might have arranged financing rather easily. However, he seems to have believed that Gibbons's asking price was far too high as compared to the value offered—especially since Vanderbilt and Sophia represented the bulk of the management expertise in the firm. Was he, Vanderbilt asked rhetorically, three decades later, to pay a premium to acquire his own talent? He thought not.

While not making an offer to William Gibbons himself, Vanderbilt at the same time let other potential buyers know that should the Union Line change hands he would be leaving the concern to pursue other opportunities. All in New York steamboating circles of course understood Vanderbilt's intimate involvement and utter importance in all aspects of the management of the Union Line operations between New Brunswick and New York, not to mention Sophia Vanderbilt's central part in the running of Bellona Hall. Thus, given Vanderbilt's pledge to leave should the Union Line's ownership change, William Gibbons found no takers for his interest. By summer he'd taken the firm off the market. Vanderbilt, however, took the episode as a sign that he should make his own plans and not, in future, be in any way dependent upon Gibbons's largesse. Since the promises of the father had come to nothing, Vanderbilt now slowly made arrangements to strike out on his own. As an old man, he'd tell an associate that the ultimate lesson he'd been taught by William Gibbons was this: *Never be a minion; always be an owner.*

11

BLACKMAIL ON
THE HUDSON

JUST BEFORE CHRISTMAS OF 1828, CORNELIUS VANDERBILT prepared to make his very last voyage from New Brunswick to New York City as captain of the *Swan*—indeed, as the captain of any Gibbons boat. He'd given formal notice one month before, and on this particular morning he was not the only Vanderbilt boarding the steamer. With him were Sophia and their eight children, including seven-year-old Billy, whom Arthur D. Howden Smith described as "a stolid, uninteresting boy, with narrow, squinty eyes that somehow minimized the effect of a nose that was a replica of his father's masterful beak." Smith added that Billy was "regarded with testy contempt by his redoubtable father."[1] But so were they all, the boy and the seven girls, equally. Given his schedule of the past decade, which had involved long days (and many nights) away from home, and abject exhaustion during the few hours he spent with them at Bellona Hall, it could not be otherwise. Then again, his temperament—brusque and businesslike—could not have helped much either. Vanderbilt, it seems, was not a nurturer, and never would be.

As the children and Sophia lumbered out of Bellona Hall and down to the pier on the Raritan, they could not have been happy. For ten years Bellona Hall had been an idyllic home for the clan. The children had grown up swimming in the river to the front of the place and playing games amid the rich and welcoming woods that swept in close on the other side of the rural hotel. Their school and school-mates were all within a mile or so. Indeed this was the only world and home any of the children had ever really known. One also guesses that Sophia must have had more than a passing affection for Bellona Hall as a successful enterprise that was uniquely and completely hers: the creation of her own sweat and smarts and industriousness. Now all of it—the familiar dwelling, the quiet countryside, the long friendships with neighbors—would become things of the past. Now, upon Cornelius's uncompromising demand, they were launching themselves away: he into the unchartered waters of enterprise, and they into the unchartered waters of unlovely New York. Smith wrote of Sophia that she would have "sought the black waters of the Raritan had she sensed a tithe of the misfortunes awaiting her. It was enough, surely, to stand on the [deck] and watch the dwindling group of friends on the wharf, the tiny smoke-puff above the chimney of Bellona Hall, with its memories of achievement that had justified her to herself in moments of mental anguish, when the remorseless hammer of Corneel's will beat, beat, beat upon a soul that was never intended for conflict."[2]

Despite Vanderbilt's relative affluence as the possessor of $30,000, he moved his family into a grim tenement on Manhattan's Madison Street, paralleling the East River in lower Manhattan, from which it sat back only a few blocks.[3] The tenement was a cramped and unhealthy space. The neighbors were the extended families of longshoremen and laborers, many of these being Irish and German immigrants. Three not very large rooms housed the entire Vanderbilt family. The rent was $100 per year. A mile or so to the north, in the area of Bleecker Street, entire townhouses, newly constructed, could be had for a rent of $300 per year. One is forced to wonder whether the $200 saved annually would have made a very large difference in Vanderbilt's fortunes, and why he chose to subject his wife and children to squalid conditions when such exposure, quite simply, was not necessary.

Vanderbilt turned thirty-five in the spring of 1829. The year before, while still in the employ of William Gibbons, he'd arranged financing and commissioned the building of his own steamboat. The *Citizen*, equivalent to the old *Emerald* and later *Swan*, launched early in the spring from a slip at the foot of New York's Water Street. Not long afterwards, Gibbons (as Vanderbilt probably expected) began having serious problems with the operation of his line. Suffering from the soaring costs that so often accompanied absentee management whenever reliable and trustworthy executives were not in control, Gibbons in June 1829 held what amounted to a fire-sale of his operation, liquidating the entire enterprise at a fraction of the original $400,000 asking price.

Vanderbilt bought two boats: one smaller vessel which he subsequently renamed *Emerald*, after the boat that had burned, and the good old *Bellona*. These, together with his new *Citizen*, he dubbed the Dispatch Line. Meanwhile, the Stevens family bought out the balance of William Gibbons's Union Line interests, including Bellona Hall and the *Swan*. (At the same time, they acquired the assets of the Citizen's Line, which they folded into the Union Line.) For the foreseeable future, the Stevenses would run the Union Line while Vanderbilt, choosing to make his first field of operations one that he knew well, targeted their trade. Vanderbilt put both the

Citizen and the *Bellona* on duty doing alternating runs from Water Street (where all the New York–based Vanderbilt boats now departed) to Staten Island, Elizabeth, and New Brunswick. Vanderbilt captained the *Citizen* personally, while he put a cousin, John Vanderbilt, in charge of the *Bellona*. At the same time, he sent the renamed *Emerald* via ocean-route to the Delaware River, there to be captained by an ambitious twenty-six-year-old navigator named William Whilldin. Wanting to offer Philadelphia/New York through-service packages that were the equivalent to those provided by the Union Line, Vanderbilt also took pains to form partnerships with several stagecoach companies making runs between New Brunswick and Trenton.

A rate war with the Stevens interests erupted immediately. This time, however, it was Vanderbilt's rivals taking the lead in slashing prices. Vanderbilt, with smaller resources, was at first hesitant to respond in kind. For a brief period of a few weeks, Vanderbilt attempted to keep his rates higher than those on the Stevens boats, positioning the Dispatch Line as the conveyance of choice for first class passengers. His ads boasted that travelers on the Dispatch Line could be assured comfortable and dignified accommodations without "the pressure of a crowd of ten-shilling passengers."[4] The approach failed, however, and Vanderbilt realized that in order to fill his boats he had no other choice but to bring his prices down. Eventually, in the autumn of 1829, both the Dispatch Line and the Union Line were offering one-dollar passage between Philadelphia and New York—a lower fare than had been asked in more than ten years. For good measure, Vanderbilt offered a six-cent fare between New York and New Brunswick, with a meal thrown in.

He could do this because he was thinking short term. Vanderbilt's ambition, evidently, was not to own the New York/Philadelphia trade, nor the New York/New Brunswick trade, but rather just to harass the Union Line into buying him off. After a year of bleeding himself, and in turn forcing the Stevens forces to bleed, he won. Although the precise amount of Vanderbilt's remuneration is not known, it seems that in 1830 he accepted about $10,000 and a royalty payable on future Union Line business in return for his retreat from the market between Philadelphia and New York. For the foreseeable future, he would focus his energies and assets on the Hudson River corridor. His only business touching upon New Jersey or Staten Island was to be a ferry service from Elizabeth to ports in Staten Island and then Manhattan that he leased from William Gibbons on a seven-year agreement, which he later renewed.

Vanderbilt allocated much of his proceeds from the Union Line blackmail, together with some leveraged money, to pay off the acquisition of yet another steamboat, the *John Marshall*. This was an older boat that had previously made runs between Manhattan and Norwalk, Connecticut. The steamer had, several years before, been commanded on its Norwalk run by Captain Noah Brooks—a young man who as a boy of fifteen, in 1810, had been apprenticed with Vanderbilt's cousin John. Brooks was soon to start commanding various Vanderbilt-owned boats on the Hudson River and the Long Island Sound. In the not distant future, Brooks would also win another distinction by becoming one of the few employees who would go against Vanderbilt on a point of principle and prevail. "While Capt. Brooks was running one of Cornelius Vanderbilt's boats," wrote Samuel Orcott, a Connecticut minister who had been an acquaintance of Brooks, "Mr. Vanderbilt made arrangements for and insisted upon Sunday trips." The devout Brooks, however, had another idea. "Capt. Brooks at once resigned his position. This occurred when he was a young man, dependent entirely upon his own labor for livelihood. From his knowledge of Mr. Vanderbilt's character, he had no doubt that all business relations between them were at an end." Nevertheless, Brooks remained true to his religious convictions whatever the cost. And in time, Vanderbilt came back to Brooks. Vanderbilt "invited him to return to his service, with total exemption from Sunday duty, with advanced position and better pay than before." Orcott marveled at this display of magnanimity from one such as Vanderbilt who, as Orcott noted, "then made no pretensions to a religious character."[5]

With captains like Brooks and John Vanderbilt in place, Cornelius brought the *Emerald* back from the Delaware River (leaving Whilldin behind in Philadelphia to fend for himself). Then, with four boats— the *Citizen*, the *John Marshall*, the *Bellona*, and the *Emerald*—he set about positioning himself for Hudson River commerce.

These were waters with which Vanderbilt was quite familiar from his sailing days. He knew all the whims of the tidal estuary: the subtle slice of water that Native Americans through millennia had described as "the river that flows two ways." Vanderbilt understood the rhythm and gradual rotation of the Hudson's tides as they flushed in and out at the whim of the ocean below. (At high tide, the Hudson was brackish as far north as Poughkeepsie, some seventy miles above Manhattan.) As well, Vanderbilt knew most of the harbormasters of the various ports on either side of the river, and still had good contacts with many of the wholesalers and shippers who had given him trade when he was running sloops and schooners between the Battery and Albany. When Vanderbilt entered the Hudson River trade, he did so with a fairly precise prior knowledge of what was to be had in the way of inbound and outbound business involving not just Albany, but also such other major Hudson River stops as the towns of Hudson, Kingston, Poughkeepsie, Highland, Newburgh, Beacon, Haverstraw, Croton, and Tarrytown—all places where he'd picked up extensive business in his sailboat days.

It was not by virtue of the decision in *Gibbons vs. Ogden* that Vanderbilt had leave to enter and compete between one New York port and another. The *Gibbons vs. Ogden* decision had impacted interstate commerce only. After the decision of the Supreme Court, the Livingston-Fulton monopoly remained intact and on good legal standing with regard to all steamers voyaging between New York ports. Neither the federal government nor the Supreme Court had disputed the state of New York's right to regulate intrastate commerce in any way it saw fit. However, the monopoly remained just as supremely unpopular within New York as it had been without. Numerous would-be steamboat entrepreneurs in cities from Albany to Manhattan and the eastern tip of Long Island felt themselves unjustly stifled and hindered. These forces soon coalesced to create a political situation which demanded remediation and the Livingston-Fulton cabal's eventual annihilation. The final blow came in 1825, when the New York Court of Errors annulled the exclusive grant to Livingston and Fulton, thus opening the waters of the state to completely unfettered trade.

One group of entrepreneurs who took advantage of the open Hudson River before Vanderbilt did was none other than the Stevens family. The father, John Stevens, was by now far more interested in locomotives than steamboats. But his sons established the North River Line on the Hudson. Their boats quickly became the dominant fleet on the same river from which Stevens and his *Phoenix* had been banned two decades earlier. Another competitor on the Hudson River was Cornelius's younger brother Jacob Hand Vanderbilt (known popularly as "Captain Jake") who owned a half interest in the *General Jackson,* which plied the route between Manhattan and Peekskill, on the river's eastern shore (a ninety-mile round trip). The other half of the boat was owned by Westchester native Stephen Van Wart, whose uncle Isaac Van Wart had been a local hero of the Revolution: one of a party of four patriots who captured the British spy Major John Andre and thus foiled the plan of General Benedict Arnold to surrender West Point, on the Hudson, to British forces.

Jacob's partner Stephen, born in 1777, had been a small child at the time.

Competition between the *General Jackson* and various Stevens boats had been fierce from the beginning and, as in so many other theaters of steamboat navigation, hinged upon speed. In the name of boosting schedules and setting record runs, safety valves and vents on the *Jackson* and other steamboats were routinely left closed, and gauges left unwatched. On June 7, 1831, just off Grassy Point near Haverstraw, the boiler of the *General Jackson* exploded in what was to be the most deadly such event on the Hudson River to date. Fourteen people (including Van Wart, who was at the helm) died immediately, and several others within days. "The boiler was lifted from its place, and the boat rendered a perfect wreck," wrote a reporter not long after. Jacob Vanderbilt, who had not been on board at the time and had no reason to know, later maintained that "the steam had not been raised to an excessive height, thus showing his conviction that the safety valves were not overloaded, and that the steam gauge had been observed."[6] Journalists doubted the claim. During the same conversation with reporters, Jacob praised the *Jackson*'s engineer, who had been killed, saying the man had been one of the finest in his profession, and had come recommended by none other than Cornelius himself.

The *General Jackson* went in for repairs and, in due course, was back plying her trade. For most of the public, the tragedy was not big news. Indeed, such hazards had come to be expected: a slight downside to the convenience and speed of steam-driven propulsion, which remained a new and imperfect technology. During the spring of 1826, a flue in the boiler of the steamboat *Hudson* had collapsed in the midst of a run—remarkably without loss of life. That same year two steamboat explosions occurred in Charleston, South Carolina, resulting in four deaths and one severe scalding. During

March of 1827 the *Oliver Ellsworth*, on the Connecticut River, experienced a major accident as the result of a collapsed flue. Two
years later, ten or twelve people died when the steamer *Tricolor*, operating near Wheeling in what is now West Virginia, suffered an
explosion caused by a deficiency of water in the boiler. And a year
after that, several people died when the boiler of the steamer *Macon*
exploded in 1830, near Sullivan's Island, in Georgia.

Occasional explosions would remain standard for quite some
time to come. At the same time, the breathless pace at which the
steamers from the various lines proceeded as they competed with
one another, continued to increase. As well, the hordes of travelers
that began to descend as boats got bigger and fares dropped lower
due to excess capacity and price wars continued to grow. Both phenomena conspired to make steamboat transport quite uncivilized
as an exercise, at least in the eyes of some. The Knickerbocker
writer Nathaniel Parker Willis, a friend of Washington Irving's
who lived on the Hudson near Newburgh and rode Vanderbilt's
boats frequently, described how the grandiose beauty of the Hudson River landscape was lost completely on most travelers dealing
with the rigors of steamboat "convenience."

With most persons, to mention the Palisades is only to recall the
confusion of a steamer's deck, just off from the wharf, with a
freight of seven or eight hundred souls hoping to "take tea" in
Albany. The scene is one of inextricable confusion, and it is not
till the twenty miles of the Palisades are well passed that the be-
wildered passenger knows rightly whether his wife, child, or baggage, whichever may be his tender care, is not being left behind
at the rate of fifteen miles in the hour.

I have often flung my valise into the corner and, sure that the
whole of my person and personal effects was under way, watched

the maniform [*sic*] embarrassments and troubles that beset the uninitiated voyager upon the Hudson. Fifteen minutes before the starting of the boat, there is not a passenger aboard: "time is money," and the American, counting it as part of the expense, determines to pay only "on demand." He arrives on the narrow pier at the same instant with seven hundred men, ladies, and children, besides lapdogs, crammed baskets, uncut novels, and baggage for the whole. No commissioner in the world would guarantee to get all this freight on board in the given time, and yet it is done, to the daily astonishment of newspaper hawkers, orange women, and penny-a-liners watching for dreadful accidents.

The plank is drawn in, the wheels begin to paw like foaming steeds impatient to be off, the bell rings as if it were letting down the steps of the last hackney-coach, and away darts the boat, like half a town suddenly slipping off and talking a walk on the water.[7]

Poets and artists had dubbed the river "the Lordly Hudson" and "the Rhine of America." Painters came from around the world to capture her beauties. Indeed, Thomas Cole, the English artist who was to found the Hudson River School, had first explored the Hudson and the Catskills only a few years before, in 1825. But to most of the paying customers who traveled upon her, just as to the steamboat entrepreneurs and crews who made their livings upon her, the river was, at turns, either an obstacle to be overcome or a resource to be exploited. There was no poetry in commerce; nor was there any in technology. Willis was not the only writer to notice how the frantic steamers seemed to suck all the charm and romance out of the Hudson Highlands with their whistles, howling engines, violent wakes, and occasional explosions disrupting the formerly tranquil riverscape in a way that could not be described as anything but ugly.

Ugly or not, the steam trade generated significant cash, even amid price wars and other facts of the competitive marketplace. During mid-1831, Cornelius Vanderbilt felt rich enough to add another boat to his collection. The custom-designed *Cinderella* was relatively small at 145 tons, but her narrow beam pierced the water with minimum resistance so that she made fast time on the Hudson. Additionally, Cornelius bought out (at a considerable discount) the half share in the wounded *General Jackson* previously owned by the heirs of poor Van Wart. In this way he became partners with his brother in that vessel. While the *General Jackson* was laid up for repairs after her explosion, Cornelius used the *Cinderella* to service the lucrative Peekskill/New York run, taking over what had previously been a small monopoly for the *Jackson*. However, Vanderbilt was able to exploit his plum position exacting fat fees for transport on that line for only two months before a serious competitor appeared.

The competition came in the person of Daniel Drew, with whom Vanderbilt was to a have a long, complex and often troubled relationship. Three years younger than Vanderbilt, Drew had been born on a farm in Carmel, Putnam County, New York, not far north of the Westchester County border. As a youth he worked as a roustabout in circuses. Then, at the time of the War of 1812, the fourteen-year-old succumbed to the temptation of a $100 sign-up bonus and joined the ranks of the United States Army. As fate had it, he never faced the enemy. Following his discharge, Drew became a drover: purchasing cattle from local farmers in Putnam and Westchester counties, then bringing them down to New York wholesalers, to whom he sold the beef. During these sojourns, Drew would routinely salt his beasts to make them ravenously thirsty. Then he'd stop in the village of Harlem to "water" his stock before selling them by the pound downtown. (In later years, Drew would develop the same subtle art into a Wall Street gambit, watering stocks in much the same way he'd always watered his cattle. He would also develop a well-deserved reputation as a liar and a swindler, this despite his numerous Bible-thumping professions of faith and his teetotal habits.)

Living in Carmel, Drew frequently used Captain Jake's *General Jackson* to get down to New York from nearby Peekskill Landing. With a nose for opportunity, he noticed the decks full of passengers and the fully loaded cargo bays. He also made note of the grumblings of local farmers, many of them his acquaintances, who complained loudly about usurious prices and how the Vanderbilt brothers were taking unfair advantage of their position as the only providers of steam service between Putnam County and the city. With this in the wind, Drew bought a half interest in the steamboat *Water Witch*, owned by James Smith, near the end of July 1831. Drew's share of the investment represented some of his own money, but also smaller sums put into a pot by the previously grumbling farmers, who advanced the capital in the interest of smashing the Vanderbilts' advantage as sole providers. On August 7, New York and Putnam County newspapers announced the schedule of the *Water Witch*, saying that no pains would be "spared to render every accommodation to the traveling community on this rout, with the hope to merit their patronage."[8]

A rate war commenced immediately. The *Water Witch* lost $10,000 in her first year. The Vanderbilt brothers suffered similarly. In the course of the war, one-way passage between the two points dropped to a single schilling (twelve and a half cents). With both Drew's line and Vanderbilt's Dispatch Line hemorrhaging cash, the situation could not go on for long. During the spring of 1832, after the *Water Witch* had been plying the Peekskill route for less than a year, Drew and Smith betrayed the farmers who had helped bank them by selling the *Water Witch* to Cornelius and Jacob Vanderbilt. In turn, the Vanderbilts immediately took the *Water Witch* off the Hudson and restored the old rates on the *Gen-*

eral Jackson, which itself had also, by now, been restored. It is said that Drew did not even pay back his farmer backers, who had naively advanced him funds on faith rather than as formal "paper," and that he had to keep a low profile in Putnam County for quite some time. As for the *Water Witch,* she eventually wound up owned entirely by Jacob Vanderbilt, who ran her on the Long Island Sound and up the Connecticut River as far as Hartford, starting in 1833.

Once he'd regained control of the Peekskill route and raised prices to a level of robust profitability, Cornelius looked to extend his trade to Albany in a grand way. He'd sold the *Bellona* and another older boat in mid-1831, and he used the proceeds from those sales to fund the construction of a substantial new vessel. At 230 tons, the *Westchester* was easily the most substantial boat on the river when she launched in late April 1832. She had been built at the yard of Smith and Dimon on the East River at the foot of Fourth and Lewis Streets, Pier 9. Commencing on May 3, she began leaving Manhattan for Albany, and Albany for Manhattan, at 7:00 A.M. on alternate days. The first voyage from New York on May 3 signaled the commencement of a three-year siege by Vanderbilt against the interests of a formidable cabal: the Hudson River Steamboat Association.

The Association was, in essence, a pool of steamboat entrepreneurs on the Hudson (one formed after the demise of the Livingston-Fulton monopoly) whose members colluded amongst themselves (in a perfectly legal manner, well before the age of antitrust laws) to shape yet another monopoly. The Association dictated routes, schedules, and fares, and thus put free trade on the Hudson into shackles yet again. Leading members included Robert and James Stevens of Hoboken, who were the sons of John Stevens, himself preoccupied with his fledgling Camden and Amboy Railroad. (Like his father, Robert was a tinkerer and inventor who innovated many steamboat improvements, including walking beams and false bows.) Another leader in the Association was one Isaac Newton, an energetic entrepreneur from Manhattan who would be the first to pioneer the use of coal, as opposed to wood, in steamboat engines. Then there was also Dean Richmond, a hard-living, hard-drinking, and hard-swearing old river hand who was well connected in New York's then-powerful Democratic Party, himself being a member of the so-called "Albany Regency" group which dominated politics at the New York State Capitol.

At first, Vanderbilt employed just the *Westchester* to engage in a price war with the Association's interests. However, one year later, in 1833, he put yet another vessel on the Albany run. Built that year in the New York yard of Bishop & Simonson (one of the partners, Jeremiah Simonson, being a nephew to Cornelius), the *Union* was equally as large as the *Westchester,* and just as grand. Both boats featured lavish amenities: comfortable seating, food service, bars, and various lounges. In the midst of the price war, fares dropped from three dollars (the preferred Association rate for passage between New York and Albany) to ten cents, and at the very end of the war, to zero. What Vanderbilt gave away in free passage, however, he seems to have made up for (at least to some extent) by charging hefty prices for food. Operating costs for a single Albany/New York run of an average steamboat in 1832 have been estimated at a mere $200. Vanderbilt easily made this much in food- and drink-service profits on any given voyage. Thus his price war was most likely a break-even proposition for him. What was more, Vanderbilt had excellent inbound cash-flow not only from his Peekskill route, but from the Elizabeth ferry which he still controlled and operated, dedicating the *Cinderella* to that purpose as of 1832.

The Association's ten boats, on the other hand, represented the sole revenue streams for many Association members. Although they, too, probably had a break-even situation on their hands, the majority of the members of the Association (the Stevenses exempted) possessed no other sources of revenue. Therefore, the ravages of the price-war were felt keenly by many in the camp opposing Vanderbilt. Meanwhile, as had been the case when Vanderbilt targeted the Stevens clan on the Raritan, and when Drew targeted Vanderbilt on the Peekskill route, Vanderbilt's ambition here was not to dominate Hudson River traffic in the long-term, but merely to make the Association desperate enough to buy Vanderbilt off. In this spirit he ran his boats and waited.

On June 14, 1833, Vanderbilt himself was at the helm of the *Cinderella* when President Andrew Jackson was a passenger. One guesses Vanderbilt was polite, even though he himself was a supporter of his acquaintance Daniel Webster as well as Henry Clay, two key players in the newly formed Whig party, which generally opposed the interests of Jacksonian Democrats.

Five months later, having to go to Philadelphia on business, Vanderbilt bowed to his curiosity about the nature of Stevens's new Camden and Amboy Railroad. Ironically, Vanderbilt's history with American railroading was not to be off to an auspicious start. Cornelius boarded an early-morning train at Amboy, New Jersey, on November 8 and (no doubt) marveled at the speed with which the contraption progressed through the meadows near Highstown, New Jersey (twenty-five miles per hour).

"There were upwards of two hundred passengers in the Amboy railroad cars," recalled former President John Quincy Adams, who was sitting in a coach ahead of Vanderbilt on the same journey. "There were two locomotive-engines, A and B, each drawing an accommodation car, a sort of moving stage, in a square, with open railing, a platform, and a row of benches holding forty or fifty persons; then four or five cars in the form of large stage-coaches; each in three compartments, with doors of entrance on both sides, and two opposite benches, on each of which sat four passengers." According to newspaper accounts, the train was maintaining its twenty-five-mile-per-hour clip when an axle in the car forward of Vanderbilt (the car carrying Adams) gave way, and the car in which Vanderbilt was sitting overturned. Thrown violently from the train, Vanderbilt then fell down a thirty-foot embankment. By the end of his fall, he'd broken three ribs and suffered a punctured lung. But he was lucky. "Of sixteen persons in two of the three compartments of the car that overset," wrote Adams, "one only escaped unhurt. . . . One side of the car was stove in, and almost demolished. One man, John C. Stedman, of Raleigh, North Carolina, was so dreadfully mangled that he died within ten minutes; another, named, I believe, Welles, of Pennsylvania, can probably not survive the day." Adams called the wreck "the most dreadful catastrophe that ever my eyes beheld!"[9]

Sophia's sister, Jane Robbins, was at that time working in the Vanderbilt household as a nurse assisting Sophia with her large and growing brood. Upon receiving word of the accident, Jane came directly to New Jersey. There she tended Cornelius for three weeks before bringing him back to the family home. Here Vanderbilt would convalesce for several months. It was now that Vanderbilt made the acquaintance of Jared Linsly, the man who was to be his primary physician and one of his few close friends for the rest of his life.[10] A native of what is now North Branford, Connecticut, Linsly had graduated from Yale in 1826. Thereafter, he studied medicine with Dr. John C. Cheesman of Manhattan. Linsly graduated from the College of Physicians and Surgeons in the fall of 1829. At the time that he came to Vanderbilt's sickbed in New Jersey, the thirty-year-old Linsly was three years into a partnership with Dr. William Baldwin of New York, to whose daughter Catherine he was engaged to be married. In addition to tending to Cornelius going forward, Linsly would also become Sophia's primary physician.

Still on the mend through the end of 1833 and into early 1834, Vanderbilt nevertheless laid plans and made deals with the object of further discomforting the doyens of the Hudson River Association. He sold the *Westchester* to Daniel Drew, and used the funds thus gathered as down payments for the construction of two new boats: the *Champion* and the *Nimrod*. These he declared the flagships of a new enterprise: the People's Line, so named because its mission was to battle in the public interest against monopoly. Or so Vanderbilt said. Both boats were launched in August 1834, long after Vanderbilt's recovery. The two day-boats operated on opposite schedules. Where Vanderbilt had previously offered day-boat service from New York to Albany and from Albany to New York on alternating days, he now offered day-boat service in both directions every day. And at bargain prices: just fifty cents one way between Albany and Manhattan, with shorter trips prorated accordingly for those who wished to get on or off at Kingston, Poughkeepsie, Tarrytown, or elsewhere. Even given Vanderbilt's lucrative Peekskill and Elizabeth franchises, many nevertheless wondered how he could afford to build newer and faster boats and run them on accelerated schedules while at the same time slashing fares. The answer, of course, was simple volume. With fast and attractive steamers offered at dramatically low fares, and with the populist appeal of the "People's Line" name working for him, Vanderbilt filled his boats and continued to break even on the Albany route; meanwhile, the Elizabeth and Peekskill franchises brought in positive cash-flow.

Of course, the Hudson River Association continued to take notice. Near the close of the 1834 season, as Christmas approached, Robert Stevens found himself delegated by his colleagues to buy

Vanderbilt off. After several conversations, Vanderbilt agreed to absent himself from the Hudson River for one solid decade in exchange for an immediate bonus payment of $100,000 and an annual fee of $5,000 for each year of the agreement. So much for Vanderbilt's war on monopoly. Somewhat to the Association's chagrin, Daniel Drew soon picked up the name of Vanderbilt's suddenly defunct People's Line and ran competitive boats in the same manner until he too was bought off, receiving a $50,000 initial bonus and a $10,000 annual fee. Several other opportunists also followed the same model—so many, in fact, that eventually the *New York Herald* editorialized on "the curious fact that there are several steamboat captains now in this city (who have been bought off the North River line by the old monopoly company) who walk about the streets with their hands in their breeches pockets, and who are each receiving from $5,000 to $10,000 annually for staying in the city doing nothing . . . suffering their boats to remain rotting at the wharves instead of running in opposition to [the boats of the Hudson River Association] and reducing the rates."[11]

Perhaps others were roaming the streets with their hands in their pockets. Vanderbilt was not.

12

THE SOUND ...
AND BEYOND

UNLIKE FACTORIES OR FARMS OR THE FLEDGLING RAILROADS, the beauty of steamboats as a capital investment was that they could be moved from one theater of operations to another with relative ease. In fact, with impunity. Thus, after Vanderbilt was bought off the New Brunswick and Hudson River routes, it was easy enough for him to set his sights on the next most likely target, the Long Island Sound, where he'd already dabbled as an owner of sailboats. (Of course, as early as 1832, he'd explored New England steam routes when he quite profitably put the *Chancellor Livingston* on the Boston-Portland run under a Maine skipper.)

As previously mentioned, Jacob Vanderbilt had, since 1833, been running his *Water Witch* between Manhattan and Hartford, Connecticut. This route took him from the Battery, up the East River, through Hell Gate, out into the Sound, and then along the Connecticut coast to Old Lyme, where he turned up the Connecticut River and headed north to Hartford. Stops along the way included

Stamford, Old Lyme, and several inland Connecticut towns in addition to Hartford. Early on, adopting the standard Vanderbilt price-war strategy for staggering the competition, Captain Jake lowered New York/Hartford fares on the *Water Witch* to $1, and garnered the lion's share of the traffic nearly instantaneously, putting a serious crimp into the operations and profitability of the previously dominant Hartford Steamboat Company.

Cornelius, meanwhile, eyed the lucrative Providence/New York route. At the start of the 1835 season, typical fares on the New York/Providence run, which ran up from the city into the Sound, thence along the Connecticut coast, and round Point Judith into Narragansett Bay, ran about $8 full fare between the starting and ending ports. On the main route connecting southeastern New England with Manhattan, the Manhattan/Providence steamer trade was growing in popularity all the time. Not only was Providence itself a thriving commercial center needing the swiftest possible connection to the metropolis of New York, but the town was also the most convenient point-of-waterborne-departure for Boston travelers wishing to get to New York. That summer of 1835, the Boston & Providence Railroad completed a four-year effort to link the two towns by rail. Thereafter, pending the eventual development of more rail lines, the swiftest way to travel between Manhattan and Boston became steamboat between Manhattan and Providence, and train between Providence and Boston.

The train depot was situated conveniently right beside the wharves at Providence's India Point. Writing years later, the journalist Benjamin Perley Poore remembered that the New York–bound steamboats "lay at India Point, just below the town [of Providence], where immense quantities of wood were piled up, for each boat consumed between thirty and forty cords on a trip through Long Island Sound." Perley further recalled that there were "no staterooms, the passengers occupying berths, and at dinner and supper the captain of the boat occupied the head of the table, having seated near him any distinguished passengers."[1] As on the Hudson, there were no varying classes of tickets: cobbler and banker sat down at the same table, although the banker was likely seated closer to the commander of the vessel.

Like the steamboats, the Boston & Providence Railroad enforced a rather raw democracy that some wealthy Brahmins and Knickerbockers found annoying. Samuel Breck, an affluent Philadelphian of Boston birth, rode the railroad from Boston to Providence shortly after it opened, and came away disgusted by the egalitarian nature of this form of travel. "Five or six other cars were attached to the loco, and uglier boxes I do not wish to travel in. They were huge carriages made to stow away some thirty human beings, who sit cheek to jowl as best they can. Two poor fellows, who were not much in the habit of making their toilet, squeezed me into a corner, while the hot sun drew down from their garments a villainous compound of smells made up of salt fish, tar and molasses." Factory girls on holiday also afflicted Breck's sensibilities, and he took it as an insult when a conductor asked that he give up his seat for them in the name of gallantry. "The rich and the poor, the educated and the ignorant, the polite and the vulgar, all herd together in this modern improvement of traveling. . . . Steam, so useful in many respects, interferes with the comfort of traveling, destroys every salutary distinction in society, and overturns with its whirligig power the once rational, gentlemanly and safe mode of getting along on a journey."[2]

Breck's sensibilities aside, Vanderbilt could not have timed his entry into the New York/Providence market any better given the concurrent completion of the Boston & Providence Railroad. Vanderbilt's first boat on the New York/Providence run was the *Lexington:* a massive vessel which he launched during the spring of 1835. Built in the New York yard of Bishop & Simonson and measuring 208 feet from stem to stern, the *Lexington* weighed 488 tons and featured enormous paddle-wheels 23 feet in diameter. She had been specifically designed to move both fast and cheaply. The boat, capable of speeds up to 20 miles per hour, routinely covered the 210 miles between Providence and New York in under twelve hours. Almost more important, she did so using roughly half the wood that a vessel of her size would normally demand. Her specially designed vertical-beam engine (built by the West Point Foundry and strategically positioned at the beam) delivered such tremendous fuel economies that Vanderbilt would be able to devour his competition when it came to pricing, and do so without jeopardizing his own profitability. After the *Lexington*'s maiden voyage on June 1, the New York *Evening Post* breathlessly proclaimed her "the fastest boat in the world." The same paper, in the same report, heaped praise on the *Lexington*'s sire. "The *Lexington* was built by Bishop & Simonson, under the direction of Captain Cornelius Vanderbilt, her owner. Her construction exhibits great knowledge of mechanical principles, and a peculiarly bold and independent genius."[3] Although Vanderbilt himself captained the *Lexington* on her initial runs, Captain Jake was soon called from the Connecticut River to take the helm. Jacob, in turn, hired a captain to command the *Water Witch* for him on the Hartford/New York route.

In addition to offering a fast and modern boat, Vanderbilt also slashed prices, going almost immediately to $4 for one-way passage between Providence and New York. For this he was hailed by the *Evening Post* as "the greatest practical anti-monopolist in the country."[4] Vanderbilt's principal competition in the Providence trade was a firm known as the Boston & New York Transportation Company, which in 1835 owned six boats on the Sound: the steamers *Boston*, *Providence*, *President*, *Benjamin Franklin*, *Massachusetts*, and *Rhode Island*, all of them being relatively small. Up until Vanderbilt's arrival on the scene, the company had been a sole provider and had charged accordingly—thus explaining the $8 fare quoted above. The firm's chairman was thirty-two-year-old Moses H. Grinnell, a New York shipping merchant and Whig politician who, like Vanderbilt, had worked himself up from nothing. Grinnell was born to near poverty in New Bedford, Massachusetts, and moved to New York when he was fifteen. When he was twenty, he journeyed to Rio de Janeiro as supercargo and, disposing of his responsibilities, next carried South American coffee of his own purchase to Trieste, where he again made a killing. After his return to Manhattan, he and a partner founded Grinnell, Minturn & Co., which by 1835 was known in ports around the world. In particular, the firm dominated two major packet routes—New York to London and New York to Liverpool. Given all this, it is clear that the business of the Long Island Sound was a secondary matter to Grinnell. However, it remained a sphere in which he was intent on succeeding.

In that spirit, during the spring of 1836, Grinnell launched the *Narragansett*—a boat with which Grinnell hoped and failed to beat both the speed and the economies of the *Lexington*. The *Narragansett* was reasonably fast, but unstable—pitching and rolling in even the slightest chop. Also, her hull was not crafted tightly enough to sustain the vibrational stress emanating from her powerful engines; visits to the dry dock for recaulking became common. Perhaps buoyed by the shortcomings of the *Narragansett*, Vanderbilt launched yet another ship, the *Cleopatra*, in 1837, which he promptly put on a mirror-run with the *Lexington*, each vessel leaving New York on alternating days. That same year, the Rhode Island Legislature shot down an attempt by the Boston & Providence Railroad, which held a small interest in Grinnell's company, to deny Vanderbilt access to the wharves near the India Point depot. The legislature insisted that the railroad honor its charter,

which called for the provision of fair and equal access to all steamers seeking to make connections.

The calculus of Boston/New York through-traffic was further
complicated in the autumn of 1837, when completion of the new
Providence & Stonington Railroad extended outbound Boston rail
service some forty-eight miles from Providence to the seaport town
of Stonington in southeastern Connecticut. In response, both
Grinnell and Vanderbilt built Stonington stops into the schedules
of their vessels, giving the railroad passengers the option of boarding or disembarking the boats at either India Point or Stonington.
Vanderbilt promptly noticed the rapid decline in Providence trade,
and somewhat darkly contemplated plans by a group of New York
businessmen to extend rails south across the Connecticut coast
from Stonington, as well as up from New York. At about this same
time, in the face of increased demand that was filling all boats,
Grinnell and Vanderbilt worked out a pricing agreement for their
Providence steamers. The two colluded to restore the old $8 one-
way rate between Manhattan and India Point, and journalists once
again stopped touting Vanderbilt as a great anti-monopolist.

Leaders in Providence's business community just as quickly became alarmed. They believed, with reason, that the restoration of the
high fare would mean the diversion of passenger traffic to Stonington arrivals and departures. (The steamboat fare between Stonington
and New York was just $6, while the railroad fare between Boston
and Stonington was only $1 higher than the fare between Boston and
Providence. Given this price structure, any traveler could save a dollar on the through-price between Boston and New York if they simply bypassed Providence and made connections at Stonington. As
well, the Stonington transfer allowed travelers to avoid the rounding
of treacherous Point Judith, at the mouth of Narragansett Bay, notorious as the site of numerous shipwrecks.) Despite these realities of

the marketplace and geography, the Providence interests formed the Atlantic Steamboat Company in 1837. One year later, they launched the 500-ton steamer *John W. Richmond* (named for the president of the company).

The *Richmond*'s hull had been built at a shipyard situated on Eddy's Point in Providence, and her boilers came from the Providence Steam Engine Company.[5] Her captain was William H. Townsend, a respected Rhode Island coast skipper, under whose direction she had been built. The *John W. Richmond* and Vanderbilt's *Lexington* (with Jacob Vanderbilt at the helm) ran a rather famous race in the spring of 1838, shortly after the *Richmond*'s launch on June 7, with the *Richmond* barely beating the *Lexington* on a run from Stonington to New York. Not long after, in that same year, Vanderbilt sold the *Lexington* to Grinnell for $60,000. Grinnell converted the boilers to burn coal and refurbished the interior. Tragically, the *Lexington* was destined to burn while abroad on the Sound during a frigid night in January 1840. Of two hundred people aboard, only four would survive. As the man who had built the boat, Vanderbilt testified at the inquest as to the sea-worthiness of the craft. Vanderbilt insisted that when he owned the *Lexington,* he had her skippers on instructions to plow right through any and all foul weather: "If only they could see ahead, they were to go ahead."[6]

The same year he sold the *Lexington* to Grinnell, 1838, Vanderbilt bought a half interest in the Staten Island Ferry. (Vanderbilt's partner in the Staten Island Ferry was Oroondates Mauran, a native Rhode Islander but now a New Yorker who, like Grinnell, had grown rich as a shipping merchant. Unlike Grinnell, however, Mauran made a specialty of the West Indies.) At forty-two years of age in 1838, Mauran was two years younger than the forty-four-year-old Vanderbilt. His chief interest in the ferry enterprise (which at that time consisted of the boats *Samson, Hercules,* and

Bolivar running between Tompkinsville, Stapleton, Vanderbilt Landing/Clifton, and New York) seems to have sprung from his recent acquisition of a summer home on the island. It appears, as well, that Mauran left the day-to-day management of the ferry to Vanderbilt, and that he and Vanderbilt, both with considerable money to invest, partnered in numerous land deals on the island, Mauran being the negotiator for these.

Along with the ferry, Vanderbilt continued to operate the *Chancellor Livingston* (later to be replaced by larger and faster boats, the *Augusta* and *C. Vanderbilt*) on the Boston/Portland route. Elsewhere, he'd for three years tasked the old *Citizen* to innovate a run between Boston and the New Hampshire towns of Portsmouth and Dover, on the Piscataqua River. Other Vanderbilt steamers developed short routes within the Sound and in other precincts. The *Nimrod* ran between New York and Bridgeport. The *Water Witch* came down from the Connecticut River and was put to work servicing the Elizabeth ferry trade, being replaced on the Hartford route by the *Cleopatra* and later by the *Champion*. And Vanderbilt's *Clifton* developed a new route via the Long Island Sound, stopping at ports on the north shore of Long Island between Manhattan and Sag Harbor. (Business on the Elizabeth ferry grew exponentially when the Elizabethtown and Somerville Railroad, later to be known as the New Jersey Central, extended rail service to Elizabeth.)

One year into his association with the Staten Island Ferry, Vanderbilt had to swat a fly of competition in the person of a cousin, Oliver Vanderbilt of Castleton. Early in 1839, Oliver purchased a small steamer, the *Wave,* and its dock from the Keyport Company, which had previously offered a ferry service but was finding competition from the Mauran/Vanderbilt organization to be too much to deal with. Oliver's cause was lost from the start—and blood did not prove thicker than water when it came to competition. Cornelius continued a price war he'd previously launched against the Keyport Company, eventually bringing fares down to six and a half cents per trip. He also lodged a motion in the courts disputing Oliver's title to the dockage he'd acquired from Keyport. While the case was being deliberated, Cornelius took it upon himself to fence the old Keyport landing and dump a large load of gravel there. Showing Vanderbiltian fortitude, Oliver managed to remain in business for several years as the Citizen's Line before folding.

By now, newspapers routinely referred to Cornelius Vanderbilt as "the Commodore." His personal income was well above $30,000 per year, and his net worth approximately $1.2 million. In addition to his steamboat interests and land speculations on Staten Island, Vanderbilt also held real estate in Perth Amboy and elsewhere. He was no longer a giant in the making. He was a giant growing larger.

13

OF AN OLD
DUTCH ROOT

As THE RAILROAD MAP OF THE EASTERN SEABOARD CONTINUED to change, so did its impact on steamboat routes. More and more, the trains appeared to be the dog, and the steamers the tail wagged by the dog. On the Sound, Stonington remained the main, undisputed transfer point for travelers between New York and Boston up until 1840, with the diminished India Point facilities at Providence filling the number two spot. However, in 1840, the Norwich & Worcester Railroad connected Allyn's Point near Norwich, Connecticut (on the Thames River above coastal New London, Connecticut) with Worcester, Massachusetts, the latter town being a thriving commercial center with a fast train connection to Boston. With the cutting of a ribbon, Norwich suddenly became the preferred transfer point for many Boston/New York travelers.

Both Norwich and New London, the latter located on the Sound some thirteen miles to the west of Stonington, had previously hosted lethargic and ill-used steamboat operations catering to New

York–bound travelers. However, the market there had not been large enough to interest the likes of Vanderbilt or other major players. Now that changed. Both Vanderbilt and Menemon Sanford, whose Hartford Steamboat Company had previously given Cornelius and "Captain Jake" Vanderbilt considerable competition on the Connecticut River, started running New York boats up the Thames to connect with Norwich & Worcester trains, and Vanderbilt cut back his service to Stonington and Providence. Vanderbilt's and Sanford's boats connecting New York with Allyn's Point were both night boats, departing Manhattan at 5:00 P.M. Passengers ate and then bedded down, being roused from their berths some eleven hours later to board trains in the wee hours of the morning. Passengers coming from Boston suffered equally inconvenient schedules. Nevertheless, the route flourished. Eventually, Vanderbilt dedicated his *Cleopatra, New Haven,* and *Worcester* steamboats to the Norwich route, the latter boat being under the command of Captain Jake.

In 1844 both the railroad and steamboat map changed again, with the railroad once more being the dictating factor. During 1836, local entrepreneurs had completed construction of a small railroad linking Brooklyn and the town of Jamaica, in Queens, on the western end of Long Island. Thereafter, the Long Island Railroad Co., established in 1835, began laying tracks east across Long Island, not so much with the idea of servicing local Long Islanders as extending rails to the northeastern tip of the island, there to connect with steamers for New England. By 1837, the line had reached Hicksville, nineteen miles east of Jamaica. Subsequent benchmarks were Farmingdale (twenty-five miles east of Jamaica, 1841), Deer Park (thirty-three miles east of Jamaica, 1842), and, finally, Greenport, on the eastern end of Long Island's "North Fork," some eighty-nine miles east of Jamaica, from which tracks had begun being laid heading west as early as two years before.

Shortly after the completion of the Long Island Railroad, both Commodore Cornelius Vanderbilt and Commodore George Law, each blandishing that honorific, found themselves invited to sit on the railroad's board of directors. Like Vanderbilt, Law had impeccable credentials as a steamboatman. Sometimes referred to as "Liveoak George," the burly Law had started his career as a common day laborer in upstate New York and then made a small fortune as a contractor servicing such large municipal projects as New Jersey's Morris Canal and the so-called "High Bridge" designed to carry drinking water over the Harlem River and into New York City as part of the Croton Aqueduct. Law also operated steamers on the Hudson River, where he was variously a partner and adversary to Daniel Drew and Isaac Newton, depending on how the wind blew and where the most money was to be made. He was also an early dabbler in railroads, having an interest in both the New York & Harlem Railroad (chartered in 1832) and the Mohawk & Hudson (chartered in 1826), the latter being the first railroad built in New York State.

Law and Vanderbilt were to have a complex and highly competitive relationship on a range of domestic and foreign fronts. Both were highly respected—indeed, esteemed. Each earned glowing tributes in the 1845 edition of *Wealth and Biography of the Wealthy Citizens of New York City,* written by New York *Sun* editor Moses Y. Beach. Of Vanderbilt, Beach wrote: "Of an old Dutch root, Cornelius has evinced more energy and 'go aheadativeness' in building and driving steamboats, and other projects, than ever one single Dutchman possessed. It takes our American hot suns to clear off the vapors and fogs of the 'Zuyder Zee' and wake up the *phlegm* of a descendant of old Holland."[1]

Beach made no mention of Vanderbilt's politics. At the time, the entrepreneur remained a fervent Whig, having followed his friendly acquaintance Daniel Webster into that movement. As a Whig, Vanderbilt supported that party's candidate for the presidency in 1844, Kentucky's Henry Clay, and expressed his agreement with Clay's conservative hesitancy over the annexation of Texas and the prospect of war with Mexico. That autumn, Vanderbilt organized a group of some five hundred Staten Islanders to march and ride horses in a torch-lit parade through lower Manhattan, all for the support of Clay and other Whig candidates. In the midst of the parade, Vanderbilt and his party found themselves confronted by a mob of Tammany Democrats, many of them Irish, all of them emerging from a saloon on Chatham Street. In the melee that followed, the fifty-year-old Vanderbilt personally throttled one James "Yankee" Sullivan: an Irish pugilist seventeen years younger than Vanderbilt who, eleven years later, would go thirty-six rounds before losing the world heavyweight title to John "Old Smoke" Morrissey, twenty years Sullivan's junior. (Later on, after the demise of the Whig Party, Vanderbilt was perhaps inspired by his altercation with Sullivan when he briefly became interested in the Know-Nothing nativist movement.)

Vanderbilt was ever pugnacious, in every sense of the word, whenever he thought necessary. The writer, attorney, and abolitionist Henry Brewster Stanton (husband of women's rights advocate Elizabeth Cady Stanton) recalled a particular episode from the late 1830s:

> In the summer of 1838 or 1839 I took passage at New York on a Vanderbilt steamboat plying through Long Island Sound. A Southern gentleman with a colored chattel and a large trunk in his train violated the rules by putting the trunk in his stateroom. Soon after passing Hell Gate the deckmaster pulled the trunk out. A scuffle ensued, and the Southerner seized the deckmaster by the collar, the Negro lowering darkly in a corner as a reserved

corps. A crowd of passengers were spectators of this sharp tussle, in which the Vanderbilt forces were getting worsted. Suddenly a well-knit man dashed into the ring with a battle-cry that sounded exactly like swearing. In an instant his coat was off and his fists doubled. Just at this point the colored contingent wheeled into line. The new-comer dealt a blow that sent the Negro spinning, and then moved at double-quick time on the Southerner's works. The affair was rapidly approaching the precincts of a rough-and-tumble fight between the four combatants when the passengers intervened and proposed an adjournment. The motion was carried. The trunk remained outside the stateroom, and the other chattel retired to repair his nose. This was the first time I ever saw Captain Cornelius Vanderbilt.[2]

But neither politics nor brawling took up the lion's share of Vanderbilt's time. Business came first, then personal pleasure, with politics following as a distant third, and pugilistics entering into the mix whenever necessary.

Not long after Vanderbilt joined the board of the Long Island Railroad, that concern purchased his *Cleopatra* and *Worcester* for use carrying railroad passengers from Orient Point to the connection for the Norwich & Worcester Railroad at Allyn's Point. Rapidly, the Long Island Railroad became the preferred route for New York/Boston travel, customers being routed to Manhattan on the east end of the journey via the Brooklyn Ferry. The Long Island Railroad partnered with the Norwich & Worcester Railroad to offer a through-fare of $4, but later lowered this to $2 in order to match price-war competition from the increasingly desperate Atlantic Steamboat Company, dedicated as it was to streaming traffic towards Providence.

Unlike the old, original Norwich & Worcester route which involved steamers departing Manhattan in the afternoon for an overnight journey to Allyn's Point, or the routes offering Stonington or Providence transfers, the new Long Island Railroad/Norwich & Worcester route between Boston and New York had the advantage of offering early morning departures which assured arrival in one's destination city by evening. Thus, for the first time, travelers passing between the two towns could avoid having to spend a night abroad. Despite the popularity of its service, the ravages of price-wars eventually, in 1846, forced the unprofitable Long Island Railroad to sell the *Cleopatra* and the *Worcester* to its partner, the Norwich & Worcester. With that sale, the Long Island Railroad gave up its ambitions to cater to Boston through-traffic. By the same time the boats were sold, Vanderbilt had already departed the board of the Long Island Railroad.

Along with his brother Jacob, Vanderbilt entered into several arrangements with the Norwich & Worcester. Captain Jake contracted to oversee the operations of the *Cleopatra* and the *Worcester*, which now comprised the property of a newly-formed Norwich & Worcester subsidiary, the Norwich & New London Steamboat Company. For his part, Cornelius in late 1845 allowed himself to be hired as the contractor overseeing the construction of a new steamer for the same firm. Built to Vanderbilt's specifications by the yard of Bishop & Simonson, the *Atlantic* came at a cost of $150,000. Her keel was laid in November 1845, and she was launched the following May. According to the 1895 directory *American Steam Vessels*, the *Atlantic* was "one of the largest and finest steamboats that had ever been constructed for Long Island Sound. Her commodious saloons and staterooms, the elegance of her fittings and appointments, the finish of her boilers and engine, and speed placed her in the front ranks of Sound boats of her day. A novelty was the introduction of gas as light on board—probably the first steamboat to be so equipped. She commenced her regular trips from New York on August 18, 1846."[3] However, just three months later, on November 27, 1846, the *Atlantic* suffered a wreck in a gale, being blown ashore on the rocky coast of Fisher's Island, off the east end of Long Island. Forty two people died.

Such episodes as this explained, in large measure, the popularity of trains. No one drowned on trains, although, as Vanderbilt knew all too well, one was risking death on a railroad just as surely as he was on the water. Nevertheless, the public's distinct inclination to choose rail travel over steamboat travel whenever such a choice was offered could not be ignored. This is perhaps why, as early as 1845, Vanderbilt had involved himself in the affairs of the Providence & Stonington Railroad, that small line that had so demolished the Providence transfer business just a few years before. Around July of 1845, Daniel Drew and Vanderbilt collaborated in acquiring a controlling interest in the publicly traded firm, picking up some 20 percent of the company's voting stock at about $40 per share. Drew and Vanderbilt immediately went on the company's board of directors, as did two recently acquired sons-in-law of Vanderbilt's for whom he was trying to find places, Daniel B. Allen and William K. Thorn. (Drew, meanwhile, gave employment to young William H. "Billy" Vanderbilt, who worked as a clerk in the former's Wall Street brokerage office, Drew, Robinson & Company.)

Still, Vanderbilt's main focus continued to be steamboats. Having abdicated the Norwich trade, Vanderbilt had also, at this point, taken a break from the Stonington trade (to which he would return) in favor of more profitable routes. Thus the way was open for Drew to bring his *Knickerbocker* from the Hudson to service Stonington/New York travelers. Drew's competition, in turn, came from George Law, who in 1845 launched the "floating palace" *Oregon*, at that time the fastest steamboat in the country. Law put the *Oregon* into the Stonington/New York market at competitive prices, which caused Drew to lose considerable trade. Given their druthers, passengers would always go for the newest, shiniest, most luxurious, and fastest boat. Since speed remained of paramount importance, one wonders whether it was as a favor to Drew, and perhaps in hope of diminishing the *Oregon*'s reputation as the world's fastest boat, that Vanderbilt challenged Law to a race: Law's *Oregon* against Vanderbilt's *Traveler*, a boat half the size of the *Oregon* that Vanderbilt had just built to service New Haven/New York traffic. On a twenty mile course, the boats ran bow to bow, leaving neither the clear winner, and Vanderbilt frustrated.

Immediately thereafter, Vanderbilt ordered yet another new vessel from Bishop & Simonson. Launched two years later in early 1847, the *Cornelius Vanderbilt* weighed over 1,000 tons and was capable of speeds up to twenty-five miles per hour. As soon as Vanderbilt had put her through enough trials and shake-down cruises to assure himself of her readiness, he issued another challenge to Law: a round-trip race from the Battery to Ossining on the Hudson River, and back—seventy miles for a $1,000 bet. Once Law had agreed, the date (June 1, 1847) was set for what was to become one of the most talked-about races in the history of steamboating, and a legend on the Hudson.

Both boats departed the Battery at 11:00 A.M. For more than thirty miles up the river they kept side by side, but then Law's *Oregon* passed the *Vanderbilt* as both vessels made their turn around the stake boat off Ossining. The *Vanderbilt*, with Cornelius at the helm, took the turn at too high a speed and overshot the mark. The maneuver put the *Oregon* half a length ahead, even though it also resulted in a small collision with the *Vanderbilt* which severely damaged the *Oregon*'s wheelhouse. Halfway back to the Battery, the engineers on the *Oregon* ran out of coal. In desperation, the crew threw chairs, tables, woodwork, berths—anything they could grab—on the fires under the boilers. In the end, the *Oregon* finished the race roughly twelve hundred feet ahead of the *Vanderbilt*. Each vessel had run the course in a mere three hours and fifteen minutes, the tide being against them going north and with them going south. One year later, Drew purchased the *Oregon* from Law, gaining her for his Hudson River trade while at the same time getting her off the Stonington route. Meanwhile, Vanderbilt himself returned to servicing Stonington in his continued friendly (for now) competition with Drew, first using the *Vanderbilt*, and later the *Commodore* and the *Plymouth Rock*.

He was, however, as the 1840s drew to a close, becoming wary of most coastal and nearly all river-borne steamboat commerce as a long-term investment. It seemed that wherever the railroads could eat into steamboat trade, they did so. Thus most coastal and river-routes began to lose their appeal for Vanderbilt. Increasingly, through the next few years, he would look to develop steamboat and, more importantly, steamship routes that could not be replaced by rail transport. This thinking formed the core of his affinity for the Staten Island Ferry, which would never, ever be replaced by rail—a railroad bridge from Staten Island to Manhattan being an impossibility. But aside from such services as the ferry, most other coastal and river routes were doomed in the long-term, and Vanderbilt knew it. For this reason, he would now start to turn his attention to ocean-going, transcontinental travel, while slowly (over the course of several years, whenever lucrative opportunities arose) beginning to divest the bulk of his domestic steamboat holdings.

14

MATTERS FAMILIAL AND SOCIAL

FOLLOWING THE VANDERBILTS' RESIDENCE ON NEW YORK'S Madison Street, they moved to somewhat larger quarters on East Broadway.[1] Then finally, in 1839, Cornelius acceded to Sophia's constant lobbying that they should return to Staten Island. On the northeast corner of the old Staten Island lands once owned by his father, who'd died in 1832, Vanderbilt built a large mansion complete with a portico and palatial Corinthian columns overlooking the Narrows and Upper New York Bay. Built at a cost of $27,000 dollars, the house stood halfway between Stapleton and Tompkinsville. Stained glass in the front door depicted Vanderbilt's steamer *Cleopatra*. Inside, awed visitors were stunned by mantelpieces made of Egyptian marble, and an elaborate grand staircase. "The stairway was a striking feature of the house," noted the *New York Times* after the place burned in 1882. "It was built in spiral form, and ran in an oval well to the top of the building. . . . The house was divided from top to bottom by wide halls which ran through the center of it on every floor. The ceilings on each floor were 12 feet high and the rooms were very large. In the roof, to illuminate the halls, was set a skylight of colored glass . . . ."[2] The Commodore's modest, though by-now slightly enlarged boyhood home, which was still occupied by his elderly mother, lay a mere three-minute walk to the south.

Seven years later, while keeping the Staten Island place as his summer residence, Vanderbilt built a four-story townhouse at 10 Washington Place, near Washington Square in Greenwich Village, with grand stables right next door, and informed the unhappy Sophia that Greenwich Village would, henceforth, be their formal year-round residence. The house Vanderbilt built at Washington Place was described by one reporter as being "a large but exceedingly plain brick mansion. . . . Everything about it is solid, substantial and comfortable. The facade is as flat and plain as the side of a dry goods box, the only attempt at ornamentation appearing in the porch, which is composed of two Corinthian columns and an entablature of classic design. . . . The house comprises four stories and a basement, the bedrooms and sitting rooms, all above the first floor, being little less ample in their dimensions and luxurious in their furnishing than the parlors below."[3]

Sophia did not like it. But then she did not much like anything with which Cornelius presented her. Sophia had, by all accounts, long been a sad, psychologically abused spouse. Given Cornelius's frequent, extended absences while building his businesses, it had been left largely to Sophia to raise their children single-handedly. On those occasions when Vanderbilt swooped in on Sophia and their brood, he was routinely critical of both her and them: the ultimate micromanager finding fault, issuing edicts, and throwing down ultimatums. As well, he seems to have made very little effort to mask the fact that, when away, he enjoyed the company of other women—most often professional waterfront wenches. (Jared Linsly diagnosed Vanderbilt with syphilis in 1839. Linsly diagnosed Sophia herself with the same ailment one year later. He subsequently treated the lesions of both Vanderbilts with mercury ointment, and mercury given orally.)[4]

Adding to Sophia's woes was the fact that in 1846, when she protested too loudly about being taken from Staten Island to occupy the new Washington Place residence nine months out of the year, Vanderbilt threatened to have her committed to an asylum in Flushing. When a trip to Canada with a daughter and son-in-law did nothing to calm Sophia's nerves or tone down her protest, Vanderbilt made good on the threat. Sophia remained incarcerated for three months until, after the apparent intercession of Phebe Hand and Sophia's surrender in the form of an announced willingness to live in Greenwich Village, she was finally released.

To his offspring, Vanderbilt was a distant, quarrelsome, and forbidding figure. Since moving to New York at the end of 1828, Cornelius and Sophia had become parents to four more children: two boys and two girls. Cornelius Jeremiah arrived in 1830, Mary Alicia in 1834, Catherine Juliette in 1836, and George Washington (named for Cornelius's greatest hero) in 1839. Of the three Vanderbilt boys (Billy, Cornelius, and George), the last seems to have been something of a favorite of the father's during his childhood. The best the other two could expect on any given day was benign neglect, although the middle boy, Cornelius, was rarely so lucky. Afflicted with a nervous disposition, a stutter, a propensity for depression, and the curse of epilepsy, young Cornelius found himself chastised with a whip as a prohibitive measure against seizures. During the late 1840s, he fled his father's household as a boy of 19, and worked his way to California before the mast, rounding Cape Horn as an able-bodied seaman. Then in California he passed checks in his father's name, beginning a life-long career of desperate and half-witted fraud, before being summoned back to the east and placed in an asylum himself. He would end as a conspicuously unhappy adult: a self-bludgeoning gambler who, disinherited, died in debt as a suicide in a hotel room he could not pay for.

The eldest son, Billy, fared somewhat better—though not much—as a child and young man. His father thought him dim-witted, and the father's estimate was evidently born out by the boy's slow progress through the Columbia Grammar School in Manhattan. In general, as Billy came of age, Cornelius seems to have thought that he lacked the drive, initiative, and mental agility one needed to succeed in the world, and that he was lucky to have his father's umbrella under which to enjoy shelter. It was in this spirit that Vanderbilt arranged for Drew, as a favor, to take Billy into his Wall Street brokerage house in 1839, when the boy was eighteen. And it was in this spirit, two years later, that the father loudly objected when, at age 20, Billy defied a parental edict and wed Maria Louisa Kissam, the daughter of upstate Dutch Reform minister Samuel Kissam.[5] At the time, Billy's salary from Drew was not only miniscule, but subsidized by Vanderbilt, who had wanted his son to be self-supporting before taking on the obligations of marriage. In response to Billy's defiance, Vanderbilt purchased a seventy-acre farm in New Dorp, close by the old Moravian Church, on lands once originally controlled by old Aris Vanderbilt back in the 1680s.[6] Then, pulling Billy out of Drew's office, he consigned both the son and his young wife to the newly acquired land, making it a gift outright, but insisting that they make their way there with no further aid from him. Not for another twenty years would Billy win his father's at first grudging respect.

The youngest boy, George Washington Vanderbilt, was much more warmly embraced by Vanderbilt than the other two. Just a year old when Vanderbilt built the Staten Island mansion and just seven when the Washington Place house went up, young George grew up experiencing a degree of parental tolerance and understanding largely unknown not only among the other boys, but amongst the balance of Vanderbilt's children as well. From the start, Vanderbilt seems to have recognized himself in the lad, and therefore adopted a different attitude towards him. The father took pride in George's resemblance to him, and was also heartened when George entered school and excelled. Eventually, the quick-witted George would enter West Point—his father extolling his conquests and forecasting the briefest of military careers, after which George would be groomed to take command of the Vander-bilt empire.

At the time of George's birth in 1839, Cornelius and Sophia's eld-est daughter Phebe Jane was twenty-five. Thus, long before Cor-nelius saw his own last-born child emerge from the womb, he himself had to be busy finding suitable husbands for a large cadre of grown daughters. Phebe Jane married one of the steamboat captains from Cornelius's staff, James M. Cross, in 1833. One year after that, the next in line, Ethelinda, married Daniel B. Allen (mentioned pre-viously) who became an agent for various Vanderbilt properties. In 1849, Elizabeth became the wife of George A. Osgood, who like Allen got made into an agent for the Commodore. Emily, in turn, married William K. Thorn (mentioned previously), another Vander-bilt captain who eventually involved himself in other Vanderbilt enterprises, in 1839. Five years later, Maria Louisa wed attorney Ho-race Clark, himself destined to rise in Vanderbilt's organization as a trusted assistant. Then Mary Alicia married Nicholas Bergasse La Bau in 1850, the same year Catherine Juliette married Smith Barker, the latter being an attorney in private practice, both men to be given roles in various Vanderbiltian firms at different points in time. Young Sophia, meanwhile, married merchant Daniel Torrance, who also eventually found employment with Vanderbilt. In all instances, the Commodore insisted his sons-in-law earn their keep. In general, they seem to have performed, and Vanderbilt seems to have been unceremoniously satisfied. (He adopted a similar attitude of gruff satisfaction when it came to his numerous grandchildren, the first of whom began arriving in the 1830s well before his own last born came into the world. Vanderbilt viewed his children's children always from a distance, inviting no informality, tolerating rather than loving them. None would remember him fondly.)

As of 1850, Vanderbilt was to spend less and less time on the water and more and more time in his personal office, located at Fourth Street and Broadway, adjacent to his stables. Also as of 1850, he began to seriously pursue the hobby that would become one of the main passions of his idle hours going forward: harness racing with trotting horses. As Elliott Gorn and Warren Goldstein have written: "By the 1850s, more spectators watched harness racing than any other sport, and there were about seventy tracks nationwide, seven in the New York metropolitan area alone. The city's greatest harness-racing venue, however, was Third Avenue; trotters raced up and down the road, and at taverns along the way, men gathered to discuss the sport and arrange new contests."[7] Not long after, the preferred venue moved uptown to Bloomingdale Road (now upper Broadway) and Harlem Lane (now St. Nicholas Avenue). But regardless of geography, Vanderbilt was always a passionate participant. Indeed, after dollars and female flesh, carriage racing soon became one of his greatest interests.

A reporter for the *New York Herald* described how, after the close of daily business and the retirement of the old Knickerbockers, who preferred to take their exercise on horseback in the mornings, the rough-and-tumble nouveau rich would emerge in their racing carriages. "It would seem as if all New York had suddenly become owners of fast horses, and were all out on Bloomingdale on a grand trotting spree. This rushing to and fro of ship commodores, book and newspaper publishers, bankers, builders, merchants, gamblers and fast men generally, continues until the sun in its daily course has gone to visit the antipodes. By this time, the extra steam is worked off, the rich and fast men all return home, thoroughly ventilated and in good condition for a comfortable supper and a sound sleep." Daniel Drew was there, along with George Law, and *Herald* publisher James Gordon Bennett Sr. The reigning champion meanwhile, was young Robert Bonner, who had emigrated from Ireland as a boy. In 1851, when he was twenty-seven, the enterprising Bonner purchased New York's *Merchant Ledger,* a financial weekly which he revised into a general interest daily and renamed the *New York Ledger* four years later. Vanderbilt could beat everyone and anyone except Bonner. "What fine looking man is that with a segar [sic] in his mouth, who is passing all those roadsters on the right?" asked the *Herald.* "He dashes past everybody but Bonner. His bays must be well trained; he handles the ribbons as though he was used to it. That gentleman with a white cravat on, you mean? Yes, sir. That is Commodore Vanderbilt, who has four of the best horses that appear on the road, every one of them exceedingly fast."[8] In time, Vanderbilt became one of the first millionaires to frequent the Saratoga region, and he eventually signed on as one of the incorporators of the Saratoga track.

Although Irish-born, Bonner was of Scotch-Presbyterian descent: an affiliation he took seriously.[9] Bonner served as a trustee of his church and, unlike Vanderbilt, as the contemporary reporter Matthew Hale Smith noted, was "a liberal contributor to the support of public worship and the various forms of benevolence and charity." At his private stables on Twenty-seventh Street, manned by three full-time employees, Bonner housed the finest specimens of horses to be found on the eastern seaboard, for some of which he'd paid as much as $30,000. "Mr. Bonner buys his horses for his own pleasure," wrote Smith. "He drives them himself, and is one of the best horsemen in the country. He will not allow his horses to be used for show or gain. . . . Millionaires mash their teeth as Bonner drives them. There are horsemen in New York who would pay $25,000 for a pair of horses that would make Bonner take their dust. If Bonner's team is beaten, the driver must do as he does, drive it himself. Of the speed of his horse he is his own judge. He will buy anything that will beat the world."[10] Of all the millionaires, Vanderbilt did the most mashing of teeth. Reporter Junius Henri Browne noted that "Cornelius Vanderbilt, after Bonner, is probably the greatest horse-fancier in Manhattan. He has long been anxious to buy [some of Bonner's] blooded stock; but he can't, with all his millions. The Commodore owns a dozen fine horses; but his best and fastest are Mountain Boy, Post Boy, and Mountain Girl, which could not be purchased at less than fabulous figures, as Vanderbilt, like the *Ledger* proprietor, is a buyer, not a seller."[11] At his private stables on Fourth Street, right next door to his Washington Place townhouse, Vanderbilt collected and cultivated horsemeat with the express purpose of defeating Bonner, whom he considered a friend and whom he admired. While Vanderbilt's townhouse was made of brick, his stable building was made of brownstone. A trade publication called the *Sanitary Engineer* singled Vanderbilt's stables out as being state-of-the-art in the way of lighting, plumbing, heating, and ventilation. "Commodore Vanderbilt's early passion for horses still survives," wrote journalist James Dabney McCabe, "and his stable contains some of the finest in the world. Nothing pleases him so well as to sit behind a fast team, with the reins in his hands, and fly along the road with almost the speed of the wind."[12] Writing years after Vanderbilt's death, jour-

nalist James L. Ford recalled seeing Vanderbilt "nearly every afternoon behind a pair of swift trotters speeding uptown to Judge
Smith's or to some other popular roadhouse. Behind his residence
on Washington Place was his stable, and between the two build-
ings a ring where he was wont to have his horses exercised while he
watched them from the piazza." Ford went on to say that the boys
of the neighborhood "used to be glad enough when they were allowed to exercise 'Mountain Boy,' and other favorite animals in the
Commodore's presence. . . . A trainer told me once that if Mr.
Vanderbilt had not been a millionaire he might have become the
leading professional horseman in the country."[13]

The friendly rivalry between Vanderbilt and Bonner was to per-
sist for decades. Eventually, both men helped found the Elm Park
Pleasure Ground Association, which established a half-mile track
just north of Nineteenth Street. A devout and pious soul, Bonner
refused to bet on his horses, or even to allow them to race. Bonner
simply ran his trotters publicly on tracks, and clocked their perfor-
mances. Meanwhile, Bonner's standing offer to Vanderbilt and all
other comers was this: Should any team ever beat the fastest speed
clocked by his own fastest team on a public course, he would place
$10,000 in an escrow account for the victor, who might then give
the sum to any worthy cause he chose. On one famous day at Long
Island's so-called "Fashion Course" (in what is today Corona,
Queens), after Vanderbilt's teams swept every race, Bonner ran his
two fastest mares and clocked them accomplishing a mile in two
minutes, thirty-two and one-half seconds, three seconds better
than the Commodore's fastest speed for the day.

Aside from the men he met through business, the men he met
through the trotters, and the whores with whom he consorted with
such frequency, Vanderbilt enjoyed little in the way of social life.
Unkempt and ill-mannered, he was routinely shunned by polite

society, as much for his lack of decorum as for his lack of benevolence. On those rare occasions when Vanderbilt found himself invited into one of New York's finer homes, he routinely outraged hostesses by spitting when and where he felt the urge after chewing a plug of his friend Pierre Lorillard's tobacco, and by drinking more than his fill of his favorite concoction: gin mixed with sugar. One friendly reporter put the best spin possible on Vanderbilt's lack of manners: "The Commodore is simple in his manners and habits. He is a representative of a former age, when men lived less artificially than at the present time, and when there was more happiness and less show."[14] But the Jays, Schuylers, Rhinelanders, and Van Rensselaers who comprised Vanderbilt's neighbors in Greenwich Village during the late 1840s were no more interested in simple manners and habits than they were in the parsimonious and vindictive Vanderbilt himself, by now as much defined in the public eye by his undisguised, undignified, and ravenous hunger for increased wealth as for his near-legendary status as a self-absorbed boor and braggart, intent on self-glorification, and devoid of generosity.

Vanderbilt's reputation in polite circles was that of a man who routinely bedded down impoverished girls many years younger than himself. Further, it was whispered that these maids and waterfront whores were creatures with whom he shared near total illiteracy: a condition in which he took a perverse pride, often boasting about how cheaply literacy's replacement could be bought. (The clerks to whom he dictated earned $5 per week.)

Most damning in the eyes of Society, however, was Vanderbilt's abject lack of charity. A man who was far more philanthropic than Vanderbilt, John Jacob Astor, died in his eighty-fifth year on March 29, 1848, after a long retirement during which he'd devoted himself to good works. After making his initial fortune in the fur trade, Astor had built a second empire in Manhattan real estate, having acquired vast swaths of the island all the way north to the Harlem River. Astor left an estate of approximately $20 million—at that time the greatest fortune in America—a portion of which he willed for the creation of the Astor Library, this to be open to the public. He also made just one son his primary beneficiary within the family, effectively disinheriting one other surviving son and three surviving daughters. Speaking to a journalist on the day Astor was laid to rest at New York's Trinity Churchyard, Vanderbilt noted with approval Astor's move to keep the fortune intact and robust in the hands of just one heir, but discounted the library as a nonsensical and inordinately expensive stab at post-mortem public relations.[15]

More than one acquaintance and clerk of Vanderbilt's remembered him taking note of Astor's maximum value, $20 million, and pledging to surpass that in short order. Thereafter he would have his clerk follow the financial press assiduously for intelligence on the wealth possessed by others of his generation, George Law and Daniel Drew among them, tallying up positions in the grand race to be the richest man in the United States. More than twenty years before, Vanderbilt, as a young upstart battling against monopoly, had gone on record criticizing Astor for his dominance of the fur business. At that time, Vanderbilt told an acquaintance he did not think any man should ever be worth more than $20 million. Now, an older, more conservative, and constitutionally dissatisfied Vanderbilt expressed a different point of view.

15

SOUTHERN ROUTE

IT WAS NO RANDOM WIND THAT HAD BLOWN CORNELIUS Jeremiah, as a seaman before the mast, to California in 1849. Gold had been discovered on the American River, in the Sierra Nevada Mountains, during January of 1848. Eight months later, James Gordon Bennett's *New York Herald* blasted word of the "mother lode" to East Coast readers. Then, in December of 1848, President James Polk officially confirmed the strike in a speech before Congress. By that time, tales were being told of California's streams being "rivers of gold." The popular music hall entertainer Jonathan Nichols wrote a song on this theme, which soon became a hit in numerous theaters across the East, long after Nichols himself had given up performing, purchased a shovel, and headed West.

I'll soon be in 'Frisco,
And then I'll look around,
And when I see the gold lumps there,
I'll pick 'em off the ground.

I'll scrape the mountains clean, my boys,
I'll drain the rivers dry,
A pocket full of rocks bring home,
Susannah, don't you cry.

To get to California, one could take off across the western plains and mountains in a train of covered-wagons: a grueling overland journey conducted under nearly constant threat of attack by Native Americans. Alternatively, one could get on a sailing ship heading round treacherous Cape Horn, at the southern tip of South America. Either means of travel took months. Nevertheless, most immigrants chose the water route as the lesser of the two evils. According to historian George Tinkham: "All of the eastern ports sent out their quota of ships, and in December, 1848, and January, 1849, sixty-one vessels left for California, each vessel averaging fifty passengers." Tinkham added that: "In February, 1849, sixty ships sailed from New York and seventy from Boston and Philadelphia. Before the spring of 1850 vessels to the number of 250 had cleared from eastern ports bound for San Francisco. In one day, forty-five vessels entered the Golden Gate."[1]

All classes of men debarked. One of the earliest and largest packets to leave Boston was a charter carrying 152 well-heeled young men from prominent eastern families. For the duration of the charter voyage, the vessel was renamed the *Edward Everett,* after the famous orator and statesman who was at that moment the president of Harvard College. Everett himself visited the ship before she left port, and brought with him a going-away gift. Everett hoped his present, a library of three hundred volumes, would help the young men, so many of them Harvard students, use the long days of the voyage productively. The *Everett* departed Boston on January 10, 1849, and arrived in San Francisco on July 7. (The trip round Cape

Horn typically took from six months to a year. The very fastest clipper ships could do the trip in about a hundred days.)

Besides going round the Horn, one other route—combining fast, ocean-going steamships with a brief overland journey crossing the Isthmus of Panama—presented itself. Before the discovery of gold, the Isthmus route between the eastern seaboard and the California coast had been established by two key firms, both working in cooperation and both enjoying healthy subsidies from Congress in return for enabling the movement of the U.S. mails to and from California. In the East, the United States Mail Steamship Company, controlled in turn by George Law and later Law's agent, Marshall ("Marsh") Roberts, received close to $300,000 a year from the Federal Treasury to conduct mail to Chagres, on the eastern Panama coast. In the Pacific, the Pacific Mail Steamship Company enjoyed similar support in return for conducting the mail from Panama City to San Francisco. (This firm was headed by William H. Aspinwall, of an old New York family that had made fortunes in shipbuilding and the China trade.) The fifty-mile journey across the malarial jungle of the Isthmus was made partly by mule-train, partly by small boats navigating on the Chagres River. (Only later, in the 1850s, would the Panama Railroad connect the port of Aspinwall, also known as Colon, on the Caribbean Sea, and Panama City.)

Early on in the Gold Rush, both the United States Mail Steamship Company and the Pacific Mail Steamship Company entered aggressively into the passenger business, charging exorbitant prices ($600, more than twice the standard price for a trip round Cape Horn) for relatively quick transport to California. Combined with fat fees for transporting freight, and the mail subsidies, the two companies seemed to have struck their own vein of gold. Indeed, the subsidies alone more than covered the baseline costs of operation for both firms. Everything else was pure profit. What was more, the two operations not only had a monopoly on government grants, but as well possessed a virtual monopoly in Panama proper, where well-subsidized government officials looked out for the interests of Aspinwall and Law, to the exclusion of all other comers.

Nevertheless, Vanderbilt believed he had an idea with which he could compete. To the north of Panama and Costa Rica, the country of Nicaragua looked attractive. Despite its width (three times that of Panama), Nicaragua offered an option that was nearly five hundred miles shorter than the Panama route. Lake Nicaragua, in the west of the country, drained via the San Juan River into the Caribbean Sea. And from the westernmost point on Lake Nicaragua, it was only eleven miles to the Pacific Ocean. While the idea of a canal through Panama had been discussed and dreamed about since the early days of Spanish exploration, Vanderbilt now came to believe that a Nicaragua canal, which he believed would require the excavation of just that last eleven miles in the nation's west country, could be achievable. Such a canal would change the map of the world forever, and be a boon to whoever controlled it. For émigrés from the East Coast of the United States to California, it would offer a route that was 4,531 miles from New York to San Francisco, rather than the 4,992 miles which constituted the same journey via Panama.

During the spring of 1849, Vanderbilt sent a protégé, Colonel David L. White, to Nicaragua to feel out local authorities. A retired career officer of the military, David White was the brother of Joseph L. White, an attorney, originally from Indiana, who'd been active in Whig politics, now in Manhattan working as an associate of Vanderbilt's. In Nicaragua, David White collaborated with the U.S. chargé d'affaires, Ephraim George Squier, to coax the government into an exclusive agreement for the construction and management of a canal. Recently appointed by President Zachary Taylor (a

Whig), Squier was a journalist and archeologist who would later write several important books about the history and culture of Central America. Although at first complicated by the presence of British investors who cherished the same ambition as Vanderbilt, the negotiations between Allen, Squier, and the Nicaraguan officials bore fruit in August, when Vanderbilt's new "American Atlantic & Pacific Ship Canal Company" signed papers with the Nicaraguans.

Formalized that September, the contract between Vanderbilt and Nicaragua called for Vanderbilt to pay the government an immediate $10,000 in cash and $20,000 in company stock, this to be followed by $10,000 cash each year until the canal opened. Construction was estimated to take twelve years. After the opening of the canal, Vanderbilt or his assigns were to pay the Nicaraguan government 20 percent of net profits for a period of eighty-five years, at the end of which period the canal would become the property of the people of Nicaragua. A rainy day clause stipulated that should the canal prove unbuildable, Vanderbilt would be permitted to construct a fall-back operation (a railroad or some other combination linking the two oceans) on the same terms.

Immediately after the signing of the agreement, Squier and Secretary of State John Middleton Clayton negotiated a treaty between the United States and Nicaragua in which the United States agreed to guarantee the neutrality of the canal (in other words, allow vessels from all countries to pass through), and, more important, to recognize Nicaraguan sovereignty over the proposed route. The swift negotiation of the treaty was at least in part a reaction to one serious potential stumbling block. Great Britain had long claimed protectorate status over Nicaragua's Mosquito Indians (actually Jamaican blacks for the most part, with a small smattering of South Ameican native blood), who lived on the country's swampy eastern "Mosquoto Coast." Early in 1848, the Nicaraguan village of San Juan del Norte, on the Caribbean Sea at the mouth of the San Juan River, had been invaded by Mosquotans at the behest of the local British consul, a close friend of the Mosquito "King." On the heels of this, Nicaraguan troops retreated in the face of a challenge from the Royal Navy. By the end of 1848, a British custom house had been built and the place renamed Greytown. Shortly after, when the British seized small Tigre Island in the Gulf of Fonseca, Squier raged against British imperialism. The Nicaraguans and Hondurans, meanwhile, decided to cede their respective claims to the tiny piece of real estate, passing these to the Americans, hoping in this way to protect themselves from further British incursions. (To complicate matters further, 1848 also saw the British sign treaties of friendship with Guatemala and Costa Rica.) Thus, even as Vanderbilt's agents formalized agreements with the Nicaraguan officials, Vanderbilt realized those officials did not at the moment possess complete authority over the eastern terminus of the proposed route. Thus also, the rush of the United States to recognize Nicaraguan "sovereignty" over the proposed route was really just a means by which to work toward U.S. sovereignty over the same terrain.

What was actually going on here? The ambition of the government of Lord John Russell was not to take over Nicaragua, nor was it to instigate hostilities between Great Britain and the United States. The British aim was, quite simply, to prevent the creation of a canal which would be under the sole authority of the Americans. Realizing this, and wishing to avoid a confrontation with the Russell government, President Taylor and Secretary of State Clayton began talks with Sir Henry Bulwer, who arrived in Washington as ambassador from Russell's government in April of 1849. As those talks proceeded, Bulwer dangled a tempting possibility. It seemed that under the right circumstances, British opposition to the Nicaraguan canal might easily be transformed into support accompanied by investment, assuming adequate language concerning sovereignty could be worked out. Upon hearing this, Vanderbilt himself instantly changed: No longer was he the frustrated and proud American entrepreneur loudly and belligerently insisting that the Monroe Doctrine be rigidly enforced; indeed, he was now a far more moderate entity. The canal would be expensive, after all. And it would be nice to acquire some of the capital by drawing credit on London's Lombard Street banks as well as to have the resources of the rich London Exchange available. Signed in 1850, the Clayton-Bulwer Treaty stated that neither nation would move to seize exclusive control of any canal across Central America or act in any way to disenfranchise the other.

Vanderbilt hired O. W. Childs, the engineer who had lately won praise for successfully enlarging the Erie Canal, to survey a route for his canal, calculate logistics, and estimate costs. At the same time, Vanderbilt made other key investments. To Jeremiah Simonson (his nephew who had by now broken off from the Manhattan firm of Bishop & Simonson and opened his own shipyard at Greenpoint, in Brooklyn) he gave a contract to build a number of new vessels, including two shallow-draught steamers designed for operation on the San Juan River and Lake Nicaragua. As well, he commissioned several ocean-going steamers.

While Vanderbilt made capital investments in the Southern Route, as he sometimes called it, he continued his program of slowly and methodically divesting the bulk of his domestic coastal and river routes whenever a good price was to be had. At the same time, as had been his plan, he sought credit and investment from Lombard Street. To this end, Vanderbilt and David L. White visited London in the autumn of 1850, arriving October 5, only to be rebuffed. A number of the town's investment bankers expressed keen interest in the concept of what one London paper described as an "interoceanic canal." However, precise feasibility studies, strategic plans, and budgets (of the type just then being researched by Childs) needed to be presented before firm financial commitments could be made. Besides, recent news from Nicaragua had not been good. One of Vanderbilt's new smaller steamers, the *Orus,* having been towed to San Juan del Norte from New York, subsequently crashed and was destroyed while attempting to run several dangerous rapids during an ascent of the San Juan River. (Her wreck was to remain on a reef in the middle of the river for more than a decade.) Following the disaster, Childs sent word that they might have to build canals beside the river at the points, five of them, where rapids made the waters treacherous.

Given this news, it is not surprising to realize that almost immediately after his return to New York from London, Vanderbilt decided he had to see the river for himself. The enormous *Prometheus,* a wooden side-wheeler launched by Simonson on August 3, 1850, departed New York on her shakedown cruise to San Juan del Norte on December 26, 1850, and Vanderbilt was aboard. The larger vessel towed a small steamer, the new *Director,* which like the *Orus* had been designed and built by Simonson expressly for the San Juan River and Lake Nicaragua. (Eventually, the small steamboats *Central America, John M. Clayton,* and *Sir Henry Bulwer* would be brought to join the *Director* in populating the San Juan River and Lake Nicaragua, the latter two vessels having been built in Wilmington, Delaware, at the Harlan & Hollingsworth Yard.)

Upon his arrival in Nicaragua, Vanderbilt himself piloted the *Director* up the San Juan River. With several reluctant, trepidations engineers in tow, the fifty-five-year-old Vanderbilt put the *Director* at full steam, with her safety valve tied down firmly, and pushed her over every single range of rapids. The *Director* "jumped" four out of five of them, her bow scraping on the rocks but the boat always moving forward. Finally, at the Castillo Rapids, the Commodore confronted a drop of eight feet in the course of just a few yards.

Earliest known daguerreotype of Cornelius Vanderbilt, 1845, age 52. COLLECTION OF THE AUTHOR.

Robert Fulton's "North River Steamboat of Clermont," 1807, depicted in an 1841 engraving. COLLECTION OF THE AUTHOR.

"Live Oak" George Law, against whom Vanderbilt competed (and with whom he sometimes cooperated) in steamboats and railroads.
COLLECTION OF THE AUTHOR.

Dean Richmond, railroad entrepreneur and New York politico, photographed in 1864.
COLLECTION OF THE AUTHOR.

Daniel Drew, crafty capitalist who sometimes allied with Vanderbilt, and just as often betrayed him. COLLECTION OF THE AUTHOR.

Cornelius Vanderbilt as portrayed on the cover of *Harper's Weekly* in 1859, after a photograph by Brady. COLLECTION OF THE AUTHOR.

William Walker, native of
Tennessee and notorious
"Filibuster" of Nicaragua,
photographed in 1855.

Vanderbilt's steam yacht *North Star*, in which he took his family
on a grand tour of Europe in 1853.

Vanderbilt's son-in-law, associate, and confidante Horace Clark photographed in 1868.

William Henry Vanderbilt photographed in 1880.

Augustus Schell, loyal Vanderbilt
protégé, photographed in 1875.
COLLECTION OF THE AUTHOR.

Vanderbilt's friend
Horace Greeley, editor
of the New York *Tribune*,
photographed in 1860.
He was one of the
Commodore's biggest fans.
COLLECTION OF THE AUTHOR.

The New York Stock Exchange photographed in 1865. COLLECTION OF THE AUTHOR.

Wall Street, New York City, photographed 1860. COLLECTION OF THE AUTHOR.

Jay Gould, who with Jim Fisk
and Daniel Drew battled
Vanderbilt for control of the
Erie Railroad in 1867 and 1868.
Vanderbilt emerged from the
battle chastened, and calling
Gould the "Smartest Man in
America." The photo shows
Gould as he appeared in 1868.
COLLECTION OF THE AUTHOR.

Jim Fisk, who partnered with
Gould and Drew to seize the
Erie, as he looked in 1875.
COLLECTION OF THE AUTHOR.

The Commodore as portrayed on the cover of *Frank Leslie's Illustrated Newspaper* in November of 1869, after a photograph by Brady. The image formed the basis for Ernst Plassmann's statue of Vanderbilt, unveiled that same month. COLLECTION OF THE AUTHOR.

Captain Albert De Groot, longtime commander of the Commodore's various steamboats, and chief architect of the "Vanderbilt Bronze" atop the Hudson River Rail Road Freight House (aka, St. John's Freight House), as portrayed in *Frank Leslie's Illustrated Newspaper*. COLLECTION OF THE AUTHOR.

The unveiling of the "Vanderbilt Bronze" in late November of 1869.

The Hudson River Railroad Freight House photographe in 1870. The pediment containin the "Vanderbilt Bronze" is visible in the distance.

Vanderbilt's New York: The lower west side of Manhattan and New York Harbor photographed in 1875. COLLECTION OF THE AUTHOR.

Cornelius Vanderbilt with crossed legs, wearing a top hat, and clutching a walking stick, is at right on the piazza of the Congress Hall Hotel in Saratoga, NY, 1870. The Commodore was one of the founders of the track at Saratoga. COLLECTION OF THE AUTHOR.

Victoria Woodhull—suffragette, free love advocate, and spiritualist who took full advantage of the Commodore's belief in séances and spirits—photographed in 1870.
COLLECTION OF THE AUTHOR.

Woodhull's sister Tennessee Claflin, who was Vanderbilt's "magnetic healer" and lover, photographed in 1868.
COLLECTION OF THE AUTHOR.

Cornelius Vanderbilt in old age, photographed 1875, two years before his death. COLLECTION OF THE AUTHOR.

Manhattan's Church of the Strangers, financed for the Rev. Dr. Charles Force Deems by Vanderbilt. The church catered to southerners displaced by the Civil War; Vanderbilt's second wife and her mother were among them. COLLECTION OF THE AUTHOR.

New York's Grand Central Depot, on the site of today's Grand Central Station, as the Commodore knew it. COLLECTION OF THE AUTHOR.

The all-glass train-shed of the Grand Central Depot collapsed beneath the weight of snow in a blizzard on the day the Commodore died. COLLECTION OF THE AUTHOR.

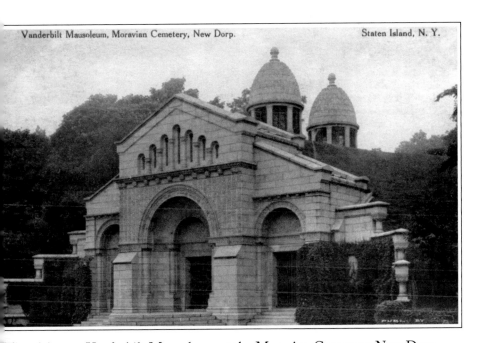

Vanderbilt Mausoleum, Moravian Cemetery, New Dorp. Staten Island, N. Y.

The elaborate Vanderbilt Mausoleum at the Moravian Cemetery, New Dorp, Staten Island. COLLECTION OF THE AUTHOR.

Ernst Plassmann's Vanderbilt as it appears today, standing outside Grand Central Station. Photo by the author.

Here he utilized trees on the shore and various capstans on the boat deck, wrapping ropes about both and dragging the vessel, an inch at a time, across the obstacle. When, on New Years Day of 1851, the *Director* finally slipped into Lake Nicaragua at San Carlos, she became the first steamer (and Vanderbilt the first captain) to have navigated the full 119 miles of the San Juan River. From San Carlos, the Commodore proceeded west for 60 miles to the place called Virgin Bay, 12 miles from the Pacific coast, and already selected by Childs for use as a terminal. Beyond this point, workers employed by Childs were already busy felling trees to clear a road to San Juan del Sur. On his way back east, Vanderbilt moored the *Director* just above the formidable Castillo Rapids and told those who traveled with him that a portage would have to be made at that spot when carrying paying customers. Other obstacles, meanwhile, were to be improved by Vanderbilt's engineers, whom he charged with blasting and otherwise removing rocks from the remaining four smaller clusters of rapids.

Upon Vanderbilt's return to New York, he delighted in a record run. He told a reporter for the *Herald:* "I built the *Prometheus* according to what I judged a sea steamer should be, having particular regard to the qualities of safety, comfort, economy in use, and speed."[2] The Commodore bragged that in a 5,590 mile round trip between Manhattan and San Juan del Norte, the enormous but highly efficient vessel had devoured a mere 450 tons of coal. During the same interview, Vanderbilt announced a new subsidiary of the American Atlantic & Pacific Ship Canal Company, the Accessory Transit Company, under which he'd do the bulk of his Nicaragua trade in future. An ad in the July 3, 1851, issues of various New York newspapers announced the new proposition for travel to San Francisco via Nicaragua. Where the Panama route providers were charging $600, Vanderbilt priced his service at $399. Within a year, in the midst of a price war, the rate would go as low as $150 for first-class accommodations, and $45 for steerage. Even at the lower prices, and in the absence of postal subsidies, Vanderbilt's profits were enormous.

Vanderbilt's second steamship for the Southern Route, one in a procession of wooden side-wheeled vessels, was launched September 20, 1851. Weighing 1,187 tons, the packet *Daniel Webster* came to be at East Boston's Donald McKay Shipyard. The *Webster* embarked upon her first voyage from New York on October 22, 1851, and was later put to work servicing a secondary route connecting New Orleans and San Juan del Norte. The *Webster* was followed by the *Northern Light,* launched from Simonson's yard in January of 1852. The *Northern Light* began service between New York and San Juan del Norte in May of 1852. Then came *Star of the West,* launched from Simonson's yard on June 17, 1852, which started on the New York/San Juan del Norte run the following October.

Each ship was capable of carrying upwards of five hundred passengers. And none ever traveled with empty places. In fact, westbound, six hundred passengers were often crammed into a vessel explicitly designed to hold one hundred less than that number. (The population of eastbound passengers was generally less than half that count. Vanderbilt made his money on the westbound trips through passenger ticket sales, whereas the eastbound trade found its profit in the transport of specie from California to New York.) Another new steamship, the *Pacific,* was sent round the Horn to run between the western Nicaraguan port of San Juan del Sur, near Panama City, and San Francisco. All of these vessels were owned not by Accessory Transit, but by Vanderbilt personally and, in some cases, by Vanderbilt in partnerships with other individuals. They were used by Accessory Transit, of which Vanderbilt operated for the moment as CEO, on lease terms that were excellent for the owners of the ships.

Via his Accessory Transit Company, Vanderbilt offered speed and economy. He did not, however, offer true luxury or courteous service, not even in first class. The westbound Vanderbilt boats on the Nicaragua route were routinely over-crowded, their staffs over-extended and weary, their food mediocre. What was worse, since Vanderbilt's larger and better boats tended to service the Atlantic route, there was sometimes not enough room on the connecting steamers, many of these (other than the *Pacific*) being inadequate second-hand vessels (such as the ancient *North America*, jointly owned by Vanderbilt and Daniel Drew, and the *Brother Jonathan*) hastily purchased or leased by Vanderbilt to take up the slack in the San Juan del Sur to San Francisco traffic. On top of everything else, the trek up the San Juan River remained grueling and treacherous, despite the best efforts of Vanderbilt's engineers. One group of east-bound passengers came away from their excursion feeling so ill-used that, upon their arrival in Manhattan, they purchased space in the *New York Times* to vent their anger in an open letter to Vanderbilt:

> There are a few trifling items which we in kindness submit to you as being unworthy of your generally enlarged views and most liberal, humane intentions toward those under your care and protection. For instance, all the meats set before us at our meals were so tainted as to be positively offensive to the smell, and, of course, unfit as food for any civilized creature. . . . Our eyes were never feasted by the appearance of a clean cloth on the table, nor did we . . . luxuriate upon a clean sheet or pillow case. Not a bathroom on the ship, and a spittoon is not an article of furniture to be found in the establishment. We regret, sir, to mention these little inconveniences as having a tendency toward complaint— yes, even instill in the minds of passengers a thorough disgust and most perfect contempt toward you, as the controller of the magnificent institution composing this company. In conclusion,

our very dear friend, we promise you that we will never burden again your superior steamer . . . with out presence on board; and in preference to another such voyage, we would each get a wheel barrow, carry our provisions on it, and thus plod across the plains to our homes on the Pacific—and there we will teach our children to revere your name as the most successful, most penurious and most heartless millionaire that ever disgraced our country.[3]

In mid-1853, one passenger who felt particularly ill-used sued in the New York courts, the result being a $10,000 fine levied against Vanderbilt and Drew as co-owners of the decrepit *North America*.[4]

Early in 1852, the engineer Childs issued a detailed survey. In his lengthy report, Childs argued for a lock canal fifty feet wide and seventeen feet deep between Lake Nicaragua and a port immediately to the north of San Juan del Sur called Brito. Additionally, Childs prescribed several small canals as work-arounds for problematical sections of the San Juan River. Childs estimated the total cost of the project at $32 million. Interest soon picked up when influential groups of topographical engineers in the United States and London declared the project, as laid out by Childs, to be feasible.

That spring, the New York Stock Exchange briefly embraced the idea of the canal. Each original investor in the American Atlantic & Pacific Ship Canal Company (primarily Vanderbilt and a few close associates and family members who had made initial investments of $2,000 per share to cover initial expenses) possessed 192 "grand" shares in the project as a whole. Each grand share represented the equivalent of 200 shares in the Accessory Transit Company: a firm with a total of 40,000 shares outstanding. (A second commodity related to the venture, Canal "Rights," rose from a base price of $800 to $3,600 during this period of exhilaration.) Shares of Accessory Transit, meanwhile, spiked from $20 to $50, causing each $2,000 "grand" share to have a value, at the market peak, of $13,600.

The excitement of the topographers and the stock traders was not, however, shared by the world's bankers. That summer, when a delegation of American Atlantic & Pacific Ship Canal Company executives visited London's Lombard Street in search of financing, they found themselves rebuffed. Leading investment banks from Baring Brothers on down flatly refused to fund the project. Joshua Bates, a native of Boston and a Baring Brothers partner who loomed large in virtually all the firm's American investments, roundly condemned the economics of the Nicaraguan canal scheme. Doing the most elementary of sums, Bates pointed out that in order to yield a 6 percent return on a $32 million investment, the canal would need to transport 900,000 tons annually—an astronomical figure. Also, further clouding the financial viability of the venture, Bates questioned the American Atlantic & Pacific Ship Canal Company's proposed toll of $3 per ton, which he thought exorbitant to the point of being prohibitive. Bates's criticisms effectively killed the Nicaraguan canal not just with Barings Brothers, but all other London banks. On Wall Street, canal "Rights" dropped back down to $800 and eventually to nothing. However, Accessory Transit, as a going-concern with positive cash-flow, remained strong. Overall, Vanderbilt continued well into the black, personally netting $1 million per year from the Nicaraguan venture.[5]

Down in South America, relations with the government and with the locals in San Juan del Norte were sometimes complicated. During the fall of 1851, the Mosquito King, backed up by the British brig-of-war *Express,* forced the payment of $123 in "port dues" for the *Prometheus,* this despite language in the agreement between Vanderbilt's company and the Nicaraguan government stipulating that no such fees would ever be imposed. Under duress from the British gunship, Vanderbilt himself (who happened to be on board at the time) went ashore and paid the demanded fee. Back in the United States, word of the event was greeted with outrage. Speaking on behalf of Vanderbilt, Joseph White demanded the protection of the United States Navy to defend against any further bullying by the British. In turn, Daniel Webster, now having replaced Clayton as Secretary of State, lodged a formal complaint with British authorities, who promptly repudiated the actions of the commander of the *Express.* (A few months later, in March of 1852, Vanderbilt joined with other New York Whigs in calling for Webster to be made the party's presidential nominee.[6] Webster died that same year, in October.) Eventually, to punish the Mosquito King, Vanderbilt relocated all his piers and other facilities to the other side of the harbor from San Juan del Norte (the Mosquito King's Greytown), thereby claiming to be out of the Mosquito King's jurisdiction while also removing quite a bit of activity from Greytown's local economy.

One year later, at the close of 1852, Vanderbilt and the Nicaraguan government got into a squabble over accounting. That year, after declaring a $2 dividend, Vanderbilt's Accessory Transit informed the Nicaraguan government that its 10 percent payment for the same fiscal period would be zero, there having been no formal profits after the deduction of expenses for the lease of steamships (from Vanderbilt and a few partners) and the payment of fees associated with the promotion of the by-now defunct canal project. Citing the $2 dividend declared for stateside investors, the Nicaraguans argued that their 10 percent should have come out before any such declaration. Subsequently, when the government sent a delegation to New York to discuss the matter, Joseph White refused to even meet with them.

The ignoring of the Nicaraguan claims by Vanderbilt and White stemmed from a complex back-story. Starting when Baring Brothers and the other Lombard Street banks killed the canal idea, Vanderbilt seems to have lost interest in Accessory Transit as a corporate entity (even though he remained an avid speculator in the firm's stock and used his unique position vis-à-vis the company to create news on which the stock would plunge and rise). Part of the reason for his alienation was almost certainly the ending of the prospects for the canal, which had been his pet project. However, Accessory Transit was also the first public corporation in which Vanderbilt had been involved in a large way. Not having total control of his brainchild seems to have been a major adjustment for him. Others on the Accessory Transit board, White among them, were men possessed of strong personalities and bold visions—men who could not be bullied by Vanderbilt, the Commodore who was so used to having his way in all things.

During the late summer of 1852, shortly after the disaster on Lombard Street, Vanderbilt briefly threatened to end the leases of his "Vanderbilt Line" steamships servicing the Nicaraguan trade, thus causing the stock of Accessory Transit to plummet at a moment when Vanderbilt was conspicuously short, and in place to reap millions on a fall in the price. With the same action, as something of a bonus, he was able to send shivers through White and others sitting about the firm's boardroom: demonstrating the strength he still possessed. One month later, in resigning the presidency of Accessory Transit, he wrote that he did so because he was "unable to act in concert with a majority of the Directors whose right it is to rule."[7]

Thereafter, in response to a request from the Accessory Transit board, Vanderbilt agreed to sell the company seven steamboats, including the *Prometheus, Daniel Webster,* and *Pacific.* The price Vanderbilt demanded and got was $1,350,000, with $150,000 of that amount being in company bonds payable one year from the bill of sale, and the balance representing cash to be paid immediately. Per Vanderbilt's agreement with Accessory Transit, he remained in place as a management agent for the vessels at a very rich commission rate: 20 percent of the gross receipts. This huge percentage even drew a protest from Vanderbilt's own son-in-law Allen, who subsequently resigned from his position as vice president of Accessory Transit, saying he did not want to appear to be in collusion at a time when his wife's father was drawing usurious compensation from the company.[8] (Allen, nonetheless, remained on reasonably good terms with the Commodore. In fact, the high rate awarded Vanderbilt was a bow of recognition to Vanderbilt's founding of the franchise. It was also a premium payment for the use of Vanderbilt's name, his good reputation, and the stability implied by his continued association with the route.) To cover the cost of the transaction, Accessory Transit floated 40,000 shares of stock at $30; most of these purchased by officers, who quickly saw the stock rise to $40 on the strength of Vanderbilt's personal commitment to the enterprise. Vanderbilt's return to the board (though not to the presidency) on Valentine's Day, 1853, also did not hurt.

Two days after Vanderbilt rejoined the Accessory Transit board, one of the antiquated steamers on the California side of the Southern Route, the *Independence,* suffered an accident while northbound off the southernmost point of California's Margarita Island. Less than three hundred yards off the rocky shore, the *Independence* struck a rock amid rough seas, in the wee hours of the morning, and immediately filled with water. The *Independence* had been licensed to accommodate 250 souls, but she carried 450 individuals, nearly all of them asleep in bunks, at the time of the accident. When rising water blocked the draft of the ship's flues, fire erupted. "Men and women, as the flames were spreading, screamed frantically," recalled one survivor, "the former smiting their breasts, the latter tearing their disheveled hair. The scene beggars description. Wealth and poverty were on an equality, and sank together to rise no more."[9]

One hundred and seventy-six died. But on Wall Street the stock of Accessory Transit remained buoyant once word spread that the *Independence,* having been leased, would not show up as a loss in the firm's account books. Two months later, the Accessory-owned *Samuel S. Lewis* sank off Duxbury Reef in Bolinas Bay, near San Francisco. All 385 passengers, among them William Tecumseh Sherman, survived. However, the ship represented a capital loss. As well, it represented a public relations problem *viz* safety in the wake of the wreck of the *Independence.* Therefore Accessory Transit's stock sank below $30.

Vanderbilt, meanwhile, planned a vacation.

16

A FINER HEAD THAN WEBSTER'S

DURING THE SPRING OF 1853, VANDERBILT TOLD AN OLD FRIEND (Jacob J. Van Pelt, a Staten Islander who had captained several of the Commodore's steamboats through the years), that after the liquidation of his Southern Route steamers and the run-up in Accessory Transit's stock, he had $11 million tucked away, invested securely in assets yielding 25 percent annually with low to no risk.[1] Given this, and given the fact that he was nearing the milestone age of sixty, Vanderbilt resolved to orchestrate a monumental celebration of his worldly success on a highly public, international scale: a grand tour (in fact, the first American grand tour) of the Old World. But he did not plan to soak up European culture so much as he intended to put American progress and wealth on display. "I have a little pride," he told New York Senator Hamilton Fish, "as an American, to sail over the waters of England and France, up the Baltic and through the Mediterranean and elsewhere, under this flag without a reflection of any kind that it is a voyage for gain—with such a vessel as will give credit to the enterprise of our country."[2] The *Herald*'s James Gordon Bennett received a similar message, and echoed it on his editorial page. "The real character of our people," he wrote, "has been misunderstood. What can the Czar of Russia know of our social life—of the general prosperity which prevails throughout the country—of the intelligence and comfortable condition of our industrial classes, and the refinement of those whose enterprise, industry and genius have placed them at the head of the social scale?"[3]

Bennett may have been overestimating the degree of Vanderbilt's refinement. However, he was right on target in discerning the message about the emerging wealth of the United States, and the meritocracy enabled by its open markets, which Vanderbilt's tour of Europe would send. The vessel Vanderbilt's nephew Simonson built for the voyage adhered to the Commodore's own precise specification and, at a cost of $500,000, spared no expense. Two hundred and seventy feet long at the spar deck and 260 feet on the keel, the *North Star* weighed in at 2,500 tons and was the largest steamship in the world. The ship measured 38 feet at the beam, where were found two massive, lever-beam engines serviced by four, 24-feet-long boilers. The *North Star* also had two masts. From the foremast fluttered a white spike flag with a red *V* in the middle, and from the mainmast waved a red flag on which "North Star" was painted in blue letters. The two flags combined to assemble the red, white, and blue of the United States.

As impressive as was the *North Star*'s engineering, it was her palatial appointments that caught the attention of the press. An artist who had previously been engaged to similarly decorate the walls and ceilings at Washington Place spent several weeks creating medallion portraits of Christopher Columbus, George Washington, Benjamin Franklin, Henry Clay, and the recently deceased Daniel Webster for the ceiling of the ship's dining room. As Croffut reported, the ship featured "ten elegant state-rooms connecting with the saloon, each with a large glass door. . . . The berths were furnished with silk lambrequins and lace curtains. . . . Forward of the grand saloon was a magnificent dining-room. The walls were covered with a preparation of 'ligneous marble,' which was polished to a degree of mirror-like brightness. . . . The panels were of Naples granite, resembling jasper, and the surbase was of yellow Pyrenees marble. . . . The china was of ruby and gold finish, and the silverware was the finest that could be had."[4]

On May 19, the day before his departure for Europe, Vanderbilt concluded a deal to sell the Staten Island Ferry, together with numerous tracts of real estate on Staten Island, for $600,000. The purchaser was Minthorne Tompkins, son of old Daniel Tompkins who'd died back in 1825. Held back from the sale was the landing, now known as Vanderbilt Landing, north of Tompkinsville in southern Stapleton. Overlooking this was the Commodore's boyhood home, where the elderly Phebe Hand Vanderbilt still lived. As part of the deal, Vanderbilt agreed to lease Vanderbilt Landing to Tompkins for ten years. Tompkins, meanwhile, set about planning a railroad that would run across the island from Vanderbilt Landing to Biddle's Grove, opposite Perth Amboy.[5]

The following morning, the twentieth, as the North Star approached the Narrows, the aged Phebe came out, stood on her front porch, and waved as Vanderbilt himself, using a small deck cannon, fired a salute.[6] Immediately surrounding Vanderbilt stood most of his extended family. Each of Vanderbilt's sons and daughters (save for the disdained Cornelius Jeremiah, and Cornelius and Sophia's daughter Frances, who was at that time in poor health), accompanied him, as did their spouses and several sets of grandchildren. The apparent congeniality of the family scene belied the fact that the children had not been invited, but rather commanded, to come.

Also in the party bound for Europe were Dr. and Mrs. Jared Linsly, Captain Asa Eldridge (commanding) along with his wife, and a Baptist cleric, the Reverend Dr. John Overton Choules, who traveled with his wife. Choules led the Second Baptist Church in Newport, Rhode Island. He had been invited personally by Vanderbilt, the latter in this way acceding to the request of his devout daughters who had asked that a minister be on board to conduct services. Seven years younger than Vanderbilt, Choules had been born 1801 in Bristol, England. He came to the United States in 1824, and three years later was made pastor of the Second Baptist Church. (Later on, he served congregations in Buffalo, New York City, and Boston's Jamaica Plain before returning to Newport in 1847.) Conspicuously devout, sober, and literate, Choules was a Whig in politics. When Webster died in the autumn of 1852, Choules preached a sermon which gained considerable attention nationwide when published as a bestselling pamphlet. "Whatever Daniel Webster was," said Choules, "belongs to the United States. . . . He was (to accommodate the language of John Quincy Adams, employed in a eulogy upon Canning) 'American through and through, American in his feelings, American in his aims, American in his policy and projects. The influence, the grandeur, and the dominion of America were the dreams of his boyhood, and the intense effort of his riper years. For this he valued power and for this he used it.'"[7]

Vanderbilt found common ground with Choules in his politics, and in his Americanism. Thus the two men clicked, despite the fact that Vanderbilt continued his habit of making no pretensions to piousness. After the voyage was done, Choules would somewhat wryly tell a reporter that while he had been in charge of all the praying on the voyage, the Commodore had been in charge of all the swearing. Luckily for history, Choules also appointed himself in charge of something else: chronicling the trip in an account which he published the following year as *The Cruise of the Steam Yacht North Star.*

Vanderbilt told Choules he had no ambition in the European tour other than to "gratify his family and afford himself an opportunity to see the coast of Europe, which he could do in no other way."[8] The voyage across took twelve days, with the ship averaging three hundred miles per day. Arriving in Britain on June 1, Vanderbilt shortly found himself invited to visit the elite Royal Yacht Club. In London, the party took in all the likely sights (Parliament, the Tower, St. Paul's and Westminster Abbey). However, Vanderbilt, with his wealth and fame making every wish achievable, appears to have sought out no artistic, literary, or political celebrities. Dickens and Tennyson were among those who went unmolested. In fact, Vanderbilt seems to have only accidentally bumped into various prominent Americans (such as the banker George Peabody, who as an after-thought threw a dinner for the Commodore, and the politician Stephen A. Douglas).

At one point, Vanderbilt and his son George, wishing to get a taste of middle-class British life, boarded a public conveyance to take them from London to see the races at Ascot. "In going over from Windsor," reported Choules, "they occupied seats in an omnibus, and the subject of conversation happened to be the American steam yacht at Southampton. One of the persons present said that he had been to see her, and gave a pretty glowing account of the *North Star.* He spoke of her elegance and accommodations at full length, and then ended by remarking that the Commodore was a wide-awake man; that he had twelve sons on board, and made them work the ship; and that he saw seven or eight of them rowing the barge ashore." Choules added that Vanderbilt and son "sitting next to the speaker, smiled and laid low."[9]

Vanderbilt had been in London only a few days when that city's *Daily News* ran a glowing editorial:

An American merchant has just arrived in London, on a pleasure trip. He has come by train from Southampton, and left his private yacht behind him at a dock in that port. This yacht is a monster steamer. . . . The building of the vessel alone cost 100,000 pounds. The expense of keeping it up is 300 pounds a week. Listening to the details of the grandeur of this new floating palace, it seems natural to think upon the riches of her owner, and to associate him with the Cosmo de Medicis, the Andrea Fuggers, the Jacques Coeurs and Richard Whittingtons of the past; but this is wrong. Mr. Vanderbilt is a sign of the times. The medieval merchants just named stood out in bold relief from the great society of their day. Mr. Vanderbilt is a legitimate product of his country—the Medicis, Fuggers, and others were exceptional cases in theirs. They were fortunate monopolists who, by means of capital and crushing privileges, sucked up the wealth of the community. They were not a healthy growth, but a kind of enormous wen on the body politic. It took Europe nearly fifteen centuries to produce one Cosmo, and she never brought forth another. America was not known four centuries ago; yet she turns out her Vanderbilts, small and large, every year. America . . . is the great arena in which the individual energies of man, uncramped by oppressive social institutions, or absurd social traditions, have full play, and arrive at gigantic development. It is the tendency of American institutions to foster the general welfare, and to permit the unchecked power of the highly gifted to occupy a place in the general framework of society which they can obtain nowhere else. The great feature to be noticed in America is that all its citizens have full permission to run the race in which Mr. Vanderbilt has gained such immense prizes.[10]

On June 13, the mayor, merchants, and traders of Southampton, that great port town, hosted an elaborate dinner in Vanderbilt's honor. During the toast, the mayor exclaimed that the position Vanderbilt and his family held in the United States was the equivalent of any ducal house in the United Kingdom. After the mayor's toast, a band loudly played the American national anthem. In responding, Vanderbilt proclaimed that the citizens of the United States and Britain were "one people" and said he hoped that "by the power of steam, our common countries will be so bound together that no earthly power can separate us."[11] After those few words, the ineloquent Commodore introduced his son-in-law Horace Clark, on whom the burden of a fuller response was thus bestowed. Clark in turn was followed by another son-in-law, Nicholas LaBau, both of them singing the praises of Anglo-American camaraderie. Captain Eldridge also spoke, as did Choules.

One day later, the *North Star* departed Southampton for a cruise along the coast of Norway and beyond: to the Baltic Sea, Russia, and Denmark. At Cronstadt, on the Gulf of Finland, Vanderbilt and his wife remained aboard the *North Star* while the balance of the party went ashore to visit *Monplasir*, the home Peter the Great lived in while overseeing the construction of the grand Peterhof, long known as the Russian Versailles. "[Monplasir] is quite small," Choules observed, "and not unlike a Dutch farmhouse. Its interior is quite like some old houses that I remember on the North River. In this snuggery Peter died. We saw the bed on which he breathed his last; the bed clothes are all preserved, as when he occupied the chamber."[12] Next they visited the Peterhof itself with its cascading gardens (the Grand Cascade) flowing down to the sea. Back on the *North Star*, Vanderbilt entertained Grand Duke Constantine, the second son of the tsar and a high admiral of the Russian navy. After inspecting the steamer, the Grand Duke put Cornelius and Sophia onto the royal yacht and used this to transfer them to shore, where one of the emperor's carriages with royal livery picked them up for a tour of the palace and grounds. Later on, the combined party visited nearby

St. Petersburg, where they enjoyed private tours of the Winter Palace and the Hermitage, as well as the relatively small palace belonging to Vanderbilt's new friend, Grand Duke Constantine.

The *North Star* steamed out of Russia on June 29 and proceeded to Copenhagen, arriving July 1. Here the party visited the Thorwaldsen Museum and made an expedition to the Palace of Rosenbergh, the ancient seat of the kings of Denmark, before departing for their first port in southern Europe: the French city of Le Havre. Here they arrived on July 5. At Le Havre they were greeted by William Henry Vesey, the American consul for the city, appointed by Millard Fillmore. (Vesey had been kept on, despite differences in politics, by the newly sworn president, Franklin Pierce.) Vesey helped the party get oriented, and placed them in first-class railroad cars aimed towards Paris on a picturesque route that ran along the banks of the Seine. "Of all railroad routes that I am acquainted with," wrote Choules, "I regard this as the most pleasant one I ever traveled. I cannot conceive of more rural happiness and comfort than appears to be spread over the glorious fields of Normandy, and between Havre and Rouen." Choules noted that all of the party boarded the train for Paris, save for Vanderbilt himself who, being "indisposed," chose to "remain for a quiet day aboard the yacht."[13] Dr. Linsly, in his diary, shrewdly noted that "the Commodore" lagged behind "complaining of lethargy, ministered to by a young servant girl who will quickly cure him better than I ever could."[14] (Vanderbilt followed his party one day later, traveling via the same riverside railroad route from the sea to Paris. Shortly after his arrival in the city, he politely rebuffed an approach by French capitalists who sought his partnership in a new steamship line linking major European ports with North, South, and Central America.)

At Paris, where they were to stay for nineteen days, the Vanderbilt group put up in several hotels: the Hotel du Rhein in the Place

Vendôme, the Hotel d'Albion, and the Hotel Windsor on the Rue Rivoli. The outgoing United States consul S. G. Goodrich (who, unlike Vesey, had not survived the change in administrations) saw to the party's needs and got them situated. Goodrich arranged trips to Versailles, the tomb of Napoleon, the Botanical Gardens, Notre Dame, the Palace of Justice, the gardens of Tuilleries, the Champs Elysées, and other landmarks. Vanderbilt and clan also spent an entire day wandering the endless corridors of the Louvre, and another exploring the region of Normandy. (Linsly, meanwhile, seems to have devoted his days to visiting the physicians and surgeons, and touring the operating theaters and hospitals, which constituted Paris's world-class medical establishment.) Finally, on July 25, the *North Star* steamed out of Le Havre, bound for the Mediterranean.

On the morning of the 29th, as the steamer pushed through the Bay of Biscay off the coast of Portugal under both steam and sail power, a crewman was lost overboard and drowned. This was Robert Ogden Flint, a twenty-year-old promoted to the rank of quartermaster only days before. Flint had been standing on the quarter deck watching other members of the crew work to shift the main sheet, which flapped up in a high gust and knocked him over the side. The *North Star* was traveling fast at the time, and thus took several minutes to slow down and come about in an effort to save Flint. A yawl boat searched for more than an hour before the quest was given up. Officers and crew shortly started a subscription for the erection of a memorial marker back home. Vanderbilt, Billy, and the various Vanderbilt sons-in-law all contributed.[15]

Arriving in Spain, the *North Star* made the port of Malaga on the 31st. After a brief tour of the town, the Baptist Choules noted, with revulsion, the heavy presence of the Roman Catholic Church both on the streets and in the corridors of government. While walking near the docks, Vanderbilt and Choules found themselves accosted by a priest who, ringing a bell and holding out a box, begged for money. "On asking what the objects of his solicitation were," recalled Choules, "we were informed that a murderer was to be garroted the next day, and the good padre was taking up alms to pay for his funeral masses. Such is Popery in Spain. They can 'pray a soul out of purgatory;' but even this poor murderer must bring fish to the priest's net." Choules noted that coastal Malaga boasted a large British Protestant community: mostly gentleman associated with the port trade, managing exports from Spain's wine country. This community had recently succeeded in establishing a small Protestant cemetery overlooking the water. "Now an effort has been made to secure one in Madrid; but the Bishop of Barcelona has fiercely denounced the measure . . . "[16]

Departing Malaga on August 2, the Vanderbilt party traveled next to the port of Leghorn, and from there went by train to Florence. Here, Vanderbilt posed for a portrait bust executed by the American expatriate artist Hiram Powers, a neo-classical sculptor who, knowing how to secure a commission, anxiously declared that Vanderbilt possessed "a finer head than Webster's."[17] Born in Vermont in 1805, Powers had not become famous in his native land until 1847, when his controversial erotic statue *The Greek Slave* toured the United States. The sculpture, as several historians have pointed out, was one that had allowed Powers to demonstrate his command of the nude figure in a way acceptable to provincial America: a country still much fettered by puritanical Calvinist conventions. The piece depicted a young Greek girl captured by the Turks and displayed naked for auction at a Constantinople slave market. Chains covered the genitals of the Powers slave. Nevertheless, since the chains formed both the thematic and literal center of the sculpture, all eyes were drawn to them, and thus to the genitals. The sensuality of the piece was made acceptable by the idea of the woman having been disrobed by barbarians against her will. At the same time, the Greek-classical style of the piece served to summon thoughts of Greece's democratic tradition, while the narrative conjured memories of that nation's recent defiant struggle against Turkish domination. (Of course, for Americans already anxious about an issue that threatened to undermine their own democracy, the theme of slavery had yet another subtext.)

Vanderbilt posed fully clothed for his portrait bust, which showed him from the shoulders up. Nevertheless, Powers draped the shoulders in such a way as to suggest a toga.[18] One presumes Vanderbilt did not mind this, for as he posed he sat close by Powers's neoclassical, full-body statue of South Carolina's late states-rights hero John C. Calhoun, who as a senator had bargained with Daniel Webster to help craft the Compromise of 1850. The former vice president, senator, representative, secretary of state, and secretary of war wore a full toga. Thus clad, Clay stood next to a palmetto tree. A scroll he held in his right hand read: "Truth, Justice and Constitution." But Calhoun was imperfect: His left arm was broken off from the elbow.

When Margaret Fuller, the author and New England transcendentalist, had visited Powers's studio in 1849, she'd described the Calhoun statue as "full of power, simple and majestic in attitude and expression."[19] Ironically, Fuller, along with her Italian husband and small son, were all drowned in the same 1850 shipwreck off the south shore of Long Island that caused the damage to the toga-clad Calhoun. The marble South Carolinian had, at that time, been en route to Charleston via New York. Now, after being fished up off the floor of the Atlantic near Fire Island, the piece had been returned to Powers for mending. (The Calhoun statue was to remain jinxed. Powers finished the repair-work in 1857, after which the statue returned once more to the United States, where it was placed on its originally intended pedestal in Charleston's City Hall. Later on, during the Civil War, South Carolina officials installed the work in the capitol building at Columbia, where it was destroyed when Union troops under General William Tecumseh Sherman burned the building on February 17, 1865.)[20]

Choules was full of praise for Powers, whom Vanderbilt evidently liked as well. "Mr. Powers's efforts on Mr. V. we all watched with great interest," he wrote. "The artist was delighted . . . and he was engaged evidently *con amore;* his subject sat charmed with the originality of his eloquent conversation. If the result was not a perfect representation of a head of rare power and command, I am no judge, and we were all of us mistaken. Long as the marble lasts will that face evince its striking force." Vanderbilt loved the result but, when the two ordered marble copies from the plaster mold arrived in New York three years later, he balked at shipping fees, which he thought usurious, and made an enemy of Powers.

While Cornelius posed for Powers, Sophia posed for a bust executed by a forty-three-year-old ex-patriot Kentuckian by the name of Joel T. Hart. In order to accommodate the sudden Vanderbilt commission, Hart briefly had to suspend work on a portrait bust of one of Cornelius's great heroes, Henry Clay. Choules wrote that he'd watched Hart at work and was convinced that Hart was, like Powers, "a genius." Choules said Hart had a "large heart," a "good head," and was "no pretender." Further, Choules came away convinced that "his head of Mrs. Vanderbilt, in four sittings, was as complete a likeness as was ever molded."[21] Interestingly, Sophia did not sit for Hart at her husband's request, but rather at the request of her sons-in-law, who had taken it upon themselves to commission the work. Vanderbilt himself, meanwhile, commissioned Powers.

Both Powers and Hart enjoyed close friendships in Florence with the likes of Robert and Elizabeth Barrett Browning, the American sculptress Harriet Hosmer (who lived in Rome but spent much time in Florence), and other literary and artistic notables. However, aside from Powers and Hart, there is no record of the Vanderbilt party ever mingling, or seeking to mingle, with any of the numerous literary and artistic elites in and around Florence. Vanderbilt retreated directly to the *North Star* at Leghorn from Florence, accompanied by Hart and Powers, who wanted to see the ship. The balance of the party went by railroad for a quick jaunt through Pisa, with its famed leaning tower, before returning to the steamer. Departing Leghorn on August 12, the yacht steered towards Rome. The *North Star* was in the harbor of that city when it was announced by the local authorities that a bureaucratic glitch in the ship's port paperwork would require a quarantine of several days. Unwilling to suffer any delay, Vanderbilt steamed away in a huff, thus disappointing many on the staff and crew, so many of them Catholics, who had particularly looked forward to this part of the excursion. No friend of the Roman Catholic Church, Choules nevertheless commented: "I really did pity the poor ladies maids, who were Catholics, and our purser, Mr. Keefe, who was also a son of the church. . . . One of the girls burst into a passionate flood of tears, and declared that all that had induced her to come on board was to go to Rome." After traveling slowly about three hours to a point about twenty-five miles from the city, the party enjoyed a good view of the dome of St. Peter's in the far distance. "All our party came on deck," Choules remembered, "and every glass was in demand."[22]

From there the group journeyed to Naples (where once again they were not permitted to debark), Capri, Stromboli, the Lipari Islands, Syracuse, Malta, and Constantinople before turning back towards Gibraltar. September 9 found the ship leaving Gibraltar, pointing towards Tangier and Madeira, departing Madeira on September 12 for home. On Sunday, September 18, the *North Star* came upon an eerie floating wreck "apparently of a brig, with everything washed away above the deckbeams: stern all washed away."[23] Choules noted the arrival home on Friday, September 23, when the *North Star* rounded Sandy Hook. "Staten Island looked as lovely as ever, and she is one of the sweetest spots on our globe. Travel where he may, the voyager fails to find a place where all the comforts and elegance of life are more profusely concentrated than on this island-suburb of the great metropolis America."[24]

Over fifty-eight days, the *North Star* had traveled a bit more than 15,000 miles. "For nearly all of the distance traveled," reported the *New York Times*, ". . . two of the four boilers only were in use, the vessel making 13 knots. With four boilers, she made 18 knots—a faster rate of speed, we believe, than any vessel of the size has yet attained. The average daily consumption of coal, during the voyage, was only fourteen tons."[25] Speaking to reporters in New York, the Commodore expressed himself as being more than satisfied with the ship and her crew, and speculated out loud as to whether he would keep the vessel for his private use or open her up for the traveling public on some popular oceanic route. That decision would come in time. More immediately, Vanderbilt let it be known that he had scores to settle: people who had gone wrong while he was overseas, who now needed to be put right.

17

I'LL RUIN YOU

SINCE VANDERBILT'S ABDICATION OF POWER AND DEPARTURE for Europe, the affairs of Accessory Transit had been largely run by two men: one on the east coast, the other on the west coast. New York's Charles Morgan and San Francisco's Cornelius Kingsland Garrison between them administered the affairs of the company. Each had his own geographical sphere of influence. Each also had a tangled and in some ways clandestine alliance with the other. This alliance, as the Commodore was soon to realize, worked to the exclusion and disenfranchisement of Vanderbilt.[1]

Born in the Hudson River Valley in 1807, Garrison came from a line of Hudson River sailors but had trained as a civil engineer. After several years being involved with construction projects in such regions as Buffalo and parts of Canada, he made a small fortune running sloops and small steamers out of St. Louis on the Mississippi River. Later on, at the start of the gold rush, he opened a banking house in Panama that did a huge business benefiting from the westbound traffic of human beings and the eastbound traffic of gold. During the spring of 1853, after the Pacific wrecks that have been previously noted in this narrative, the board of Accessory Transit recruited Garrison to become the San Francisco agent for the firm with a salary of $60,000 per year. Indeed, it was Vanderbilt himself who put Garrison forward as a candidate best suited to reorganize the Pacific route, and it was he who encouraged Garrison to accept the post. (One wonders if Vanderbilt ever heard what was commonly said of Garrison, whom many considered ruthless. Popular wisdom in most boardrooms held that Garrison was such a genius that it took twenty men "to watch him.") Since arriving in San Francisco, Garrison had demonstrated a remarkable hyperactivity. In addition to administering the western affairs of Accessory Transit he'd also, in a matter of months, gotten himself elected mayor and founded a bank (Garrison, Fretz) in which William C. Ralston, well on his way to becoming the west coast's most prominent banker, played a role as partner.

One year younger than Vanderbilt, Charles Morgan had been born in Killingworth (today's Clinton), Connecticut. He left there when he was fourteen and moved to Manhattan, where in time he developed successful businesses retailing ship chandlery and buying and selling imports. From that small start, Morgan branched out into merchant-shipping as both an owner and a manager overseeing various lines of sail and steamships conducting trade between ports of the American South and the West Indies. During 1837, Morgan pioneered a steamship route between New Orleans and Galveston, eventually extending service to Matagorda Bay eleven years later, then Brazos Santiago, and Vera Cruz. At first a rival who hoped to beat Cornelius Vanderbilt in attempts to establish a route across Nicaragua, Morgan later became an ally who enjoyed Vanderbilt's confidence enough that the Commodore recommended him for Accessory Transit's board of directors, of which he eventually became chairman.[2]

Morgan also signed on as the eastern agent for Garrison, Fretz. He began that position in May of 1853, just as the *North Star* steamed out past Sandy Hook. Ten days later, Morgan appointed himself as New York agent for Accessory Transit, thus canceling Vanderbilt's contract to provide the same service. Not long after, Morgan moved to restore several directors whom Vanderbilt had previously identified as enemies and maneuvered out. These men, in turn, elected Morgan president of the firm. Once in that perch, Morgan manipulated Accessory stock just as feverishly and adroitly as Vanderbilt ever had. These machinations, however, meant little to Vanderbilt. He now owned a relatively small slice of the company stock, though he remained the company's largest bondholder. Overall, Vanderbilt seems to have remained cheerfully either oblivious to the goings-on at Accessory Transit, or preoccupied with his grand tour, until significant sums owed him by Accessory Transit went unpaid. "Trouble is anticipated upon the return of Commodore Vanderbilt," intoned the *New York Herald*. "It appears that when he agreed to put boats upon the route, the Transit Company contracted to pay him twenty percent of the gross receipts of the Transit across Nicaragua. This payment was made regularly to Mr. Vanderbilt up to the time he left in his yacht for Europe. Since, the Company has refused to make payments to Vanderbilt's agent, and there is very little doubt but that upon the Commodore's return, summary measures will be taken to collect his demand."[3] Officially, the argument was a complex one over accounting: remuneration for coal and other supplies advanced by Vanderbilt, and other gray areas of easy dispute. Unofficially, Garrison and Morgan, buccaneers suddenly enjoying complete control of the firm, simply saw no point in paying the Commodore one single dime until a court, God Almighty, or both compelled them to. Reading the facts for what they were shortly after his return to New York, Vanderbilt took out ad space in the leading dailies wherein he published an open letter to Messrs.

Morgan and Garrison: "Gentlemen: You have undertaken to cheat me. I won't sue you, for the law is too slow. I'll ruin you.—Yours truly, Cornelius Vanderbilt."[4]

But how? Garrison and Morgan were hardly babes in the woods. In fact, they were quite confident predatory capitalists who had accomplished what few others ever had or would. They'd gotten the better of Vanderbilt, and were continuing to do so. The men grew richer with every Accessory Transit voyage. Perhaps even more troubling to Vanderbilt was the fact that Morgan and Garrison had won high praise from both the press and the public for improving the conditions aboard the ships Vanderbilt had previously owned and managed. The pirates provided exemplary customer service, fine meals, and sanitary conditions, where Vanderbilt had not. Further turning the tide of public opinion in favor of Morgan and Garrison was a generally accepted sentiment that Vanderbilt's 20 percent deal had been grossly unfair to Accessory Transit shareholders, who'd been overpaying for his services. (Morgan let it be known that the firm, Morgan & Garrison, which he'd put in place to replace Vanderbilt charged a mere 10 percent of the gross receipts.)

Despite the disdain for the courts that Vanderbilt voiced in his open letter, he nevertheless used them to the extent that he could—that is to say, not very strenuously or effectively. Accessory Transit was a Nicaragua corporation. This fact greatly complicated all domestic judicial proceedings. At one point, when the *Prometheus* tarried for a layover in New York Harbor, Vanderbilt made a vain attempt to attach her via writ of the New York Chancery Court. In their appeal, Vanderbilt's attorneys insisted that a Nicaraguan corporation had no authority to operate vessels within the United States. This argument failed, however, when it was realized that the *Prometheus* and other Accessory Transit steamers were registered not in the name of Accessory Transit, but rather under the names of various officers of the firm and, further, that Vanderbilt himself had approved this arrangement at the time of his transfer of the vessels.

While Vanderbilt contemplated his options and his next steps, he also dealt with a personal loss.

Early in the new year of 1854, on January 22, Phebe Hand Vanderbilt, who had been failing for months, passed away. Vanderbilt commanded the entire clan to gather at the old home on Staten Island for the funeral service, after which Phebe's bones were taken to the old Moravian Cemetery and laid beside those of her husband. Family members recalled the Commodore being sad but businesslike as he supervised his mother's final arrangements and saw her into the ground. The tomb was one of his own making, prepared several years before, to which the bones of his father had already been transferred. "The subterranean chamber," wrote journalist James Dabney McCabe Jr., "is about 30 feet square, and is surmounted by a lofty shaft, and a statue of grief adds a peculiar finish to the spot. The cemetery is on an eminence, from which one gets a fine view of the ocean, dotted with ships."[5] The family name in the archaic form familiar to his father, VAN DERBILT, was chiseled on the monument.

Through the years, he'd offered his mother mansions and trips and jewels, but she'd refused most such gifts, always insisting on keeping to her own little house overlooking the Narrows, which Vanderbilt had enlarged slightly for her. Now Vanderbilt made plans to keep the house in the family: part retreat, part memorial to his parents and to his distant youth. The décor of the place consisted of several decades' worth of elaborate gifts from a generous but self-absorbed son. Thus the cottage had long seemed to most visitors to be something of a small Vanderbiltian museum. Paintings of the Commodore's favorite horses and steamers adorned the walls, as did portraits of his daughters and his one most favorite son: George Washington Vanderbilt. Knick-knacks about the place included one of the sweeps from his first periauger, this hanging from a wall. The most recent additions were souvenirs from the grand tour: British silver, Spanish caftans, Russian dolls. All of it would remain, relatively untouched and hardly ever visited, for many decades: a time machine.[6]

After he'd bid his mother goodbye, Vanderbilt distracted himself from his grief by targeting Morgan and Garrison in the marketplace. He was still, despite being robbed, a very rich man equipped with enormous resources which he could leverage to comfort, or discomfort, anyone he chose. Now he did so: slowly, almost furtively. Throughout the autumn and early winter he'd let it be known that he was bearish on the stock: a pessimist. During January, he sold a substantial number of Accessory Transit shares: 5000 units, most at prices hovering around $25, and all on "seller 12 months" terms. This meant Vanderbilt had up to a year to deliver the promised stock, in which he was now conspicuously short. Word on the street had it that Morgan was the primary buyer. At the same time that he went short in Accessory Transit, Vanderbilt put the *North Star* (now remodeled to accommodate hundreds of passengers in considerably less spacious luxury than he and his family had enjoyed) on runs to Panama. In order to facilitate transcontinental traffic between the east coast and California, he made an alliance with steamboat-man Edward Mills, a New Yorker who'd previously embarked upon the Panama trade with very limited success. Mills's two wooden side-wheel steamers, the *Uncle Sam* and the *Yankee Blade,* had between them serviced the Pacific and the East Coast end of the Panama route, with the *Yankee Blade* operating between

New York and Chagres. In February of 1854, Mills sent the *Yankee Blade* round the Horn from New York to San Francisco. As of May he had the two boats at work servicing the western leg of Vanderbilt's new route.

Although Mills's boats left much to be desired in the way of comfort and speed, the remodeled *North Star* offered acceptable comfort and superlative speed. (As well, after the grand tour, the vessel herself was something of a celebrity. Not a few would-be ticket buyers sought to ride on Vanderbilt's "famous" *North Star*.) The record runs of the *North Star* quickly made Vanderbilt's new "Independent Line" more than competitive from a speed point of view. (The firm set the record for transit between California and New York that summer, with a run of just twenty-one days and fifteen hours.) In addition to this, Vanderbilt returned to his time-honored practice of making his boats more than competitive when it came to price. Vanderbilt's son-in-law James M. Cross, acting as agent for the line, initially offered transit between New York and California at $150 for first class accommodations and $75 for steerage, then lowered fares to $100 and $30. "For a very small sum," Vanderbilt advertised, "passengers will be guaranteed to arrive in San Francisco ahead of the Nicaragua line."[7]

Morgan and Garrison struggled to keep up with Vanderbilt's aggressive pricing, but found it utterly impossible to best his speed. At the same time, they confronted problems in Nicaragua, where a revolution erupted in the spring. Travel there became dangerous, inducing many would-be sojourners to make their way via Panama. Things became especially complicated, and tense, for Accessory Transit interests in Nicaragua when, during May of 1854, a captain of one of the Accessory steamers shot and killed a black resident of Greytown in a dispute after a collision on the San Juan River. When authorities attempted to arrest the captain, they were blocked from doing so by Solon Borland, the American minister to Nicaragua who happened to be on board at the time. Borland was rewarded for his trouble by being hit in the head by a thrown bottle. On the heels of this altercation, the United States sent a sloop of war, the *Cyane*, which lingered menacingly in Greytown Harbor. The *Cyane*'s captain, Commander George N. Hollins, was following orders that came directly from President Franklin Pierce when he made the following demands. Hollins insisted on a payment of $24,000 in damages for Accessory Transit. He also insisted on an apology for Borland, and assurances of safe passage for all Accessory Transit vessels, and their passengers, in future. After about a month, when these demands were not acceded to, Hollins announced twenty-four hours in advance that he would begin bombarding Greytown as of 9:00 A.M. on the morning of July 13. Early on the morning of the 13th, he sent a steamer to collect evacuees and their belongings. This was followed by four separate, prolonged bombardments, after which the crew of the *Cyane* torched the town.

The bad press, and the uncertainty it indicated, caused Accessory Transit's passenger trade to evaporate even more than it had already. (After all, Vanderbilt had been offering lower fares, faster service, and safe passage via Panama for several months.) At the same time, in light of the tensions in Nicaragua and the firm's well-publicized loss of revenue, Accessory Transit stock dropped to $21 on Wall Street. Becoming desperate, Morgan and Garrison soon sought a settlement with Vanderbilt. (In doing so, they acted in collaboration with Marshall O. Roberts's United States Mail Line and John Aspinwall's Pacific Mail Line, both of which had suffered collateral damage from Vanderbilt's price war with Accessory Transit.) In the final agreement, Accessory Transit agreed to pay Vanderbilt virtually all of the monies he claimed as having been owed him. In return, the Commodore withdrew completely from Isthmian transit. As a part of the broader deal, Vanderbilt sold the *North Star* to the United States Mail Line for $400,000 cash, and Mills sold the *Yankee Blade* and *Uncle Sam* to the now cash-strapped Accessory Transit for a similar total price, part in cash and part in stock. (The firm would fail to declare a dividend come January of 1855.)

Vanderbilt was not yet done, however. After all, his enemies were not yet utterly ruined. He remained loudly bearish on the already-depressed Accessory Transit stock, and took other actions as well. During March of 1855, Vanderbilt dispatched Daniel Allen (who, it will be remembered, was a former vice president of Accessory Transit) to level serious charges against the officers of the company. In court papers filed in Manhattan, Allen alleged misappropriation of funds, incompetence, and the illegal issue of 40,000 new shares. Courtesy of John Duer, a friendly New York State Supreme Court judge on the Vanderbilt payroll, Allen won an injunction forbidding the issuance of more stock and a further court-order restraining Accessory Transit from entering into new contracts with firms controlled by Morgan and Garrison. When Wall Street received word of Duer's decision, the stock dropped to $15.

In this environment, and at this price, Vanderbilt and several key allies now began, furtively and slowly, to accumulate Accessory Transit stock. Further political unrest in Nicaragua brought the stock lower, as did news in November that significant sums needed to be borrowed to make payroll and to purchase coal. Given Accessory Transit's poor financial profile and prospects, a new bond issue sold at a discount that reflected the company's miserable risk-rating: 15 percent. In December of 1855, Vanderbilt and his clique pooled their shares and seized control. A newly devised board appointed Vanderbilt as general agent. Two months later, the Commodore assumed the presidency, leaving Morgan and Garrison nearly completely out in the cold, although Garrison remained temporarily in

place as Pacific agent. One might have expected, given the resur-
gence of Vanderbilt, that Accessory Transit's stock would instantly
rise, but this did not happen. Mismanagement had been only one
part of the firm's trouble; unrest and uncertainty in Nicaragua remained an issue.

That country's largely illiterate population of 263,000 was divided
into several ethnic blocks. Roughly half the population sprang from a
mix of Mosquito Indian and Spanish blood, while a third was pure
Mosquito, a tenth Spanish/Creole, and the balance blacks a generation or two removed from Africa. On the political front, a so-called
"Liberal" or "Democratic Party," based in the city of Leon, dominated the north of the country, while the conservative "Legitima-
tists," based in Granada, held a majority in the south. The clashes
between these two parties were, generally, far less political than they
were military. Insurgent movements and counterinsurgent movements abounded; a condition of undeclared civil war prevailed. In six
years, the country had seen fifteen presidents under a constitution
that officially called for a two year term. During 1854, when the
reigning Legitimist president rewrote the constitution extending his
term from two to four years, Democratic Party leader Francisco
Castellon planned a coup and began searching for aid from abroad.

That aid came during May of 1855, in the form of one William
Walker. The self-proclaimed "General" Walker commanded a
small, fifty-eight-member army he would later dub "the Immor-
tals." Born in Tennessee in 1824, Walker had graduated from the
University of Nashville. A restless spirit, and evidently a supreme
egotist, he pursued rather mediocre careers in the law, journalism,
and medicine before deciding on a career as a revolutionist and ad-
venturer desirous of possessing his own country. Two years earlier,
in October of 1853, he'd led an expedition of forty-eight men intent on expelling Mexicans from their lands in the southern Cali-

fornia towns of Baja and Sonora. Walker never in fact succeeded in taking Sonora. Nevertheless, he declared both towns to be parts of something he called the Republic of Lower California (a name he changed three months later to the Republic of Sonora), while at the same time proclaiming himself president. In short order, Mexican forces chased Walker and his tiny band back from whence they had come. Put on trial for conducting an illegal and unsanctioned war, Walker was quickly found innocent by a jury of his peers: southern westerners who, like him, were eager to see white American dominion over the lands in question.

In Nicaragua, Walker quickly seized San Juan del Sur. There he squatted for several months, sending word of his conquest back to San Francisco, and awaiting the reinforcements he knew that good news would recruit. By October, his "Phalanx" (as he called his army) numbered several hundred men. With these, and with the help of transport on an Accessory Transit steamer, Walker seized the Legitimist capital of Granada. Afterwards, nearly instantly, Walker broke with his ostensible allies in the Democratic Party, showed his conservative colors, and set up his own government. Walker installed an elderly Legitimist politician, Patricio Rivas, as a puppet president while Walker, the actual strong-man leader, took the title of Commander in Chief of the Nicaraguan Army. Garrison and Morgan, who still controlled Accessory Transit as of October 1855, were delighted. Anxious for political stability in Nicaragua, they'd been encouraging Walker from the wings for quite some time. They'd provided free transport to Nicaragua for Phalanx members. They also helped finance the new government with an infusion of $20,000 in gold bullion: an "advance" on future payments due to the government from the firm. (Accessory Transit confiscated the bullion from an eastbound shipment in its holds, and reimbursed the owners with notes of credit.)

Two months later, in December of 1855 when Vanderbilt showed his hand and took control of Accessory Transit, Garrison (who, it will be remembered, still had a little time left on his contract as Pacific agent) evidently contrived to use his previous alliance with Walker to exact revenge. Late that month, a contingent of would-be Phalanx members journeyed from San Francisco to Granada on an Accessory Transit steamer. With them traveled Garrison's aide and business associate C. J. McDonald, Walker's friend and attorney Edmund Randolph (of the Virginia Randolphs), and Garrison's son William. Once in Granada, this trio rather easily convinced Walker, with whom Garrison and Morgan already had a close relationship, that his government should cancel the charter of Accessory Transit and confiscate its ships in Nicaraguan waters. (The pretext, despite the $20,000 in bullion recently given the government by the firm, was unpaid debts owed by the corporation to government of Nicaragua.) The trio further convinced Walker to give a new charter to attorney Randoph, as agent for Messrs. Garrison and Morgan, and to award the new company any and all assets seized from Accessory Transit. Once this deal was agreed, William Garrison proceeded on to New York via an Accessory Transit steamer to apprise Morgan of the scheme. (At the request of Garrison's representatives, the timing of the announcement of the government action was delayed so that Morgan would have time, once briefed, to maximize his and Garrison's advantage on Wall Street.)

Vanderbilt at first had no reason to believe Walker would be working against his interests. Political stability in Nicaragua was just as desirable a thing for a Vanderbilt-controlled Accessory Transit as it had been for the firm when dominated by Morgan and Garrison. Early in his tenure, Vanderbilt allowed several contingents of Walker supporters to debark for Nicaragua via Accessory Transit boats. As late as February 27, 1856, nine days after the publication of the charter revocation and asset confiscation by the Walker government but well before word of this reached New York, an Accessory Transit vessel departed New Orleans for Greytown carrying 250 mercenaries. At the same time, Morgan in New York went heavily "short" in the stock of Accessory Transit. Morgan sold shares he did not own at the going price of $23, with a promise of delivery within three months. Word of the nullification of the Accessory Transit charter reached New York on March 12, at which point the share price plummeted to $13, allowing Morgan to cover his thousands of shorts with a profit-margin of $10 per share.

Five days later, on St. Patrick's Day of 1856, Vanderbilt published a statement in the major New York dailies indicating Accessory Transit's withdrawal from the Nicaraguan route. Vanderbilt said he took the action "in consequence of the difficulties . . . growing out of the extraordinary conduct of General Walker, in seizing or taking by force the property of American citizens." Vanderbilt said he would let "the ships of the company lay at their wharves, until our government has sufficient time to examine and look into the outrage. . . . In the meantime, as I do not consider passengers or the property of American citizens safe on the transit of the isthmus, I cannot be instrumental in inducing either to take the passage."[8] Writing to Secretary of State William L. Marcy in the same week, Vanderbilt produced records debunking Walker's claim of substantial sums owed by Accessory Transit. Marcy, however, was less than helpful. The secretary pointed out something which Vanderbilt had heard before, and of which he was more than well aware. Accessory Transit was not an American but a Nicaraguan corporation. Although federal authorities would respect the properties of the firm in American waters, they would not intervene in disputes involving real-estate or maritime properties abroad. Vanderbilt was on his own.

As a first step, Vanderbilt dispatched his son-in-law James M. Cross to San Francisco, there to oust Garrison and take possession of all Accessory Transit steamers as they returned, one by one, on their routes from Nicaragua. (In New York, Vanderbilt did the same thing. At the end of the day, no ocean-going Accessory Transit vessel left the control of Vanderbilt and his allies.) Garrison and Morgan's new Nicaragua line, meanwhile, struggled along with two hastily acquired steamers. Garrison ran the *Sierra Nevada* between Nicaragua and San Francisco, while Morgan ran the *Orizaba* between New York and Greytown. As had long been the case, passengers paid additional side-fares for the railroad and lake steamers that now connected Nicaragua's two coasts. The Garrison and Morgan ocean-steamships made their first runs in April of 1856. The total assets of the new firm were those two vessels, the several lake steamers which Walker's government had seized and handed over, plus all the real property in Nicaragua that had formerly been in the hands of Accessory Transit. The total value of these assets amounted to only about $400,000, all told.

Initially, a briefly and artificially tranquil Nicaragua, with Rivas removed and Walker newly installed as president, invited a slight up-tick in trade for Garrison and Morgan. By summer of 1856, they had three ships (the *Calhoun, Texas,* and *Tennessee*) running on the Atlantic, and two (the *Sierra Nevada* and the relocated *Orizaba*) on the Pacific. Morgan and Garrison got an average through-fare price of $175 per head. The dormant Accessory Transit, meanwhile, saw its stock price sink to $5, then $4: a wildly low number considering the assets of the firm and significant positive cash-flow. From where did the cash-flow come? As he'd done more than once before, Vanderbilt managed to wring dollars out of inaction. As of mid-March Vanderbilt exacted $40,000 per month from William H. Aspinwall's Pacific Mail and Marshall O. Roberts's U.S. Mail as a fee for keeping his ships, now idle, off the Panama route, where Pacific Mail and U.S. Mail dominated.

The following autumn, while leaving the Accessory Transit vessels at their moorings, Vanderbilt personally started a war against Morgan's proprietary Gulf shipping interests with an eye toward crushing him. During September of 1856, Simonson launched the *Opelousas* and the *Magnolia,* side-wheelers of under 100 tons. Vanderbilt quickly put both vessels into direct competition with Morgan-owned ships servicing cotton exports out of the Gulf ports of Galveston and New Orleans. A price war was promptly launched, and Morgan instantly began to bleed. As regards Walker, Vanderbilt used his formidable position in financial markets, particularly the New York financial market, to make sure that loans desperately needed by Walker's fledgling government were not forthcoming. During January and February of 1856, Vanderbilt had gotten to know Domingo de Goicouria. A wealthy Cuban exile and a devoted Liberal Democrat, Goicouria had supported Walker on the latter's promise that he would one day take his revolution from Nicaragua to Cuba, liberating that island from Spanish dominion. At the time, Goicouria had been Walker's agent in New York. In November of 1856, Goicouria, now Nicaragua's newly appointed Minister to Great Britain, stopped in New York on his way to London. During his stay in Manhattan, he endeavored to secure loans for Nicaragua that, largely because of Vanderbilt's antagonism, did not materialize. In an unpublicized meeting with Vanderbilt, Goicouria received an assurance that the Commodore himself would personally provide $100,000 in credit if only Walker's government would restore Accessory Transit's charter. When Goicouria urged Walker to accept this offer, the president refused and fired Goicouria. During that same week in late November, Edmund Randolph, in New York for consultations with Morgan, gave a statement to the press in which, somewhat ironically, he attacked Goicouria as a foreigner who wished to intrude upon the business of Nicaragua "with a dishonest and treacherous intent."[9] (Goicouria subsequently demanded a duel, which never came off because of Randolph's poor health.)

Walker's position now began to look perilous. Goicouria was a popular leader, and a true idealist, whom many respected and all were sorry to see leave Walker's government, in which he had been expected to be a moderate voice of reason. As well, Walker still desperately needed the financing, which was not to be had. And he faced other issues. The Tennessean had outraged many former supporters two months before Goicouria's firing, when he'd revoked Nicaraguan laws banning slavery. Even more backers fell away in December, when Goicouria published Walker's memorandums to him written at the time he'd been selected as minister to Great Britain. Walker's memos revealed the president's radically conservative vision for South America. In written instructions, Walker had urged Goicouria to make the British leaders see that "the only way to cut the expanding and expansive democracy of the North is by a powerful and compact Southern federation, based on military principles." In other words, Walker dreamed of a military dictatorship in Central America designed to inhibit if not ban American expansion: a blasphemy against the dominant American doctrine of Manifest Destiny. While secessionist Southerners applauded Walker's map for the future of the Isthmus, northern bankers and industrialists did not.

Vanderbilt's old competitor George Law for a time chose to aid Walker, and thus gain a foothold in Nicaragua. Law forwarded guns to Walker for a short while, but this effort died away after just one shipment, once Law himself realized that in the long-term Walker would be bad for business. At the same time, Vanderbilt worked to induce neighboring countries unfriendly to Walker, especially Costa Rica, to move to close the mouth of the San Juan River at Greytown, on the Caribbean side of Nicaragua, this being the port farthest away from the main concentration of Walker's forces, the bulk of them being on the Pacific. The Costa Ricans had in fact been technically at war with Walker since early 1856, when that country's congress empowered President Juan Rafael Mora to drive Walker and his "filibusters" from the continent. After several successful incursions, the Costa Ricans had only retreated due to a cholera outbreak. That same summer, Honduras, Guatemala, and San Salvador signed a treaty of alliance to guard against incursions by Walker, and extended military aid to Rivas when the latter attempted (and failed in) a coup against Walker.

Vanderbilt urged all this on, and applauded in November of 1856 when, again, Costa Rica advanced against Walker. At Vanderbilt's urging through agents, and with his direct support in the way of guns and money, Mora in December mounted a major expedition to block the mouth of the San Juan. Early in that month, some 120 Costa Ricans under the command of Vanderbilt's agent Sylvanus H. Spencer (an Accessory Transit engineer with military training inspired by a large interest in the company's stock and the promise of a $50,000 cash bounty for success in the mission) approached the upper reaches of the San Carlos River (running parallel to the San Juan). The group macheted their way through jungles and rain forests in a grueling march. Taking some of Walker's soldiers by surprise above the mouth of the Serapiqui River, they killed the unlucky and captured the lucky. Then, descending to Greytown, the little army seized control. Moving up the river, the Costa Ricans captured the lake steamers *Virgin* and *San Carlos,* along with Fort San Carlos. At that point, Mora reinforced with more troops who boarded the steamers and made quick work of taking Virgin Bay, thus putting the entire eastern transit of Nicaragua under Costa

Rican dominion. When news of all this reached New York, Accessory Transit shares doubled in price. Vanderbilt and those allied with him quietly became sellers.

With no access to the Caribbean Sea, Walker's position was untenable. No new recruits could join him from the east, and few from California were inspired to join what was seen as a lost cause. Walker lasted until May 1, 1857, at which point he surrendered to an army led by Mora which had surrounded San Juan del Sur. (Six months later, it seemed something of a joke when Walker and a handful of supporters attempted to seize Greytown. Walker's ragged crew wound up disarmed by American sailors before their little war could even begin. But Walker could not be taught. On September 12, 1860, after attempting to interfere in the affairs of Honduras, he died before a firing squad.)

The future of Accessory Transit remained murky. Through different legal and political machinations, Morgan and Garrison briefly continued to challenge Vanderbilt for the right to the Nicaraguan charter. So too did the Commodore's onetime ally Joseph L. White, who had picked up a majority interest in Accessory Transit's "parent" company, the nearly forgotten American Atlantic & Pacific Ship Canal Company, for pennies on the dollar years before, after the collapse of the canal scheme. Complicating things further were Costa Rican territorial claims within Nicaragua. During December of 1857, Morgan and Garrison, fast running out of money, reached a settlement with the victorious Vanderbilt. Morgan and Garrison officially abandoned their Nicaraguan interests, such as these were. Morgan at the same time purchased the boats Vanderbilt had been running to compete with him on the Gulf out of Galveston and New Orleans. As part of the same deal, Vanderbilt took over Morgan's *Ocean Queen*, then nearly finished in a New York shipyard and ready to launch. Vanderbilt also received a half interest in the *Sierra Nevada* and *Orizaba* on the Pacific.

White was not so easily disposed of. White bribed the new Nicaraguan Minister to the United States (A. J. de Yrisarri, representative of the new government that had replaced that of Walker) with $5,000 in cash and $80,000 in company stock. After this payment, in July of 1857, White was actually able to secure a conditional charter for the transit, only to see this revoked early in 1858 after extensive lobbying by Vanderbilt and Vanderbilt's agents in Nicaragua. By the fall of 1858, Yrisarri had been replaced as minister by the Liberal politico and army general Máximo Jerez, a man who, like the government he served, was known to be friendly to Vanderbilt interests. When White and his associate H. G. Stebbins, a New York investor whom White had named president of the American Atlantic & Pacific Ship Canal Company, tried running a boat from New York to Greytown without a charter, Nicaraguan officials refused docking privileges to their vessel. The steamer *Washington* wound up being forced to go on to Panama.

Thus, as of late 1858, the way was clear for Vanderbilt to reopen the Nicaragua transit. But he didn't. In fact, he seems to have come to the conclusion that Accessory Transit itself was a lost cause. Satisfied that he had defeated those who would oppose him, he did not feel it worthwhile to make the investment necessary to shore up the Accessory Transit's broken infrastructure: building more boats and doing necessary repairs at Greytown. Besides, there was still good money to be made by remaining inactive in Isthmian transport, and continuing to exact lucrative non-compete payments from Aspinwall and Roberts. Once Vanderbilt's competitive advantage in Nicaragua stabilized, Vanderbilt was able to raise his non-compete price from $40,000 to $56,000 per month. Of course, Accessory Transit stock was now, again, worth practically nothing. But the Commodore and his associates had been sellers at healthy prices, and Vanderbilt still had his cash-flow from Aspinwall and Roberts. That money would continue to come for several months into 1859, and the corporate corpse of Accessory Transit would linger on spread-sheets for another four years after that.

But as of 1858, Vanderbilt's ambitions for Accessory Transit, and for Nicaragua, were at an end. He would have probably wrapped them up well before that, save for his need to chastise Morgan and Garrison. While seeking his Nicaraguan revenge, he'd also been quite busy in another theater of operations: the transatlantic trade. This was where his real interest, outside of ruination, had lain for quite some time.

18

ATLANTIC CROSSING

IT WILL BE REMEMBERED THAT VANDERBILT HAD BEEN approached in Paris about partnering in a steamship service connecting North America with the Continent. At the time, keeping to his pledge that his grand tour was to be devoid of business, he politely refused to consider the proposal. However, shortly after his return from Europe, he began to ponder the possibility of a transatlantic venture—though not one in which he'd partner with others.

The *Savannah*, a steam and sail vessel, had first crossed the Atlantic in 1819, but the trade had only begun to seriously open up after 1839, with the voyages of the steam and sail *Sirius* and *Great Western*. Although sailing vessels without engines continued to dominate the transatlantic trade as of 1853, steam was just as ascendant on the North Atlantic as anywhere else in the world. Samuel Cunard of Nova Scotia had begun planning his line of steamers in 1838, launching his first vessel in 1840. Cunard's simple steamships averaged about 160 feet in length and at first ran only between Liverpool and Boston, with stops in Halifax. Then, in the mid-1840s, Cunard doubled the size of his fleet and began an additional route between Liverpool and New York, with no Halifax stop. The Cunard ships operated with an average annual subsidy from the British government of 145,000 pounds, this in return for carrying mail and specie between Liverpool and the ports of Halifax, Boston, and New York.

Although Cunard was a Nova Scotian, his line was viewed widely, and not inappropriately, as a British venture. Not a few Americans complained about Britain's apparent dominance in what one writer called "the merchant marine of steam." Editorials noted Parliament's role in funding the Cunard Line, and asked that Congress do something similar to encourage American entrepreneurs. In 1845, Congress responded with a policy of mail subsidies for American steamship lines not unlike what the British Parliament had offered Cunard. In that year, with the federal government's encouragement and backing, Vanderbilt's future Nicaragua ally Edward Mills started a single-ship route connecting New York with Bremen, Germany. At the same time, Mortimer Livingston (a member of the old New York steamship monopoly clan) established a single-ship venture connecting New York with Le Havre. Of course, neither of these concerns posed any significant threat to Cunard, with whom they did not directly compete.

This situation remained the status quo until 1850, when American Edward Knight Collins launched three fast steamships designed specifically to compete with the Cunard steamers running between New York and Liverpool. Born on Cape Cod in 1802, Edward Collins moved to New York when a young man and went into merchant shipping with his father. During the 1820s Collins ran packets between New York and Vera Cruz. During the early 1830s, after his father's death, he made a fortune transporting cotton between New Orleans and New York. Then, in 1836, he founded the Dramatic Line of transatlantic packets on a route between New York and Liverpool, each of his ships being named for a popular ac-

tress or actor of the day. Two years after the first Congressional subsidies had inspired Mills and Livingston, Collins announced his
plan to build four large and swift mail steamships to run on the
New York/Liverpool route: this in return for a federal mail contract
assuring Collins a subsidy of $385,000 annually.

Organized as the United States Mail Steamship Company, the
firm soon became popularly known simply as the Collins Line.
Collins's contract with the federal government demanded that his
newly built vessels be of at least 2,000 tons. In fact, upon their
launch in 1850, the *Atlantic, Pacific, Baltic,* and *Arctic* each weighed
2,856 tons. The identical side-wheelers, with their side-lever engines, were 282 feet long: nearly twice the length of any Cunard
ship. They also boasted luxuries and amenities unknown on the no-
frills Cunard steamers. As one marine historian has noted, the
Collins ships featured "marble-topped tables, mirrors, paintings,
thick carpets, carved and upholstered furniture, and not a few startling innovations—automatic signals from bridge to engine room
and from staterooms to stewards' quarters, a French maître de cui-
sine, steam heat in the passenger areas, wide 'wedding berths' for
honeymooners, and a glorious barber shop with patent reclining
chair."[1] More important, in the way of hull design, the new Collins
ships took a large step away from the lines of the traditional
steamship and towards those of the modern ocean liner. (Despite
hull innovations, the Collins ships remained side-wheelers. They
also remained wooden, because America's rolling mill infrastructure
was not yet capable of producing iron sheets of a size large enough
to form reliable hulls—although that day would come soon.)

More elegant and faster than the Cunard ships, the packed-
vessels of the Collins Line seemed successful at first glance. But as a
business, the line was a disaster. Speed came at a high cost, especially when it was associated with 2,856-ton vessels. So too did luxury. From the start, expenses vastly outstripped revenue. Raising

prices was not an option, as fares needed to be competitive with those of the Cunard Line, which operated with much lower overhead. Even when Congress in 1852 increased Collins's annual subsidy to $858,000, the firm still operated at a deficit: its investors with no hope of ever seeing a dividend, and its stock price stagnating. Things went downhill from there. During 1854, Collins's *Arctic* suffered a collision off Cape Race and sank, taking 318 passengers and crew with her. Two years later, the *Pacific*, under the command of the *North Star*'s old captain Asa Eldridge, was lost at sea in winter while returning to New York from Liverpool. Eldridge and all others on board, including Collins's wife and children, went down with the ship.

Vanderbilt had evidently decided upon entering the transatlantic business even before the first Collins ship went down in 1854. Less concerned about the inefficient Collins as a competitor than he was about the highly profitable Cunard, Vanderbilt had seen an opening when the Crimean War of 1854 forced the British Navy to confiscate several Cunard ships for the war effort. This caused Cunard to suspend his Boston/Liverpool route; he maintained the New York/Liverpool route for the most part, the exception being the winter of 1854/55, when no Cunard ships ran between Liverpool or any other U.S. port. With this being the landscape, near Christmas of 1854 Vandebilt gave Simonson a commission for a new sea-going steamship, the *Ariel* (2000 tons, with a beam engine crafted by the Allaire Works). At the same time, Vanderbilt arranged to repurchase the *North Star*, most recently in the hands of Marshall Roberts.

The subsidy granted to Collins averaged to about $33,000 per round-trip, while the subsidy granted by Parliament to Cunard translated to about $16,000 American per trip. In priming the pump for his own transatlantic line, Vanderbilt let it be known that he thought the sum being given Collins to be absurdly high. He also told all who asked, and many who didn't, that as a point of national pride he would render the same service, reliably carrying mail and specie between New York and Liverpool, at a rate less than the subsidy paid Cunard by the British government. During February of 1855, while the Cunard Line remained absent from both Boston and New York, Vanderbilt formalized his offer in a letter to the Postmaster General:

> Sir:
> The Cunard line between New York and Liverpool having been withdrawn, and a frequent and rapid communication with Europe being so essential to the interest of our commerce, I submit the following proposition to the Postmaster General: I will run a semi-monthly line, which, by alternating with the Collins Line, would form a weekly communication. And I will perform this proposed mail service for the sum of $15,000, the voyage out and home— the contract to exist for five years. . . . Good and sufficient steamers shall be put on the line within thirty days after the contract is signed.[2]

Vanderbilt's proposal made complete business sense. Not only did he offer to do the job of carrying mail and specie for less than half of the subsidy being received by Collins, he was also a known quantity whom the government could count on. However, Collins possessed strong lobbyists and many friends in Congress who, instead of approving the smaller subsidy for Vanderbilt, voted an extension of the large subsidy already in effect for the inefficient Collins. President Franklin Pierce vetoed the measure on the grounds that it flew in the face of logic and ran contrary "to the soundest principles of public policy."[3] Humiliated, Collins floated a rumor that Vanderbilt had bribed Pierce with $50,000 to enter the veto. Writing to denounce that charge in the pages of the *New York Tribune*, Vanderbilt used the same forum to condemn the concept of subsidies as practiced in Washington and exploited by the likes of Collins. At the same time, Vanderbilt spoke-up for laissez-faire capitalism as opposed to federal welfare for dysfunctional corporations. It would be better if all steamships were "sunk in the ocean than that it should be permitted by our system of commercial policy that private enterprise may be driven from any of the legitimate channels of commerce by means of bounties," Vanderbilt declared. "The share of prosperity that has fallen to my lot is the direct result of unfettered trade and unrestrained competition."[4]

Congress proved unable to pass the original Collins bill over Pierce's veto; nevertheless, subsequent legislation assured continued payments to the Collins Line. Meanwhile, as if to prove the point he had made in his *Tribune* letter, Vanderbilt made plans to proceed without subsidies. That spring of 1855, the Cunard Line returned to the New York/Liverpool route. Knowing formidable competition when he saw it, and wanting to leave Collins to duke it out with Cunard for the New York/Liverpool trade alone, the Commodore chose to go up against easier prey: Livingston's Le Havre route. Vanderbilt's son-in-law Daniel Torrance, with offices at 5 Bowling Green, served as agent for Vanderbilt's European Line of Steamships. New York papers carried an announcement on April 4: "The first class steamer *North Star*, 2300 tons, Wamack, master, will leave New York at noon, precisely, April 21, for Havre, direct. First class passage, $130; second, $75. The *North Star* will be followed by the new steamship *Ariel* in May. . . . Letters prepaid, fifteen cents per half ounce . . . will be carried in strong India rubber bags, under lock; and on arrival at Havre, will be immediately deposited in Post Office there."[5] Vanderbilt later advertised stops at Cowes, on the Isle of

Wight, and in time dropped his prices to $110 and $60 between New York and Cowes, in order to compete with the lowest Collins fares of $130 and $75.

Although unprofitable, the Collins ships continued to do a brisk business for some time. For a few dollars more than what Vanderbilt and Cunard charged, they offered the heights of luxury. Like Cunard, they also offered direct delivery to the most popular and convenient British port, Liverpool, rather than to remote Cowes. Hoping to at least compete with both Collins and Cunard on the score of luxury, Vanderbilt commissioned yet another ship from Simonson. Launched in the early summer of 1856 from Simonson's Greenpoint yard, the *Vanderbilt* was the largest vessel to have ever floated on the Atlantic. At 4,500 tons, she was larger than any Collins or Cunard ship, even Collins's new *Adriatic* (fifty-five feet long, 3,670 tons) which was still abuilding in a New York yard, and the Cunard Line's most recent entry of equivalent size, the iron-hulled *Persia* (3,300 tons, launched 1855 and put into service in January 1856). When Vanderbilt brought the new ship to the Potomac to show her off that summer, the result was not that Congress voted a subsidy for him, but instead that it slashed what it was paying to Collins, cutting him back to his 1854 level of a mere $385,000 annually. This proved Collins's undoing. Launched in 1857, Collins's grand *Adriatic* made only one round-trip run before the company suspended operations. One year later, the assets of the firm were auctioned off by the New York sheriff to satisfy debtors.

Vanderbilt weathered all storms without a subsidy. During the winter of 1856 he pared down operations and briefly put the *Ariel* to work servicing the Southern Route in order to keep his spreadsheet balanced. Then, as of early 1857, he delighted in watching his fortunes improve once the Collins Line ceased to be. Still wary of direct competition with Cunard, Vanderbilt continued to avoid the New

York/Liverpool route. He put the *Ariel* and *North Star* on alternating trips between Manhattan and Bremen, thus attacking the somewhat antiquated Bremen Line, whose ships the *Hermann* and *Washington* were each showing signs of age. Vanderbilt made short work of the under-funded Bremen Line, driving them from business by July. No other serious competition emerged on that route with any immediacy. At the same time, the Commodore confronted Livingston with the *Vanderbilt* by putting that ship to work servicing New York, Southampton (a far more convenient port for most travelers than Cowes), and Le Havre. The *Vanderbilt* left New York every forty days. During 1857, the Commodore's three Atlantic ships carried a grand total of 4,863 passengers between them. (Cunard carried 5,534 passengers during the same period.) Also during 1857, the *Vanderbilt* beat by two hours the *Persia*'s best time to England.

As of late 1856, Cunard, Collins, and Vanderbilt all faced formidable competition for New York/UK traffic from the recently renamed Liverpool, New York and Philadelphia Steam Ship Company, better known as the Inman Line. Founded by Britain's William Inman in 1850, the company had since that time been quite successful running steamers between Liverpool and Philadelphia. Early on, while plying the Philadelphia route, Inman leveraged the advanced manufacturing technology of Britain to roll out the first large iron-hulled, screw propeller–driven steamers. The vessels Inman put on the Atlantic were the *City of Manchester,* the *City of Baltimore,* the *Kangaroo,* and the *City of Washington.* Near the end of 1856, the Inman Line shifted its primary western terminus from Philadelphia to New York, thus providing both Vanderbilt and Cunard with formidable, though not fatal, competition. Of the three players, however, the Inman Line did the largest trade by far. Inman carried 11,294 passengers across the Atlantic in 1857. Of the total 54,746 passengers who crossed the Atlantic on steam vessels

that year, 8.8 percent were carried by Vanderbilt, 10.1 percent by
Cunard, and 21.7 percent by Inman—the three largest players. The
balance of 59.4 percent was divided between such smaller, periph-
eral players as Livingston's Le Havre line, the gasping Bremen and
Collins Lines. (The bulk of transcontinental voyagers still preferred
sail packet ships. Some 204,000 souls came to New York City via
the Atlantic in 1857. Only 27 percent traveled on steam vessels, the
balance preferring traditional clippers.) Much of Inman's trade
consisted of Irish immigrants, as in 1857 his firm had added a stop
at Queenstown (Cobh) between Liverpool and New York. Inman
also made a point of featuring cheap berths in expanded steerage
sections of his large vessels.

Meanwhile, many of Vanderbilt's first-class passengers still came
away feeling as if they had been traveling in steerage, and they still
complained bitterly in the press. "I have made ten voyages on the
Cunard, Collins and other steamers, and one, in August last, in
the *Vanderbilt*, on which occassion there was a comparatively small
number of passengers," wrote one correspondent in a letter to the
editor of the *New York Tribune* published November 30, 1857.
"Several of these passages were extremely boisterous, having been
made in the winter months; but in no instance have I ever wit-
nessed so much distress among the passengers or heard such loud
universal and continued denunciation of the internal arrangement
and general management of any ship."[6]

Conditions aboard Vanderbilt vessels did not improve at all in
1858, even though that was the year when Vanderbilt, as the dominant American in transatlantic steamships, finally got a grudging
stipend from Congress. Vanderbilt's grant, for which he carried U.S.
mail and specie, amounted to approximately $90,000 per year for
four years, ending in 1861. Throughout 1858, Vanderbilt's combined Atlantic vessels carried 6,814 passengers on the *Vanderbilt*,

North Star, Ariel, and *Northern Light,* which continued to link New
York, Southampton, Bremen, and Le Havre. Cunard carried 5,349
souls on its New York/Liverpool line during the same period, and
Inman 10,576. In 1859, Vanderbilt abandoned Bremen as a port of
call in the face of stiff competition from the rising north German
Lloyd Line, and added the *Ocean Queen* (purchased from Morgan)
on his Southampton/New York route. That year, Vanderbilt carried
5,840 passengers versus 5,794 transported by Cunard and 14,544
transported by Inman.

1859 also saw Vanderbilt reenter Isthmian transit. When federal authorities tightened subsidies to Aspinwall's Pacific Mail Steamship
Company and Roberts's U.S. Mail Steamship Company, those entrepreneurs were forced to stop making their non-compete payments to Vanderbilt. At the same time, Roberts, as trustee for the
U.S. Mail Steamship Company, gave clear indications that he would
put that unprofitable firm out of business in short order. The sus-
pension of the payments from Aspinwall and Roberts freed Vanderbilt (who believed Aspinwall would have trouble operating in the
long term without the large subsidies of the past) to once again become competitive in transcontinental transport. That March, Vanderbilt took the *Northern Light* and *North Star* off what had come to
be called the "Atlantic Ferry," and put them in service linking New
York with eastern Panama. In the Pacific, he put the *Orizaba, Sierra
Nevada, Uncle Sam,* and *Cortez* to work plying the waters between
western Panama and San Francisco.

After buying out Garrison's lingering half-interest in the *Orizaba*
and *Sierra Nevada,* Vanderbilt formed the publicly traded Atlantic
and Pacific Steamship Company with himself as President. He then

leased the *Northern Light, North Star, Orizaba, Sierra Nevada, Uncle Sam,* and *Cortez* to that firm, and sent his longtime associate, Captain John T. Wright, to manage things on the California side of the equation. Besides the Commodore, the company's small board of directors included Vanderbilt's sons-in-law Clark and Thorn, the U.S. Mail's Marshall Roberts, and one Moses Taylor (a shipping baron who had lately come to dominate much of the trade in the Caribbean, and who would have posed a nagging competitive threat had he been left outside the new company).

Vanderbilt and Roberts had long been on friendly terms outside of business, and Clark had recently served as Roberts's associate trustee in administering the final affairs of U.S. Mail. The Atlantic and Pacific Steamship Company would eventually acquire several U.S. Mail steamers when these were auctioned. Vanderbilt also commissioned an iron, 1,419-ton steamer, the *Champion,* from Wilmington's Harlan & Hollingsworth, which he added to the Pacific fleet. Taking a tour of the new ship, a reporter for Bennett's *Herald* noted Vanderbilt's large portrait hanging over the entrance of the steamer's main saloon; the Commodore looked "as smiling and amiable as if he had just brought 'them fellers on the corner of Wall and Water Streets' to terms."[7] (The intersection of Wall and Water Streets was the location of the Pacific Mail's office in New York, whereas the office of the Atlantic and Pacific Steamship Company, manned by Vanderbilt's son-in-law Daniel Allen as agent for the line, was at West and Warren.)

Having learned a serious lesson from the board-room machinations that had defined Accessory Transit, Vanderbilt took pains to make sure his most reliable family and friends held a clear majority on the board of the new firm. But having done that, he subsequently sold large blocks of stock to pools of wealthy investors, raising capital quickly through the strength of his reputation for ruthlessness, efficiency, economy, and long-term profit. As Vanderbilt girded for war, so too did Aspinwall. Working in partnership with the highly profitable Panama Railroad, Aspinwall acquired three ships from those auctioning the remains of the Collins Line: the *Baltic*, *Atlantic*, and *Adriatic*. Aspinwall paid $300,000 apiece for the vessels, then set them up to run between New York and the eastern port of Aspinwall in Panama as a subsidiary line to Pacific Mail.

Throughout the summer and fall of 1859, a predictable price-war waged between the two providers. Vanderbilt started at a $250 fare for first class, and an $88 steerage fare, inclusive of one-way transit over the Panama Railroad, the latter having a $25 value. In short order, however, Vanderbilt dropped the steerage fare to $20, with the railroad as an extra item to be paid in Panama. Aspinwall quickly matched Vanderbilt's proposition. At those prices, all ships of both lines were easily packed, with both Aspinwall and Vanderbilt losing money on each and every passenger, and only the Panama Railroad benefiting from the boom. With both steamship firms hemorrhaging cash, the question—as usual—was which would first reach a financial precipice and be forced to come to terms.

Both Vanderbilt and Aspinwall were playing close enough to their financial limits that in August, with the old eleven-year government mail contracts set to expire in October, they bid aggressively for that business. The newly offered contract was for just nine months, however, as the federal postal authorities were at that time engaged in slowly easing away from oceanic delivery of transcontinental mail in favor of overland routes, and wanted no longterm commitments. Both players were stunned when neither got the nod, which instead went, however briefly, to Wall Street broker Daniel H. Johnson acting as agent for Joseph L. White. Though he currently owned no steamers, White still dreamed of reopening the Nicaragua route. He promised to charter the necessary vessels, but his promise was doubted from the start. Although White's bid of $162,000 for nine months was the lowest of the three, Postmaster General Joseph Holt concluded, after careful investigation, that White would be unable to deliver reliable service. Thus Holt in the end wound up accepting the next lowest bid. This belonged to Vanderbilt, who had come in at $187,500, exclusive of Panama Railroad costs. (A brief congressional investigation into charges of collusion between Vanderbilt and Holt came to nothing; and indeed there seems to have been none.)

During November of 1859, Marshall Roberts and William Aspinwall met to try to hammer out a peace between the two lines. These talks failed, however, due to the members of both boards flagrantly manipulating stocks, the prices of which ebbed and flowed according to leaked news from the negotiations. Three months later, in early 1860, another attempt at arbitration, this one successful, was made with Vanderbilt himself representing the Atlantic and Pacific Steamship Company. The peace that was made involved Vanderbilt selling to the Pacific Mail all of his steamers on the Pacific save for the *Champion*. In return, Vanderbilt was to receive 5,000 class D shares of Pacific Mail, of which Daniel Allen now became a director as Vanderbilt's representative. Vanderbilt also received Pacific Mail's pledge to vacate the New York to Aspinwall route, thus leaving the now-misnamed Atlantic and Pacific Steamship Company dominant on the Atlantic side of the Panama transit.

According to the agreement which was set to last for five years, the firms were to act in unison, splitting receipts 30 percent for the Atlantic and Pacific Steamship Company and 70 percent for Pacific Mail, which took responsibility for all transit west of Aspinwall. The new monopoly immediately raised rates to $200 for first class and $100 for steerage. Stock prices for both firms spiked along with profits. The Pacific Mail's common stock, which had hovered around

$75 during the war, shot to $100 on word of the peace, and within a year reached $325. Vanderbilt's equity in that firm alone came to be worth more than $1.6 million, while he still possessed enormous holdings elsewhere. As the Civil War began, Vanderbilt's interests in the Atlantic Ferry and other concerns, including several railroads in which he'd been investing slowly and quietly for some time, came to total a value of some $20 million.

19

THE SPECIOUS
NAME OF ENTERPRISE

WITH THE DECLINE OF THE WHIG PARTY, WHICH WENT OUT of business in 1856, Vanderbilt found himself without a political home. His friend Daniel Webster had died in 1852, the same year as the party's other great leader, Henry Clay. Before those two giants went to their graves, debate concerning the Compromise of 1850 had already severely strained the base of the party, dividing it into bitterly opposed pro- and anti-slavery factions. The landslide presidential election of 1852 (in which the Democrat Franklin Pierce trounced the Whig candidate Winfield Scott, capturing twenty-seven out of thirty-one states including Scott's home state of Virginia) was widely seen as a stiff repudiation of the party. During 1854, energetic debate over the Kansas-Nebraska Act further fractured the Whig move-ment, with southern Whigs supporting the defacto repeal of the 1820 injunction barring the spread of western slavery anywhere north of the Missouri Compromise line, and northern Whigs walking away outraged. The party mounted no presidential candidate in 1856.

Many of the northerners who left the Whig organization (men such as Lincoln) rolled themselves into the emerging Republican Party. But a small balance of former northern Whigs went instead into the nativist, anti-immigrant, anti-Catholic Know-Nothing/ American Party. Vanderbilt, despite the fact that his own Atlantic Ferry carried more than its share of German Catholic immigrants to New York through its Bremen connection, was one of these, along with such other entrepreneurs as Collins and George Law. During the spring of 1855, as the new party began to ponder whom its 1856 presidential nominee should be, Know-Nothing sympathizer James Gordon Bennett editorialized in the *Herald* that a proven man of business was needed. Although quietly unenthusiastic when it came to Law (who, after all, came from Irish stock), Bennett recommended either Law, Collins, or Vanderbilt for the nomination. Bennett applauded each as being "identified with the great material and moral agent of advancing civilization, the steam engine." This being the case, said Bennett, the three entrepreneurs stood "in the front rank of the progressive moment of the age. Talk of such men being unqualified for the White House!"[1]

Bennett's editorial appeared on March 25. Two weeks later, speculation about Vanderbilt's candidacy reached such a crescendo that he felt compelled to issue a statement formally and emphatically removing himself from consideration. In a letter written on April 12 but published by Bennett on April 17, Vanderbilt foreswore any interest in the nomination. "I can at once assure you," he wrote in a missive that, like all his public notes these days, was much tidied and assisted in its articulation by a host of clerks, "that I am not now, and that I have never at any time been, in any degree desirous of political . . . distinction." Despite this disavowal, Vanderbilt went on to vent his own political views, these being defined by a total disinterest in the moral question of slavery and a bias towards states' rights and limited federal government overall. In this, he seems to have turned 180 degrees from the politics of Webster, and from the Federalist sensibilities that had driven him in the old fight against the Livingston/Fulton monopoly. As well, despite his current interest in international shipping, and despite his own meddling in Nicaraguan affairs, Vanderbilt expressed an isolationist view of foreign policy. In this he echoed George Washington's insistence that the country should avoid unnecessary foreign entanglements. "We should be as careful," he wrote, "not to make encroachments upon the rights of other nations as to resist, at any sacrifice, any and all which may be attempted upon our own."[2]

The *New York Times* despised the idea of the likes of Law or Collins or Vanderbilt being the national candidate of any party, and criticized the political landscape in which such a notion could take root:

Statesmanship, whether acquired by profound of philosophic study in the closet, or trained by long years of practical experience in the Senate, is out of the question, and a reasonable knowledge of the politics and party history of the country, is deemed a positive drawback to the pretensions of the candidate. Successful, mammoth speculation in steam contracts and ferry privileges under the specious name of enterprise is made one— and of late the favorite—standard of qualification; but whether from the hope of making "available" the individual wealth thus acquired, in the canvass of 1856, or the expectation of turning to account the confessed or boasted ignorance of the candidate on all subjects of public and political moment, is not exactly made manifest. . . . It is about time for New York to declare that when she wants a president—Whig, Democratic, or Know-Nothing— she will ask for him in the person of some really eminent citizen, entitled by statesmanship or political experience, or at least by enlarged intelligence, to the distinction.[3]

Unlike Vanderbilt, Law actually tried to get the Know-Nothing nomination, but that white elephant went to old Millard Fillmore. The former Whig vice-president had succeeded to the presidency upon the death of Zachary Taylor in 1850, and then had outraged northern anti-slavery Whigs by signing the Fugitive Slave Act, a key element in Webster and Clay's Compromise of 1850. Those same northern Whigs later worked to deny Fillmore the nomination in 1852. Of course, in the election of 1856, Democrat James Buchanan wound up achieving the White House, easily defeating not only the Know-Nothing/American Party candidate Fillmore but also John C. Frémont, the first presidential nominee of the fledgling Republican Party.

Throughout the next four years, as the nation ticked inexorably towards disunion and Civil War, Vanderbilt tended to his affairs in the North Atlantic and on the Southern Route while also engaging in speculations involving eastern railroads. Once war broke out, and genuine fears that Confederate raiders would shortly destroy all the merchant marine of the Union became rampant, Vanderbilt sought the most profitable way out of what he thought of as a tight corner. The Commodore offered to lease his largest, swiftest, and most valuable ships to the Union Navy. Vanderbilt (who, despite his attraction to the Know-Nothings, wound up supporting Democrat Stephen A. Douglas in the general election) had met and breakfasted with Lincoln at Moses Grinnell's New York home shortly before Lincoln assumed office. Probably because of this acquaintance, he copied Lincoln on his proposal to the Navy Department. Thereafter, Vanderbilt was perhaps surprised when Secretary of the Navy Gideon Welles did not immediately seize upon his offer. Navy admirals advised Welles that Vanderbilt's ships, with their large exposed side wheels, would be particularly vulnerable to enemy fire. In the end, relatively few Vanderbiltian vessels were used by the Navy for short periods, and most of these for no more critical a purpose than transporting troops down the American coast.

One other flirtation, this one between Vanderbilt and Secretary of War Edwin M. Stanton, came to a bit more. On March 9, 1862, the Union ironclad *Monitor* confronted the similarly fortified Confederate raider *Merrimac* in an altercation at Hampton Roads. The famous battle between the *Monitor* and the *Merrimac* resulted in a tactical draw, after which the *Merrimac* retreated to the Confederate stronghold of Norfolk. Six days later, fearing that the Union ironclad would not in future be able to inhibit the movements of the *Merrimac,* Stanton made a decision to privatize the operation. He telegraphed Vanderbilt to ask what sum the Commodore would require for a commission to sink or destroy the Confederate vessel.

Vanderbilt responded by journeying immediately to Washington where he convened a meeting with Stanton and Lincoln. Vanderbilt, whose son George was then serving in the Union ranks, insisted that he could indeed sink the *Merrimac,* but that he would take no money for doing so. His plan, as he laid it out for Lincoln and Stanton, was to use the *Vanderbilt,* the forward hull of which he intended to reinforce while fitting her bow with a battering ram and covering her exposed machinery with five hundred bales of cotton. At the same time, the Commodore proposed to remove unnecessary deck houses, and fit the ship with cannon. Then he would rush her full steam at the Confederate ship, sinking the *Merrimac.* Vanderbilt, who had already leased several of his other vessels to the government for short stints as troop-transports at rates ranging from $900 to $2,000 per day, intended his free offer of the *Vanderbilt* as a display of patriotism. It was accepted as such by Stanton:

Sir:

The President desires to return to the utmost account your patriotic and generous offer to the Government of the great steamship *Vanderbilt*. . . . And to that end, having accepted your gift of the *Vanderbilt*, he authorizes and directs me to receive her into the service of the War Department, and to use and employ the said steamship and her officers and crew, under your supervision, direction, and command, to aid the protection and defense of the transports now in the service of this Department on Chesapeake Bay, Hampton Roads, and adjacent waters.[4]

The *Vanderbilt*, fully fortified and moving under the personal command of the Commodore, arrived at Fort Monroe in Hampton, Virginia, on March 23. Thereafter, he kept the vessel steaming away, prepared to launch at a moment's notice should the *Merrimac* emerge from Norfolk. She did not. Whether her captain remained fearful of the *Vanderbilt*, the lingering *Monitor*, or both, no one knows. The Confederates withdrew from Norfolk on May 9. Before they did so, they blew up the *Merrimac* lest she fall into Union hands. Subsequently, the Commodore returned to New York, leaving his fortified vessel behind. The Navy refitted the *Vanderbilt* a bit more and sent her South, to the West Indies, there to hunt the *Alabama* and other Confederate commerce raiders: a task in which she enjoyed no success.

At the beginning of 1864, Congress passed a resolution thanking the Commodore for the "free gift" of his "new and staunch ship *Vanderbilt*." The resolution further instructed President Lincoln to strike a Congressional Gold Medal "which shall fitly embody an attestation of the nation's gratitude for this gift, which medal shall be forwarded to Cornelius Vanderbilt." Ironically, it was not until

he received this thanks of a grateful nation, in the form of the resolution pending delivery of the medal, that Vanderbilt realized
there'd been a misunderstanding between Stanton, Lincoln, and
himself. The Commodore had meant his "gift" of the *Vanderbilt* to
be for the duration of the national emergency, and no longer.
"Congress be damned," he reportedly told the messenger who
brought the good news. "I never gave that ship to Congress. When
the Government was in great straits for a suitable vessel of war, I
offered to give the ship if they did not care to buy it; however, Mr.
Lincoln and Mr. Welles think it was a gift, and I suppose I shall
have to let her go."[5]

Too add insult to injury, it would be two years before the medal,
an ornate gold one, would even show up.[6] The reason for the delay
may well have related to Vanderbilt's role, during late 1862, in the
outfitting of troop transports for some 10,000 men bound for New
Orleans from New York under the command of General Nathanial
P. Banks. Providing his own logistical services for free, Vanderbilt
in turn gave extensive authority to T. J. Southard, an unscrupulous
agent who chartered several ancient, inadequate vessels at exorbitant prices. Banks and others traveling on such reliable boats as the
North Star easily made it to New Orleans that December. However, many other ships had to turn back lest they sink mid-passage.
The debacle triggered a congressional investigation. Although
Vanderbilt came away, appropriately, without being accused of
thievery or fraud, he was thoroughly criticized for negligence.

By the time of the Banks debacle, the Commodore's youngest,
smartest, and favorite son George Washington Vanderbilt, a West
Point graduate who'd served most recently as a captain in the Union
infantry, had already been granted permanent leave due to the tu-
berculosis he'd come down with during the Shiloh campaign earlier
in the year. George was to spend most of 1863 nursing in New York

at various hospitals and in his father's Greenwich Village town-house. Later that year, during October, he debarked for the warm breezes of the Riviera with his older brother Billy and Billy's wife, Maria, tending him. Among the party were also the five youngest of Billy's and Maria's eight children. These included George's toddler namesake, George Washington Vanderbilt II. Both Billy and Maria were at the elder George's side when he passed away in Nice on January 1, 1864. He'd not yet turned twenty-five. The clan returned with the corpse, which was duly interred with the Commodore's parents in the tomb at the Moravian Cemetery. The *New York Times*, maintaining its recent stance of hostility toward the Commodore, took no notice. Wheaton Lane and several other chroniclers have maintained that in the year before George's death, the Commodore made a $100,000 donation to the Sanitary Commission, which was then earnestly working to improve the conditions in Union Army camps. However, a check of the records of the Sanitary Commission in the Special Collections of the New York Public Library reveals evidence of no such gift.[7]

The Civil War seems not to have much inhibited and or constrained Vanderbilt's steamship businesses. All his Panama boats had long been armed due to the fact that they routinely carried specie on their eastbound trips, and were thus tempting targets for pirates. Probably because of this, only one was ever directly harassed. On December 7, 1862, the *Alabama* briefly detained the *Ariel* off the coast of Cuba as she headed south and west. That being her direction, the *Ariel* carried no specie and was thus not a terribly lucrative triumph. Although tempted to evacuate the passengers and sink the vessel, Captain Raphael Semmes of the *Alabama* was eventually convinced to release her upon receipt of a $250,000 bond signed by the *Ariel*'s captain. This was to be payable by Vanderbilt immediately after such time as the Union government recognized the legitimacy of the Confederacy.

During June of 1864, Jeremiah Simonson launched a new ocean-going steamer, the *New York,* from his Greenpoint yard. Vanderbilt then ran the wooden side-wheeler for just two trips between New York and Aspinwall before selling her to the Pacific Mail. (Vanderbilt at the same time sold the balance of his Panama ships to the newly formed Atlantic Mail Steamship Company, which was to operate henceforth as the East Coast partner of the Pacific Mail, just as Vanderbilt had of late. The leaders of the new Atlantic Mail were Vanderbilt's son-in-law Daniel Allen, who served as the firm's president, and Vanderbilt's former nemesis, Cornelius Garrison.) Elsewhere, on other waters, Vanderbilt embarked upon similar divestitures.

Despite the continued general profitability of the steamship trade, as of 1864 Vanderbilt was looking to get out of that business. With more and more mail moving overland between California and the eastern seaboard, related steamship subsidies had continued their fast fade. More to the point, in recent letters and memoranda to colleagues and associates, Vanderbilt had observed that waterways generally were conspicuously open (too open) to anyone afloat who cared to enter into competition. Railroads, however, tended to be unique lines of transit between such "ports" as Albany and New York. One could not own an ocean or a river exclusively, but one could own, entirely, a set of tracks on a thin state-sanctioned right of way.

There was also a family dynamic involved in Vanderbilt's growing affinity for railroads. Beyond Allen, Vanderbilt's other sons-in-law had all demonstrated themselves to be shrewd men of business who could be effective in any realm: whether administering water-borne commerce, railroads, or the mechanics of Wall Street. They were excellent and reliable, one and all. But, as Vanderbilt observed more than once to the various clerks who surrounded him in his Greenwich Village office (and to his sons-in-law themselves), *they were not Vanderbilts.* Neither were their children. Of the two surviving

Vanderbilt men of the next generation, Cornelius Jeremiah remained not only a disappointment, but a disaster. Gambling, drinking, and fraud continued to mark him: a desperate, furtive, inept swindler who, by virtue of his famous name, seemed more ironic and absurd than tragic. ("You delude yourself that you can be productive," Vanderbilt wrote him at one point in a dictated letter. "You can't. A score of failures have proved this: myriad disasters. Put simply: You have not the aptitude, nor the discipline, to make your way in the world of men. Yet still you dare to ask why I shall not bank you.")[8]

In 1856, young Cornelius had been married: an event after which the father briefly staked him $200 per month to support himself and his wife, Ellen Williams of Hartford.[9] But the Commodore eventually cut that money off when he learned the son was dropping large sums at betting parlors in Connecticut and Manhattan. Vanderbilt had already, as of 1860, strictly forbade the young man to call himself Cornelius Vanderbilt Jr.—insisting that he present himself always as Cornelius Jeremiah Vanderbilt so that they might be clearly and easily delineated. On occasions, the Commodore went so far as to take out pro-active advertisements in the New York papers, announcing his unwillingness to shoulder responsibility for Cornelius Jeremiah's debts.

With George Washington Vanderbilt dead and Cornelius Jeremiah unreliable, Billy now became the Vanderbilt on which the Commodore focused his dynastic ambition. But there was more to this than mere attrition among the brothers. Asking little or nothing from his father, Billy had worked steadfastly through the years to make his Staten Island farm a going concern. He'd generated excellent profits with crops of oats, timothy, potatoes, and corn. He'd also invested in additional acreage, and established himself as a respected businessman and community leader on the island. (Unlike his father, Billy was quite devout: a pious trustee of his local Episcopal Church.) Forty-three years of age in 1864, Billy had already worked closely with his father for several years in at least one key venture.

During 1860, the Commodore had extended funds for the completion of the then stagnant Staten Island Railroad. Originally started in 1851, the railroad (consisting of just three locomotives and six passenger coaches) went only from Vanderbilt Landing to Tottenville on the western end of the island: a distance of only about fifteen miles. The short line was one in which Vanderbilt had become interested purely because he wanted it to serve as a feeder for the Staten Island Ferry, which he shortly merged with the railroad. Concurrent with the Commodore's investment, both Jacob Hand Vanderbilt and Billy Vanderbilt went on the board of the combined companies. Billy, in particular, took an active hand in the management, and got both the trains and profits on track.[10] (At the same time, Jacob cashed out his interest in the old Stonington Line of steamboats intending, as one of his brother's aides-de-camp, to fix his sights on railroads in the future.) Railroads were to define Billy's life going forward as well.

20

HARLEM CORNERS

SINCE THE 1840S, VANDERBILT HAD BEEN PERIPHERALLY INVOLVED, on and off, with several railroads, including the Stonington Railroad, the Long Island Railroad, and the Hartford & New Haven Railroad, all of which dovetailed with and fed his various steamboat enterprises. In the decade preceding the Civil War, however, his interest in railroading had slowly increased. During 1849, Vanderbilt began speculations in the stock of the New York & New Haven and became a director of the firm. A few years after that, he acquired a significant interest in the New York & Harlem Railroad (which ran from lower Manhattan up to Harlem and beyond to Chatham in Columbia County, the tracks of which the trains of the New York & New Haven used to exit and enter Manhattan). Vanderbilt became a director in 1857. Three years prior to his New York & Harlem directorship, Vanderbilt had also become involved in the affairs of New York & Erie Railroad (running from near Buffalo on Lake Erie to Jersey City), on the board of which Drew sat at the time. The company was experiencing a financial crisis.

Vanderbilt personally endorsed notes for the firm to the tune of $400,000, taking a lien on all Erie rolling stock as surety. Two years later, in 1856, Vanderbilt acquired a significant interest in the stock of the Delaware, Lackawanna & Western, which extended through central New York into Pennsylvania and Ohio. Then, in 1859, Vanderbilt joined Drew on the board of Erie.

Vanderbilt learned early that railroading represented even more of a viper's den than did steamships. During 1854, New York & New Haven president and general transfer agent Robert Livingston Schuyler (yes, another scion of the Livingstons, also a nephew of Alexander Hamilton's) was forced to flee to Canada and then Europe when it was revealed he'd fraudulently created 20,000 shares of company stock, which he in turn awarded to himself. In the course of converting those bogus issues into roughly $2 million in cash, he'd used 2,210 shares as collateral for a large loan he'd received from Vanderbilt.[1] (Schuyler had previously served as president of the Illinois Central Railroad, where he pulled off a similar flim-flam.) After the New York & New Haven Railroad repudiated the stock and Schuyler proved a deadbeat, Vanderbilt had to go to the courts to be made whole: an exercise that would not wrap up until 1866, when the New York Court of Appeals would finally agree with Vanderbilt's attorneys that the railroad was bound by the promises, however fraudulent, of its agents and assignees. (Robert Schuyler died at Nice, France, in November of 1855. A coffin was returned to New York and a funeral held at Green Ridge Cemetery in Saratoga Springs. Still, speculation remained rampant that the disgraced Schuyler had orchestrated yet another fraud in faking his own demise. This seems unlikely, however, since Schuyler's wife Phebe accompanied the box home, and lived alone as a widow in Saratoga until her own demise in 1861.)

At the time when Schuyler absconded, he and his younger half-brother George Lee Schuyler, who between them constituted the two chief officers the New York & Harlem Railroad, had recently concluded yet another deal with Vanderbilt wherein the Commodore purchased $1 million in Harlem Railroad first mortgage bonds at .93. Subsequently, George resigned the Harlem in the midst of Robert's scandal.[2] Soon thereafter, Robert was found to have over-issued Harlem stock in the same way he had defrauded New York & New Haven shareholders. Here a problem arose when it was discovered that an initial payment of $93,000 made by Vanderbilt had evidently been confiscated by Robert Schuyler before his fast exit from the country, and the firm refused to give Vanderbilt credit for the payment. The complications arising from this fiasco took three years to solve, culminating in an agreement whereby Vanderbilt was made partially whole through a carefully orchestrated stock transaction which left him with a major interest in the Harlem. As part of the deal, Vanderbilt also received three spots on the Harlem board, where Horace Clark and Daniel Drew promptly joined him in May of 1857.

Soon thereafter, Vanderbilt received full credit of $100,000 with interest from the cash-strapped Harlem in full consideration of the old disputed first mortgage bonds. In return for this consideration, Vanderbilt (joined by Drew) pledged to make up to $650,000 in capital available to the Harlem over the course of the next twenty months (no small commitment, considering that the financial panic of 1857 was then in full sway). In fact, the Harlem management ran through the originally pledged $650,000 within a matter of months. At that point, a $1 million bond offering had to be floated at a massive 50 percent discount, with Vanderbilt doing much of the buying. Thus committed to the Harlem bonds, Vanderbilt subsequently made frequent small acquisitions of the common stock. By mid 1863 he would own some 8,801 shares in his own name, and plenty more in the names of men serving as his brokers. Nevertheless, not until a fateful day in 1863, did he bother to attend many board meetings. He generally left the latter work to Clark, and seems, as well, to have relied heavily on reports and advice from Drew, who chaired the firm's finance committee. (Aged Allen Campbell, who had served as the Harlem's first president back at its founding in 1831, returned to replace the disgraced George Schuyler. But the real power lay in the hands of Clark and Drew.)

At its northern terminus in Chatham, the Harlem connected with the Western Railroad connecting Boston and Albany. New York City was the only industrial center the route touched. The only freight it transported was agricultural produce moving from Columbia and Westchester counties into Manhattan, while most industrial and agricultural products originating in Albany traveled either to Boston on the Western Railroad or directly to Manhattan on the Hudson River Railroad, the latter having opened for business in 1851. All in all, the Harlem was little more than an asterisk lingering in between the two more major routes. Passengers bound for Boston out of New York started off on the New York & New Haven, and then connected through to the Connecticut coastal route that turned north at Providence, Rhode Island, while passengers bound for Albany from Manhattan found the most direct route in the Hudson River Railroad, which possessed a station at Tenth Avenue and Thirtieth Street, and a small extension down to Chambers Street.

The only specially valuable thing about the Harlem was its southern terminus in Manhattan, and its monopoly position on that island. The Harlem possessed horse-car tracks running up Centre and Broome Streets as well as Fourth Avenue (today's Park Avenue), with a large main station located at Twenty-sixth Street and

Fourth, and numerous other satellite stations located at City Hall and elsewhere. All cars south of the Twenty-sixth Street Station were pulled by horses, but from Twenty-sixth Street north the combined cars were pulled by locomotives which carried riders through the Murray Hill Tunnel and across the Harlem River at 135th Street, thence to Williamsburg where connections with the New York & New Haven might be made, and on up to White Plains and other stops so far as Chatham: approximately 140 miles in sum.

Throughout early 1863, Harlem common stock rose significantly on speculation that city officials would shortly grant the Harlem lucrative exclusive licenses to operate horse-car tracks down Broadway from Union Square to the Battery. On the last day of trading in December of 1862, shares closed at 27. By early April of 1863, the same commodity was engaged in a bubble-like floatation well above fair-value at more than 50. At that point, with no imminent action on the part of New York's Common Council being hinted at, a number of speculators (Vanderbilt not among them) went short in Harlem: selling thousands of shares at around 50 that they hoped to pick up well-below that price before a delivery date several months hence. Those plans dissolved when, on April 22, the Common Council approved the Broadway Railroad Project and Harlem's involvement, the Harlem to pay the city a modest 10 percent of gross revenues as well as an annual licensing fee ($25) for each car. The next day, Harlem shares went over 70 as Mayor George Opdyke (a millionaire dry goods merchant, and a Republican) signed the legislation and Harlem crews commenced frantic work on the project—all much to the chagrin of the many traders, George Law among them, who were conspicuously short in the stock.

Ever an activist, Law acted quickly to change the situation in his favor. At the capitol in Albany, then controlled by a generally corrupt Democratic political machine, he fervently greased the palms of legislators and lobbyists, who quickly passed a key measure. The new legislation gave a group of investors led by Law license to form a new company to which exclusive rights for a Broadway line were unconditionally granted by the State of New York. A battle of jurisdictions seemed likely to ensue, and Law had even started on his own hasty construction, when he received an unexpected blow from Democratic governor Horatio Seymour. On the heels of protests from such prominent New Yorkers as William B. Astor and Pierre Lorillard, also on the advice of his friend and fellow Democrat Samuel J. Tilden, and in defiance of the wishes of New York's Tammany machine, Seymour vetoed Law's bill. Following the veto, the price of Harlem shot to 100. A few days later, when Vanderbilt was elected president of the Harlem and other major associates such as Augustus Schell and Addison G. Jerome joined the board, the shares went to 116 on the strength not only of the Broadway franchise, but the revelation of Vanderbilt's controlling interest in the firm. (Jerome was a native of Rochester: a former dry goods merchant lately hailed as the "Napoleon of the Public Board" because of his many successes as a stock trader and manipulator.[3] Schell was an attorney and Tammany politico active on Wall Street.)

Now it was that Drew, who'd long had a reputation as an unreliable partner with a nose for treasonous opportunity, made a move. Drew had realized enormous profits on the run-up of Harlem stock, but he also held a significant short position at 50 that would soon come due. So it was that Drew approached a well-connected Tammany official—Street Commissioner William Marcy Tweed (soon enough to be "Boss" Tweed)—with a scheme. A majority of common council members would be recruited to short Harlem stock at the current price. Once those sales were finalized, the council would vote to repeal the grant of the Broadway franchise to the Harlem, thus causing Harlem shares to plummet and enabling a massive profit by all who were "in the know." Vanderbilt, however, who'd gotten wind of the scheme, stood prepared.

The council made its move on June 25, rescinding the Broadway license. The stock, which started in the morning at 110, closed at 72. A further collapse was expected in the following days, but instead the stock rose with Vanderbilt himself cornering the market. He and several associates (including an old Staten Island Ferry gatekeeper, John M. Tobin, now a broker and speculator who'd grown rich collaborating with Vanderbilt in recent years), bought up each and every share that came up, buoying the price. The price stood at $97^1/4$ on June 26, and 106 one day later. When the men of the common council asked Vanderbilt to please stop buying, and allow them to purchase shares from him to cover their short positions before the stock rose any higher, he refused. In due course, hoping to calm him, the councilmen repealed their repeal, and reinstated the Broadway rights of the Harlem. This happened on the last day of June. But still Vanderbilt bought.

Finally, near the end of the summer, he allowed Drew and others to cover their short positions at $180 per share. This transaction ruined many of the council members, but not Drew, who always had more than one deal ongoing. Drew lost about a million dollars and derived a couplet from the episode: "He that sells what isn't his'n, must buy it back, or go to prison." But otherwise, as shall be seen, he had not learned his lesson.[4] Vanderbilt, in turn, derived more than $5 million from what would be called the First Harlem Corner—chiefly by allowing panicked short sellers to drive the price of Harlem up, limiting his own buying at the highest prices, and going short at the top. More important, Vanderbilt succeeded in transferring to Wall Street his previously water-borne reputation as a shrewd and cut-throat competitor, intrigues against whom could prove dangerous. Drew, however, was not intimidated.

Certain obstacles remained before the Harlem could proceed with the Broadway project. In October, Judge Henry Hogeboom of the New York Supreme Court—a Tammany judge of Columbia County who was friendly to and in the pay of interests opposed to Vanderbilt—issued an injunction against the Harlem. Hogeboom said that the Broadway line was a violation of the Harlem's charter, as it constituted a new route rather than an extension of the original line. To proceed, said Hogeboom, the Harlem would need an act of the New York Legislature amending and revising the Harlem's original 1831 charter.[5] Early in March of 1864, Horace Clark and other directors went to Albany and arranged to have an appropriate bill introduced. After Clark returned to Manhattan, however, Daniel Drew (still a Harlem director, by the way) emerged in the same town.

There he formed a pool of Democratic politicos, mostly senators, who agreed to talk both the measure and the stock up in the coming days, then sell Harlem short and refuse the measure. (Drew also recruited his fellow Harlem director Addison Jerome, who had recently taken a financial bath in a failed attempt to corner the stock of the Michigan Southern & Northern Central. New York Central directors Chauncey Vibbard and Erastus Corning were likewise involved in the pool that planned to short the Harlem. Another participant was John "Old Smoke" Morrissey, a former New York gang member and bare-knuckle fighter who had once—like Vanderbilt—tangled with "Yankee" Sullivan, and was now a Tammany politico. Despite Morrissey's role in this little escapade, he and Vanderbilt were generally on friendly terms due to their shared interest in the trotters and the track at Saratoga, where Morrissey owned a casino.)[6] With all looking rosy for the legislation in the Senate Railroad Committee, Harlem stock rose from about 89, where it had hovered after leveling off from the artificial August 1863 high of

180, to 149. Drew's cabal then shorted the stock at 149, just before the committee, on March 23, reported negatively on the bill. After that, the stock went nearly immediately to 101.

Given recent experience, neither Drew nor those who had thrown in with him should have been surprised by what happened next. Once again Vanderbilt and a pool of allies bought hungrily, cornering the Harlem and driving up the price. (Ironically, Vanderbilt's pool included Addison Jerome's brother Leonard, a newspaper publisher lately interested in Pacific Mail stock, a frequent business partner of Tobin's, and the future maternal grandfather of Winston Churchill.) At the close on April 6, Harlem stood at 150, and legislative speculators were evidently worried because they soon approved a bill allowing the Harlem to increase the amount of its outstanding capital stock by $3 million. (The suggestion that more stock will be issued generally depresses prices; but in this case, with Vanderbilt and friends buying, it did not.)

By the last trading day of April the stock stood at 235. By May 17—at which point Vanderbilt and his friends controlled what amounted to the full capitalization of the firm—the issue stood at 280. In due course, Vanderbilt finally allowed the short sellers to buy at 285, once the legislators approved the consolidation. Nearly all of them nonetheless wound up losing their shirts and their homes, while Drew lost between a million and a million and a half, and remained rich. Vanderbilt, by his own account, personally pocketed about $2 million at the close of the transaction.[7] Vanderbilt now held 29,607 shares of Harlem in his own name. His friend and broker Abraham B. Baylis controlled 31,993 shares, many of these in fact owned by the Commodore. (With offices on Exchange Place, Baylis had been a member of the New York Stock Exchange since 1841. He had done much business with Vanderbilt through the years, and was a trusted insider.)[8] Smaller blocks were controlled by Horace Clark, Augustus Schell (rewarded for sticking with Vanderbilt during the corner, rather than with Tammany), James H. Banker (vice president of the Bank of New York), John Tobin, and Billy Vanderbilt.[9]

At mid-year, when the Harlem elected new officers, both Drew and Addison Jerome were, predictably, dropped from the board. (Addison Jerome died within months, nearly penniless.) Billy Vanderbilt came on, as did Tobin and New York state senator John B. Dutcher, who had remained loyal and worked effectively for Vanderbilt in Albany throughout the period of the second corner. Billy Vanderbilt was also, at his father's command, made vice president and (more important) operating executive of the Harlem. At this point, Billy and Maria moved with their brood to a large mansion at 459 Fifth Avenue, so that Billy would have convenient access to the offices of the Harlem. The couple kept their Staten Island home as a retreat. And with that, father and son entered American railroading full throttle up.

21

HUDSON RIVER & NEW YORK CENTRAL

BILLY, ACTING AS SUPERINTENDENT, PROVED A MORE THAN capable manager of the Harlem, which had previously suffered a reputation as a sloppy, crowded, and dangerous line where lax schedule-keeping reigned supreme. Billy made carefully considered capital improvements, cleaned up the trains and the look of staff, and enforced timetables strictly. *Tribune* editor Horace Greeley, an old fan of the Commodore's who in season used the Harlem daily to commute into the city from his summer home in Chappaqua, sang the line's praises in November of 1867, after three years of Billy's stewardship.

"The Harlem Railroad this day puts its trains on a Winter footing and we, as a paying customer, return thanks to the managers for the excellent accommodations we have enjoyed throughout the past Summer. . . ." Greeley wrote. "We lived on this road when it was poor and feebly managed—with rotten cars and wheezy old engines that could not make schedule . . . and the improvement

since realized is gratifying."[1] Already, as of 1868, the previously unprofitable route had managed to pay a dividend for the first time: 8
percent. That was to continue to be the dividend rate until 1873,
when the Vanderbilts leased the Harlem to the New York Central,
after which the New York Central would make similar annual payments. During late 1867, Billy was granted seats on both the executive and finance committees of the Harlem Railroad: bodies
previously dominated by Cornelius himself, and by Horace Clark.

In 1863, a year before Billy's initial ascendance to management of
the Harlem, Cornelius had quietly begun to accumulate shares in the
Hudson River Railroad (HRR), running between Manhattan and
East Albany just below Albany on the east side of the river. At the
time, after a decade of malaise, the HRR labored under the compe-
tent management of Vanderbilt's friend Samuel Sloan, whom the
Commodore knew as a fellow major shareholder in the Delaware,
Lackawanna & Western. The common stock of the HRR had hovered around 3 in 1857. Under Sloan, the HRR paid its first dividend
(3 percent) in 1862, and delivered 10 percent in 1863. By the end of
1863, the stock was at 100. Earlier that year, probably at Sloan's request, but likely also at the behest of Tobin and Leonard Jerome
(both of whom served on the HRR board), Vanderbilt had helped de-
fend the stock against a bear raid mounted by a pool who hoped to
short HRR in quantity and cash-in while wrecking the capital value
of the firm. In response, Vanderbilt, Tobin, and Jerome set a "bear
trap" of the same variety Vanderbilt had sprung in defending the
Harlem. Vanderbilt, Tobin, and Jerome cornered HRR stock and
"bulled" the price to 180, to the ruination of the "short" bears. "Wall
Street has never known so successful a corner," noted the *Herald* on
July 13. Vanderbilt and the other members of his pool sold at the
heights, once their job of defending was done, but maintained enough
stock between them to exert control over the company.[2] (Vanderbilt

eventually came to personally control approximately 17,000 of 69,000 outstanding shares, with friends controlling much of the balance.)

In the HRR election of 1864, Tobin came in as president, replacing Sloan, with whom Vanderbilt remained friendly and who seems to have been happy to pursue other ventures of greater interest. Also joining the board were Horace Clark, Augustus Schell, James H. Banker, and Cornelius himself. (The remaining minority of the board included several directors of the New York Central Railroad, which ran between Albany and Buffalo.) One year later, Vanderbilt himself assumed the presidency of the HRR, replacing Tobin, and Billy joined the HRR board as operating vice-president. Henceforth, Billy operated both firms in unison, doing all he could to maximize economies and profits between them. Agreements whereby the Harlem used sections of the HRR's tracks approaching Albany from the south (and to the north of Albany as far as Troy) were renewed on equitable terms; and parallel train schedules were designed so as to complement, rather than undermine, each other.

The Commodore invested significantly in both railroads, especially the HRR. During 1865, Vanderbilt personally subscribed the entirety of a $600,000 third mortgage issue at 105, much of the money from which was earmarked for a railroad bridge at Albany. Up to that time, passengers had been forced to detrain and cross the Hudson by ferry at Albany to connect with New York Central going to and coming from Buffalo, while freight cars went eight miles north to Troy for a bridge crossing. Now the HRR formed the Hudson River Bridge Company in association with the Western Railroad (connecting Albany and Boston) and the New York Central. The combined firms built a two-hundred-foot-long truss bridge via which Western Railroad and HRR (and, for that matter, Harlem Railroad) passengers could connect seamlessly as through-traffic onto the New York Central, transferring at that line's Albany station.

Assembled from the knotting together of nine smaller railroads linking Albany and Buffalo, the New York Central had been founded in 1853. It owned a monopoly along its route, had an impressive $25 million capitalization, and was a reasonably well-managed company paying regular dividends of 6 percent. For years, even though several leaders of the New York Central sat on the board of the HRR, relations between the two firms had been tenuous at best. Numerous major holders of New York Central stock, among them Erastus Corning and Dean Richmond, were also owners of steamboat interests on the Hudson River. (Most officers of the company, including Corning and Richmond, were as well firmly entrenched Democratic Party stalwarts with excellent connections in Albany.) Thus the New York Central preferred (at least in season) to route its Manhattan-bound traffic to steamboats rather than to the HRR. Only in winter, when the river iced up, did the New York Central route through-traffic via the HRR. Prior to the building of the bridge, this through-traffic connected via horse-drawn sleds moving across the iced Hudson, with porters seeing to the luggage.

Relations with the New York Central improved in 1864, just as Vanderbilt came into control of the HRR. At that time, a rift on the board of the Central had caused Corning and Richmond to seek new allies with which to populate that body. Coming to terms with Corning and Richmond, Vanderbilt purchased several thousand shares of New York Central stock and threw all his votes behind Corning for president in that year's election of officers. (Corning and Richmond stood in opposition to an increasingly militant minority wing of the board, headed by the New York banker Frederic P. Olcott, who were fairly instantly intimidated by Vanderbilt's arrival on the scene.) In return for Vanderbilt's trouble, his representative Banker took a seat on the Central's board, and the two railroads came to amicable terms regarding through-traffic. Early in 1865,

Corning resigned the top spot in favor of Richmond, whose movement opened up a seat for Horace Clark. Meanwhile, Richmond went onto the HRR board. Amid this cozy atmosphere, the Albany truss bridge was erected.

Things grew complicated, however, in August of 1866, when Richmond died unexpectedly while visiting the New York home of Samuel Tilden. The sudden vacuum in leadership caused a new group to develop an interest in the Central, and heatedly begin to buy stock. This group was headed by Buffalo's William G. Fargo (the founder of both American Express and Wells Fargo), together with the banker Legrand Lockwood (proprietor of Lockwood & Co.) and Henry Keep, former president of the Michigan Southern & Northern Indiana Railroad. Assiduously accumulating New York Central stock, these three drove the price from 90 to 132 by the time of the December annual meeting, at which point they controlled approximately 121,000 out of 188,000 voting shares. The trio kicked Clark and Banker off the board, elected Keep president, and made Fargo vice-president. More important, perhaps with an eye toward putting a squeeze on the HRR as a possible long-term acquisition target, they instantly stopped cooperating with the Vanderbilt organization on a range of fronts.

A $100,000 annual bonus payment that Vanderbilt, acting for the HRR, had recently negotiated from the New York Central was instantly cancelled. (That payment was supposed to cover the summer maintenance of the extra rolling stock the HRR needed to handle the Central's through-business in the winter months, when the river closed.) Other smaller matters of dispute were settled in an equally high-handed manner by Keep, who had timed his insurrection poorly. The Hudson froze up just before Christmas, locking the friendly steamers of the People's Line tight against their piers for the duration. On January 14, 1867, President Cornelius Vanderbilt of the HRR published a notice in the newspapers of Buffalo, Albany, and Manhattan announcing that, starting on January 17, representatives of the HRR would "only sell tickets and check baggage over their own road and will only recognize tickets sold at their own offices and by their own agents. Passengers will after that date be ticketed and baggage checked to and from Greenbush or East Albany, the terminus of the road. The same rule will be observed for freight." Those rules applied for the Harlem also. Vanderbilt added the following after his signature, as if it were an afterthought: "By the above notice passengers will observe that the ERIE RAILWAY is the only route by which they can reach NEW YORK from Buffalo without CHANGE of coaches or RECHECKING baggage."[3]

The new bridge sat idle. Manhattan/Buffalo passengers who took notice of Vanderbilt's announcement traveled via the Erie (on the board of which, it will be remembered, Vanderbilt sat, and in which he held a substantial interest). Those who did not were forced to lug their suitcases across the Hudson's frozen ice in order to connect between HRR and New York Central trains. (In acknowledgement of the new bridge, the teamsters and porters who had previously facilitated transfer were no longer on the payroll.) Meanwhile, for a grand total of two days, the New York Central's freight bound for either Manhattan or Boston accumulated in the line's Albany yards. Initially, a desperate Keep endeavored to negotiate with the Housatonic Railroad to create a new through-route to Bridgeport, making connections from there down to Manhattan via lines linking into the New York & New Haven. However, under the Commodore's influence, the board of the Housatonic proved uncooperative. (Besides, the New York & New Haven needed to cooperate with the Harlem, on the tracks of which it enjoyed its only access to Manhattan.) Once that option closed, Keep realized he had only one viable alternative. Keep surrendered to Vanderbilt on

January 19—restoring the $100,000 bonus payment, and making other adjustments as necessary.

Within weeks, the Railroad Committee of the New York State Senate mounted hearings to probe the corporate dispute that had so inconvenienced New York travelers for several days. The investigation led to a bill requiring New York railroads to maintain through connections. It also produced interesting testimony from Billy Vanderbilt, Horace Clark, and others—most notably, the Commodore himself. When asked whether the public did not have rights to security and travel that superseded Vanderbilt's control of the HRR and Keep's control of the New York Central, Vanderbilt replied: "I have always served the public to the best of my ability. Why? Because . . . it is in my interest to do so, and to put them to as little inconvenience as possible." When asked whether he could not have gone to the courts to see that the New York Central honored its previous pledges, he answered: "The law, as I view it, goes too slow for me when I have the remedy in my own hands." Then he added: "I for one will never go to a court of law when I have got the power in my own hands to see myself right. Let the other parties go to law if they want, but by God I think I know what the law is; I have had enough of it."[4]

General trust in the management of the Central had been badly shaken by the recent episode. In this environment, Vanderbilt evidently made a decision to take control of the railroad. "The Vanderbilt interest," reported the Albany *Argus* in early July of 1867, ". . . is steadily absorbing large amounts of stock with a view to the ultimate control of the line. Indeed a league of companies (if not a positive consolidation) reaching from New York to Chicago, including the Central and its two debouchees, the Hudson River and the Harlem, is a subject of much speculation. It is needed. The idea is based on the necessity of counteracting the consolidation of the lines from the West through Pennsylvania."[5] Later in the summer, the Erie Railroad and the Pennsylvania Railroad mounted a strenuous rate war against the New York Central, the former two firms cooperating to seize both passenger and freight trade from the Central. The consequent damage to the Central's bottom line did nothing to help prop up Keep's sagging prestige.

The stock transfer books of the New York Central closed in early November, several weeks prior to the company's annual meeting and the election of officers. (The firm at that moment had a total stock capitalization of $28,537,000.) Shortly thereafter, on November 12, a number of major shareholders in the Central, all of them former Keep allies, published an open letter to Vanderbilt in the leading New York dailies. The letter was signed by Edward Cunard, John Jacob Astor Jr., Benkard & Hutton (a French dry goods importing firm holding a significant position in the Central), the New York banker John Steward, "and others representing over thirteen millions of stock." These parties announced that they were giving Vanderbilt their proxies, with which they hoped that he would enact "a change of administration of the company and a thorough reformation in the management of its affairs."[6]

At the December 11 meeting in Albany, the majority stockholders retired all the current Central officers and retained only one director: H. Henry Baxter. Elected to the board and executive committee were Vanderbilt (as president) and Billy, together with son-in-law Torrance (vice president), son-in-law Clark, James Banker, Augustus Schell, and Billy's brother-in-law, the financier William A. Kissam. Also elected to the board (though not to the executive committee) were various railroad professionals with interests either in the Central or in connecting routes. These included Chester W. Chapin of Springfield, Massachusetts, Amasa Stone Jr. of Cleveland, James F. Joy of Detroit, and Joseph Harker and Samuel Barger of New York.[7]

Chapin served on the executive committee of the Western Railroad. Joy was president of the Michigan Central.[8] Stone had long been one of the prime movers behind the Lake Shore & Michigan Southern. Closer to home, the financier Joseph Harker owned large investments in both the HRR and the Harlem, and also raced trotters with the Commodore. Samuel Barger was an attorney active with the Central. As for the lone board holdover Baxter, this banker from Rutland, Vermont, had proved quite helpful to Vanderbilt of late, providing inside information about the dealings of the old Central board.

Daniel Torrance and Billy Vanderbilt took operational control of the Central. Annual through traffic shared by Central, the HRR, and the Harlem more than doubled in the first year of the new management, once Billy permanently did away with all the Central's steamboat connections. Profits exploded on all routes. By the end of 1868, the balance sheet looked so good that the Central's executive committee increased the annual dividend by two points, raising it to 8 percent. At the same time, the Vanderbilts (with Billy, Horace Clark, and Augustus Schell increasingly taking the lead in day-to-day operations throughout the late 1860s and into the early 1870s) eyed opportunities for similar consolidations.[9] The Vanderbilts would officially lease the HRR and the Harlem to the New York Central in 1869, forming the New York Central and Hudson River Railroad. In these railroads, and all the roads the Vanderbilt group came to be involved with in future, the modus operandi would be to consolidate towards maximum economic efficiency and profitability, water stock whenever possible, and increase dividend yield. This would be the constant pattern of business going forward.

22

THE VANDERBILT
BRONZE

DESPITE THE DEATH OF GEORGE WASHINGTON VANDERBILT, the Commodore appears to have harbored no resentment against the South following the Civil War. Through his lieutenants Clark and Schell, he joined Horace Greeley, the former abolitionist Gerrit Smith, and others in posting bond for Jefferson Davis in 1866. Like many conservative Northerners, he generally opposed Reconstruction and viewed the newly liberated blacks of the South with suspicion. At first friendly to President Andrew Johnson because of the latter's stance on these same issues, he subsequently abandoned him in the days leading up to his 1868 impeachment. During December 1867, Vanderbilt (probably at the prompting of his friend Thurlow Weed) joined such leading New York financial elites as Alexander Stewart, Peter Cooper, Moses Taylor, William Aspinwall, Daniel Drew, and a slew of Astors in endorsing General Ulysses Grant for president on the Republican ticket. In this the former Know-Nothing Vanderbilt was simply joining an unstoppable groundswell akin to the post-war surge that would elect Dwight Eisenhower nearly a hundred years later. Vanderbilt liked to back winners.

At a New York dinner for Grant held shortly before Christmas of that year, Vanderbilt, as rarely happened, briefly rubbed shoulders with the above-named millionaires, all of whom thought themselves his social superiors. And he was unimpressed. Vanderbilt had not followed them a decade before when they had moved their fine homes out of Greenwich Village to the more fashionable thirties. He'd remained cloistered at Washington Place, and there he pursued social life as he chose to know it. Despite the fact that he'd once had Sophia institutionalized over her refusal to make the Greenwich Village residence her main home, he'd in recent years practically banished her to the Staten Island mansion, so that he might enjoy himself in the Village as he saw fit.

Rough trade was known, on occasion, to go in and out of the Washington Place house. Workers in the stable brought girls around for their boss, who was now too well-known, and perhaps too old, to go solicit them himself. At the same time, Vanderbilt, slowly showing signs of sporadic dementia stemming from his long-standing syphilis, became reckless in what he allowed to happen on his premises, and who he allowed himself to associate with. (At one particularly low point, the crowd Vanderbilt assembled about him in the Village engaged in several hours of debauchery that included a black stable-worker of the Commodore's attempting the rape of a woman of the street, this followed by continued drama that included the shooting of a policeman—all of it hushed up by Clark and Schell as best as possible.)[1]

Mid summer of 1868 found Vanderbilt making an extended stay at the United States Hotel in Saratoga. There he enjoyed the trotters and licked his wounds after losing "the Erie War"—a long and publicly humiliating contest with the upstarts Jay Gould and Jim Fisk for control of the Erie Railroad. In the course of a classic Vanderbilt attempt to corner the Erie, Gould and Fisk had wantonly manufactured new shares of the firm through secret votes of the Erie's executive committee. Working for a time in collusion with Vanderbilt's old but traitorous friend Drew, Gould and Fisk blatantly issued thousands of additional Erie shares, thus sewing utter confusion in the marketplace as to the actual total capitalization of the firm. At the same time, they made the free-spending Vanderbilt, anxiously bulling up Erie, look a fool, while also costing him approximately $7 million. The episode marked Vanderbilt's last bold cornering bid on Wall Street, after which he loudly pronounced Gould the smartest man in America, and not so loudly handed the reins of his enterprises to Billy.[2]

Vanderbilt was still at Saratoga on August 17 when he received word of the death of his wife Sophia. She'd long been failing, having suffered several strokes in rapid succession. Her death was not unexpected. For several weeks, Sophia had been attended by Jared Linsly at the Manhattan home of her daughter Maria Louise Clark, the wife of Horace. Upon receiving word that Sophia had succumbed, the Commodore returned to the city via private train. By all accounts, the seventy-four-year-old mogul was brusque and businesslike in dealing with the death of the woman to whom he'd been married for fifty-five years, and with whom he'd been acquainted since they were both children. As was by now the custom in most things, Billy Vanderbilt saw to all the details.

An Episcopal funeral service was held in New York, after which the family en masse (including even Cornelius Jeremiah, by now otherwise banished from his father's presence) accompanied the casket by boat to Staten Island, thence to the tomb at the Moravian Cemetery that the Commodore had constructed for his parents years before. Here Sophia joined her in-laws as well as her son George Washington Vanderbilt. One of her pall-bearers, Horace Greeley, wrote an editorial the next day in which he praised Sophia as a woman who had lived nearly seventy-four years "without incurring a reproach or provoking an enmity."[3] Greeley did not point out that nothing of the kind could be said of Sophia's husband who, two days following the internment, returned to Saratoga, where the trotters still trotted.

Once Vanderbilt got himself back to Manhattan in early September, he quickly made the acquaintance of two sisters with whom he was to have a complex and absurd relationship for several years going forward. Victoria Woodhull was a thirty-year-old clairvoyant and spiritualist. She was also a onetime prostitute. Victoria's nubile, twenty-two-year-old sister, Tennessee Claflin, known as Tennie, shared a similar professional history. Tennie claimed expertise as a practitioner of medicinal magnetism and manual manipulation of the limbs. The two had been born in Ohio. They spent their early years traveling in a medicine show with their gypsy-like parents, who promoted the girls as psychic healers, spiritualists, and fortune-tellers. In time, the menu of services grew, and the father—Reuben Buckman ("Buck") Claflin—seems to have become something more than just a side-show barker for his daughters. He also became their pimp.

At the tender age of fifteen, Victoria began the process of suffering marriage to the much older Canning Woodhull, a Cincinnati "physician" of sorts who deployed Victoria as a saleswoman for his various quack medicines. Victoria had given birth to two children by the time she finally escaped the tender embraces of the alcoholic, womanizing Woodhull. She divorced him when she was twenty-six, after travels that had taken the couple as far west as San Francisco. Subsequently, she married Colonel James Harvey Blood: a man closer to her own age who (like the brilliant, precocious, charismatic Victoria herself) had come to believe in the doctrine of free love. (The couple also professed allegiance to a variety of other then-radical ideals, including socialism and women's suffrage.) Blood and Victoria settled in New York City in 1866, where she joined her father and her sister Tennie already in residence. In short order, Victoria opened a salon where she, joined by Tennie, practiced a variety of profitable trades. Sometimes the sisters were magnetic healers, sometimes spiritualists, sometimes fortune-tellers, and sometimes whores brandishing their wears under the reform banner of "free love," for a price. Both, however, harbored great ambitions. Victoria, in particular, claimed a special impetus for her presence in Manhattan. She told anyone who would listen that the Greek orator Demosthenes had appeared to her at a séance in Pittsburgh during which he insisted she go to New York. There she was to make her fortune and, eventually, rise to rule her country.[4]

Vanderbilt had, for some time, been a believer in spiritualism. Through the years he'd regularly made pilgrimages to the Staten Island home of a "Mrs. Tufts" through whom he believed he could commune with a variety of spirits from the nether world: his mother and George Washington among them. Tufts eventually exacted large fees from Vanderbilt in exchange for ridding him of two spirits by whom he believed he was haunted. One was a young boy he'd accidentally crushed beneath the hooves of his trotters as he'd raced around the Central Park Reservoir. The other was a railroad worker who'd been decapitated beneath the wheels of a New York Central train called, ominously, the *Flying Devil*. With what she made on those two exorcisms, Tufts was able to retire to Vermont. Tufts appears to have removed to Vermont not long before Sophia died. Thereafter, though he felt no need to raise the specter of his dead wife, Vanderbilt was nevertheless in the market for a new spiritualist advisor to help him connect with General Washington, Phebe Hand, and various dead financiers of the past with whom he was in the habit of communing.

At about this time Vanderbilt, much to Jared Linsly's annoyance, also developed an interest in the quack science of magnetic and massage healing. Hearing of Vanderbilt's fascination with these various "sciences," Buck Claflin sensed an opportunity. Thus, in the autumn of 1868, Buck paid a call on the Commodore, who was just one year his senior. Buck pitched Victoria as a spiritualist and clairvoyant, and Tennie as a healer. "She [Tennie] was experienced at the laying on of hands," writes Victoria's biographer Mary Gabriel, "which was supposed to magnetize the patient and act as a kind of electric prod to jolt his system back into shape. No doubt it did. With her full, sensuous mouth, teasing eyes, and expert hands, Tennessee was just the lighthearted hellion to work wonders on the Commodore's aged body and revive his sagging spirits." As Gabriel reports, Tennie soon began spending much time with Vanderbilt outside of their medicinal sessions, "even bringing her to his [downtown] office [adjacent to his Washington Place home], where he would sit the 'little sparrow,' as he called her, on his knee and bounce her up and down as he talked railroad business. She told him jokes, read him the newspapers, and, pulling his whiskers, called him 'old boy.'"[5]

The two had clearly become lovers. "Tennessee was the one [of the sisters] who captivated the Commodore most completely," writes Johanna Johnston. "She liked to talk with the same colloquial vulgarity that he did. She knew how to liven her magnetic treatments with unexpected tickles, squeezes, or slaps. Before long, Vanderbilt . . . was reaching for the magnetic hands of the healer to draw her into bed with him. Naturally obliging, Tennessee did not protest unduly." For several months throughout the winter and spring of 1869, Tennie became a regular fixture at Washington Place. "The servants grew used to finding her, rosy and tousled, in the Commodore's bed in the morning."[6] The worldly Jared Linsly,

writing in the privacy of his journal, expressed qualified approval of
Tennie's "invigorating" presence, about which he harbored no delu-
sions; but Linsly also noted the slow, inevitable decline of the Commodore's mental acuity. "He is often childish," wrote Linsly, "and
therefore lucky to have so attractive and willing a plaything as Miss
Tennessee to divert him, while others, more capable, go about his
material affairs."[7]

So far as Victoria Woodhull's stock market tips from the dead
were concerned, lieutenants such as Billy Vanderbilt, Horace Clark,
and others in Vanderbilt's uptown office, seem to have done a good
job of blunting the effect of any market orders Vanderbilt may have
sought to generate based on her advice. Indeed, it seems that after a
certain point Billy even colluded with Victoria, giving her tips he
wanted passed on to his father. Thus, in actuality, the most valuable
market intelligence flowed from the Vanderbilt camp to the sisters
and to Buck Claflin, rather than the other way around, with the
Woodhull/Claflins in turn reaping significant rewards on Wall
Street. At the same time, in large measure because of her connection to Vanderbilt, Woodhull developed a large following of investors who were interested in her market insights from beyond.
Whether Victoria's clients thought she really spoke to the ghosts of
John Jacob Astor and Alexander Hamilton, or just assumed that she
benefited from information supplied by the Vanderbilts, they came
in droves for her knowledge, and profited.

Despite Billy's cooperation with Woodhull when it came to stock
market information, he was not altogether delighted with his father's connection to Tennie. Of course, the Commodore having a
dalliance with a young girl was nothing new, and normally should
have been no cause for excitement. But, given the Commodore's recent widowing and increased mental imbalance, Tennie's residency
at Washington Place posed the possibility of metastasizing without

warning into an unwanted and wholly inappropriate marriage. Writing in his diary, Linsly noted Billy's fears, which the son and presumed-heir had evidently voiced to the doctor. Linsly further noted that Billy had the staff at Washington Place on orders to warn him of any nuptials that might suddenly threaten. At the same time, Billy began beating the bushes for someone who might be a more likely (or, rather, safe) match for the old man.

Professionally, the Commodore himself remained distant from Wall Street. Likewise, he remained distant from the expansion of his own New York Central through the acquisition of western railroads. Billy, Horace Clark, and Daniel Torrance, along with several other trusted stalwarts, now spearheaded those efforts, and the Commodore seems not to have challenged their assumption of authority. So far as railroads were concerned, Vanderbilt's one focus through 1868 and early 1869 was nothing so complex as stock manipulations or acquisitions in the West. No, the Commodore preoccupied himself in Manhattan with a building project that was part investment, part monument.

Early in 1867, Vanderbilt had acquired from Trinity Church a large tract on the lower West Side. The tract was the rundown and vandalized St. John's Park—hub of a formerly fashionable neighborhood abutting Hudson Street, where today the Holland Tunnel rears up into Manhattan. The site offered convenient access to the same Hudson River piers Vanderbilt had known so well as a young man. It was also located conveniently for the laying of tracks connecting to the HRR. During the autumn of 1868, an elaborate three-story structure (two top floors for service as a warehouse, and the lower floor for service as a terminal with tracks running in and out) began building. This was the Hudson River Rail Road Freight House, for the next sixty years to be better known as the St. John's Freight House.

There is no record of Vanderbilt arguing when, in February of 1868, Albert De Groot proposed that an elaborate monument to the Commodore be mounted on the building's roof.[8] Nor did Vanderbilt quibble or second guess when De Groot, who had previously captained various Vanderbilt steamers, announced a massive public effort to raise $800,000 for the grand tribute he envisioned. Such newspapers as the *New York Times,* however, offered only half-hearted support. "The project meets with great favor," the *Times* observed on St. Patrick's Day of 1868, "and is being pushed rapidly forward. It has the active cooperation of a very large number of our leading citizens, besides those who are connected with the railroads for which the Commodore has done so much, and there is no doubt it will be carried out in a style and on a scale worthy of the object and its promoters." The *Times* editors added that it was the businesses Vanderbilt had built in shipping and railroading that "constitute for him a monument at once more durable and more imposing than any which his personal admirers can possibly erect."[9]

De Groot's scheme called for a 3,215-square-foot bronze pediment (150 feet long and 31 feet high at its widest vertical point) weighing nearly 100,000 pounds, all focused around a bronze statue of the Commodore. Both the statue and the pediment were to be executed by the German émigré sculptor Ernst Plassmann after a rough and chaotic design sketched by De Groot himself. Cast in square sections for easy mounting on the roof of the terminal facing Hudson Street, the massive pediment was to be a bas-relief which *Frank Leslie's Illustrated Newspaper* described as being "ingeniously contrived not only to illustrate most admirably the career and achievements of the Commodore, but also to represent the marvelous inventions of the nineteenth century, and at the same time to portray allegorically the growth and prosperity of the great American republic."[10]

The castings required for the work were so large that Plassmann and De Groot had to innovate a new foundry at the Manhattan firm of Fischer & Brother expressly designed to handle a project of this heft. In September of 1868, after many months of design work on the part of Plassmann, the casting was begun. With childlike glee, the Commodore made frequent trips to the Manhattan shop where Plassmann and two castors, under De Groot's careful watch, shaped the monument. Upstate politico and businessman Webster Wagner, with whom Vanderbilt was partnered in the New York Central Sleeping Car Company, accompanied Vanderbilt on one such excursion. Wagner chronicled in his diary the Commodore's "embarrassingly juvenile delight" in the "cogs and contraptions" of his past as represented in the bronze. "The extent to which he appears to crave this focus is, at times, most unbecoming. Where is the old, mature Vanderbilt who, though always self-referencing, at the same time sought and needed no other confirmation than that of his own net worth? The Vanderbilt I've long known craved no monuments, and cared not for the good opinion of his fellow citizens." Wagner added that the Commodore's sudden "lust for worldly acclaim" was "unseemly." But Wagner had noticed other subtle changes in his colleague: a general dulling of response, a new and unexplainable infatuation with trivial details that meant nothing to profit, and business decisions made for the cause of spite rather than capital appreciation.[11] All of these things would have been an anathema to the old Vanderbilt, and were probably key reasons why his son and sons-in-law now insulated him from decision making.

One year following the start of the casting process, on September 2, 1869, the *New York Times* reported that "a strong scaffolding having been erected and enclosed" at the freight house, "the various parts of the work were securely boxed up, transported to the depot and hoisted to the roof, where they were duly erected against a

massive brick wall, three feet thick, to which they were firmly fastened with iron anchors, more than 2000 in number, and weighing
above four tons." The *Times* added that "the strictest secrecy was
enjoined from the outset upon all connected with the work; watch-
men were employed during its erection to see that no unauthorized
person obtained a view of it before its completion; and Captain De
Groot may well be congratulated on his success in keeping his secret so well for so long a time."[12]

"The base upon which it is erected is formed of a narrow tier of
blue-stone, in the centre of which, solidly inserted in the wall of the
building, appears a huge carved block of native granite, weighing
eleven tons or more, and serving as a support for the pedestal . . ."
reported an observer working for Frank Leslie. A granite cornice
surmounted the pediment proper, sloping upward from each end,
thus forming an oval over the head of the bronze Vanderbilt. "Ornamental work in bronze decorates the middle of the granite cornice,
the bas-relief terminating at either end in a colossal scroll-work of
leaves and plants. On either hand of the statue, between it and these
terminant scrolls, appears the allegorical biography of the subject."

The bronze Vanderbilt was dwarfed by the bas-reliefs around and
behind it. Many aspects of the piece were absurd. To the far right of
the Vanderbilt statue lounged a large King Neptune with a flowing
beard, a head-wreath of leaves, and one hand clasping a rudder.
From behind the rock upon which Neptune lounged there peeked,
inexplicably, a raccoon. Other elements on the right side of the relief
included the Palisades of New Jersey beneath which floated a little
two-masted periauger, the steamer *North Star*, and the steamer
Vanderbilt, all fully-rigged. To the extreme left, balancing Neptune,
sat the figure of Liberty. Her left hand clutched a sword, and her
right hand rested on a shield from behind which an eagle half
emerged. "In the middle foreground of this left bas-relief," Frank

Leslie's man noted, "a railroad official, flag in hand, is just emerging from the little caboose or lilliput house near the track, along which, tugging from the depot a long train of cars, appears the locomotive *C. Vanderbilt* in the background."[13] Across the front were mounted assorted knick-knacks. The shipping side of the memorial included a capstan, an anchor, and a chain, along with a ferocious dog crouching on a bale of hay, and piles of tropical fruits. The railroad side included an immense boiler, a derrick with pulleys, a large cogs-wheel, and other innovations. In short, the piece was a chaotic mess centered round a larger-than-life rendition of the Commodore that most observers, including Horace Greeley, thought remarkably wooden, static, and un-lifelike.

On November 10, 1869, traders in the Long Room of the New York Stock Exchange held a mock unveiling for a memorial of their own. Solemnly, and with great fanfare, they lifted the curtain on a small statue of the Commodore. The old man was clutching a watering can and staring into the distance. Not many blocks away, on Hudson Street, more than 10,000 spectators stood by as the dedication of the *real* "Vanderbilt Bronze" proceeded. With music supplied by the Seventh Regiment Band, twenty-five U.S. Navy sailors from the *Vermont* pulled on halyards to lift a curtain and reveal the bronze to the world. Mayor A. Oakley Hall—with such dignitaries as Horace Greeley, Thurlow Weed, Daniel Drew, and James Gordon Bennett Jr. looking on approvingly—gave a brief and tepid speech that could be interpreted in more than one way. "Stand there," said the Tammany operative who was on the best of terms with Vanderbilt's recent nemesis Jay Gould, "familiar image of an honored man! Stand there and breast the storms or glitter in the sunshine of coming centuries. . . . Stand there and tell those whose industry has been crowned by wealth that the honors of life and the praise of future generations follow those, and those only, who make the world better for their living in it."[14] Following Hall's remarks, the poet and attorney William Ross Wallace (most famous today for his poem "The Hand that Rocks the Cradle Is the Hand That Rules the World" and for his friendship with Edgar Allan Poe) recited a specially composed ode to Vanderbilt. Once the poem was read, a man of the cloth said a short benediction, and the crowd dispersed, leaving the elevated monstrosity to the pigeons who would roost and defecate there for the next sixty years.

Writing in the 1880s, William Croffut commented: "Tens of thousands of residents of the great city have never seen this unique memorial, for it is masked by high business blocks on a street which they never traverse. As a monument for the public eye, it might almost as well be in the depths of the Adirondacks."[15] But this was perhaps for the best. A few days after the unveiling, *Scientific American* ran its coverage under the headline "A Huge Joke in Brass." Noting that there had been only "a few straggling hoorays" once the crowd finally saw the long-anticipated work, the editors of that journal went on to criticize the execution of the statue, saying that Vanderbilt's overcoat seemed "ample to protect from frost a Siberian sledge driver." They also described the bas reliefs as "absurd, in many respects ridiculously so," and said that the few birds depicted at the very top of the work were obviously "struggling to fly away with the whole design."[16]

23

FRANK

The seventy-five-year-old Vanderbilt did not attend the unveiling of the Vanderbilt Bronze alone. He had on his arm a new wife of three months. On August 21, at the Tecumseh House Hotel in London, Ontario (half way between Niagara Falls and Detroit), the Commodore had married a woman whom the *New York Times* identified simply as "Miss Frank Crawford, daughter of Robert L. Crawford" of Mobile, Alabama.[1] While the newspaper nearly correctly specified the bride's age as "about 30" (she was thirty-one), it failed to note a key aspect of "Miss Crawford's" history. The presumed maiden had in fact been married once before, to a John Elliott of Mobile. The "union was not a happy one," the *Times* observed in Frank's 1885 obituary, finally getting the story right, "and did not last long. It is said that Mrs. Crawford [Frank's mother] wished the young couple to live with her, but Elliott objected and built a house of his own. Mrs. Elliott refused to leave her mother, and Elliott withdrew to his own house. For a time he visited his wife at her mother's house, but his visits became less frequent and finally ceased altogether. Mrs. Elliott obtained a divorce, and Elliott went to New Orleans." The *Times* added that "Mrs. Elliott's marriage to Commodore Vanderbilt is said to have been brought about largely through the instrumentality of her mother."[2] All of these facts, gleaned from the mother who survived Frank in 1885, could not have been truer.[3]

Frank Armstrong Crawford hailed from a venerable but impoverished Southern family with New York connections. One of Frank's great-grandfathers had been Samuel Hand, the brother to the Commodore's mother, who had been whisked south when young. This made the Commodore and his bride first cousins twice removed. Frank's father, the late Robert L. Crawford Sr., a merchant and onetime federal marshal of Mobile, had been a distant relative to William Harris Crawford (Georgia senator, ambassador to France, secretary of war, secretary of the treasury, and unsuccessful presidential candidate in 1816 and 1824) and George W. Crawford (secretary of war and Georgia governor). One of Frank's first cousins was married to Nashville's Methodist Episcopal bishop, Holland Nimmons McTyeire, who had once ministered the Crawford family in Mobile.[4] Although scattered across Alabama and Georgia, the Crawfords, as a clan, hailed originally from Virginia.[5] They were slaveholders and, immediately prior to the Civil War, die-hard secessionists. After the war, the widow Martha Everitt Crawford and her daughter arrived, virtually penniless, in New York City following the confiscation of their property by Union forces. Thereafter, Frank supported both herself and her mother by giving piano lessons to the children of affluent New Yorkers, not a few of them the Commodore's own grandchildren, whom she had come to know better than he.

The Commodore first met Frank and her mother in the autumn of 1865, but did not see them regularly, or with any frequency, until after the death of Sophia Vanderbilt in August of 1868. After Sophia's demise, he entertained the Crawfords on occasion at Saratoga, and seems to have encountered the two ladies at the homes of his various daughters, who were trying to encourage a connection. At the time of the marriage, newspapers would speculate that the Commodore's children were lukewarm about the match, and that this discord within the family accounted for the remote Canadian geography in which the nuptials took place. Nothing could be further from the truth. It seems clear that Billy, his sisters, and his brothers-in-law actively encouraged the Commodore's marriage to either one of the Crawford women—the thirty-one-year-old daughter or the forty-nine-year-old mother, they really did not care which—as a welcome antidote to the continued presence of Tennie Claflin at Washington Place. Without citing a source, Arthur T. Vanderbilt II (not a descendent) claims in his book *Fortune's Children* that the very day after Sophia's death in 1868, Vanderbilt invited Mrs. Crawford and Frank "to live at his house, free of rent, as visitors. They accepted his kind offer."[6] This, however, would not have been done by the very proper Methodist duo—especially with the rosy-cheeked Tennie Claflin lying rumpled in the Commodore's bed every morning. Arthur Vanderbilt also postulates a prenuptial agreement providing Frank with half a million dollars in Hudson River Railroad first mortgage bonds. But here again he is wrong. In fact, a postnuptial agreement negotiated many years later by Billy Vanderbilt left Frank with the bonds in exchange for her agreement not to dispute a will in which the Commodore left virtually everything to Billy.[7]

In discussing Vanderbilt's second marriage, Smith, Lane, and other writers have echoed a number of canards advanced originally by Croffut in 1886, one year after Frank's death. Croffut's sources included Frank's mother and Frank's hard-drinking brother, both of whom lived at Washington Place and in the Staten Island mansion following the marriage in 1869. (In fact, the impoverished brother held a job in the Vanderbilt stables during the Commodore's lifetime.) Seeking to present Frank and her marriage in the best light possible, mother and brother sold Croffut on tales of a happy and affectionate union. Both painted the pious Frank as a wholesome presence fawning over the formerly heretical but suddenly devout Commodore. They also depicted Frank as the one person who could influence the normally cantankerous and obstinate mogul. But in fact the marriage was cold and business-like from the beginning. Frank, who did not share a bedroom with the Commodore, served as Billy Vanderbilt's insurance and place-holder against the possible encroaches of Tennie Claflin. Meanwhile, for the Crawfords, the Vanderbilts served as insurance against destitution. After the marriage, while Cornelius continued to spend much time in the Washington Place house, his bride and her mother took up more or less permanent residence at the Staten Island mansion, making only occasional forays to Manhattan, where they spent most weekends. In the early years of the union, the only one of the Crawford clan to spend much time in Greenwich Village was the son and brother Robert who, as has been mentioned, worked in the stables.

The marriage took Tennie Claflin by surprise. According to sworn testimony offered several months following Vanderbilt's death, Tennie made a visit to the Commodore shortly after his return from Canada. Tennie was accompanied by John J. Ogden, an old Ohio acquaintance. During the visit, Tennie asked Vanderbilt, apparently to illustrate a point for Ogden's benefit, if he had not promised to marry her prior to his elopement with Frank Crawford. To this, according to Ogden, the Commodore replied that he "certainly had so promised, and would have done so, but the family otherwise arranged it."[8] In his testimony, Ogden portrayed Vanderbilt as being afflicted by what Ogden took to be the benign and amusing simple-mindedness of old age. (In fact, according to Linsly's diary notes, this was syphilitic dementia.) Ogden recalled how the apparently senile Commodore displayed New York Central stock certificates bearing his likeness, and bragged about how scores of pretty young ladies flocked to his downtown private office every day to buy shares, so enamored were they of his portrait. In the next breath Vanderbilt talked about his current, quite ridiculous scheme: a proposal to finance a 625-foot-high obelisk in Central Park celebrating himself and George Washington.

Tennie of course feared that she and Victoria's place in the Vanderbilt circle was now tenuous, given the appearance of Frank. And she was right to have that fear. However, both sisters were to remain large presences in Vanderbilt's life for about two years more. Despite later assertions about Frank's Christian influence on the Commodore, he continued to consult with Woodhull for séances and routinely asked Tennie to minister to other needs. On the many nights when Frank was not in residence at Washington Place, Tennie could still often be found rumpled and happy in Vanderbilt's bed. Even when Frank was on site, Tennie visited to administer magnetic healing. Indeed, far from conforming to Frank's Christian distaste for such things as spiritualism, Tennie Claflin, liquor, and tobacco, the Commodore seemed at times to glory in Frank's outrage over such matters, defying her (just as, for decades, he had defied proper Society). Armed with her financial security and the confidence that the old man could not live forever, Frank persevered, even when Cornelius's involvement with Victoria Woodhull and Tennie Claflin reached absurd proportions.

On February 5, 1870, the sisters opened their own brokerage office at 44 Broad Street—space previously occupied by a disgraced broker who had swindled his clients out of more than $300,000.

Chronicling the launch of Wall Street's first female firm, the *New York Times* headline noted that the financial district had found itself "aroused" by the two "adventurers." The *Times* said the scene at the opening of Woodhull, Claflin & Co., "beggered description. . . . The place was thronged from early morning until late at night by a crowd of curiosity hunters, who gazed at the females and besieged them with questions." Not a few of the questions concerned the women's recent history. "About a year ago, at 17 Great Jones Street, the parties who compose the stock brokerage firm of Woodhull, Claflin & Co., were magnetic physicians and clairvoyants. They charged $25 in advance for their services, advertised largely, and guaranteed wonderful cures. For a time business went on swimmingly. But at last a turn came in the tide. The clairvoyant powers becoming exhausted or discovered to be all humbug, they took another tack and have anchored their craft on Broad Street." Near the end of its piece, the *Times* duly reported a denial by "friends" of Cornelius Vanderbilt that he had any involvement in subsidizing the new operation. The *Times* also issued an injunction and a prediction: "The scenes of yesterday are, to say the least, disgraceful in the extreme. Insulting remarks and shameful allusions were carried to the ears of the women . . . by the throng that curiously gathered . . . and who sang and whistled after the fashion of a Bowery pit. A short, speedy winding up of the firm of Woodhull, Claflin & Co. is predicted."[9] Speaking to a *Herald* reporter who seemed to delight in interviewing the women he called Wall Street's "bewitching brokers," Tennie was less dogmatic than others in denying Vanderbilt's involvement. "Commodore Vanderbilt is my friend," she noted, "but I will not say anything more concerning that matter."[10]

The *Times* was accurate in predicting a short life for the brokerage, because within months the sisters were onto something else altogether, administered out of the same office. First published in

early May of 1870, *Woodhull & Claflin's Weekly* focused on the themes
of women's suffrage and free love, but also sought to advance "knowledge" of spiritualism as well as to explore trends in political and economic reform. The paper lobbied for vegetarianism and legalization
of prostitution, and on December 30, 1871, made history by hosting
the first American publication of Karl Marx's *Communist Manifesto.*
Backed by the Commodore, Woodhull and Claflin rolled out their
publication nationwide. In 1872, Woodhull used the paper to support her role as the new Equal Rights Party's candidate for president
of the United States. (The party's announced vice-presidential con-
tender, Frederick Douglass, refused the draft to the extent that he did
not even acknowledge receipt of notification of his nomination, and
instead served as a presidential elector for the Republican ticket in
New York State.) Tennie ran for Congress on the Equal Rights ticket
in the same election, campaigning in a Manhattan district.

Ironically, both Woodhull and Claflin spent election night of
1872 in Manhattan's Ludlow Street jail. Several days before, they
and Colonel Blood had been arrested on a charge of having sent ob-
scene literature through the U.S. mails. The November 2 issue of
the *Weekly* featured salacious details of an alleged affair between the
renowned minister Henry Ward Beecher and one Elizabeth Tilton.
Beecher, the internationally famous rector of Brooklyn's Plymouth
Church, was a longtime critic of Victoria's. He was also an outspoken, perhaps hypocritical, opponent of free love. The woman in
question was the wife of Beecher's longtime assistant, Theodore
Tilton, who was himself, coincidentally, one of Victoria's many
lovers. The sisters and Blood were to spend nearly a month in jail
before being released. Eventually, Theodore Tilton sued Beecher for
alienation of affections, leading to a sensational 1875 trial. This trial
ended in a hung jury while at the same time exhausting what little
public good will Woodhull and Claflin still enjoyed.

By that time, however, the sisters had long been out of Vanderbilt's life. As of mid-1871, at Frank's insistence, the sisters were denied access to Washington Place, and Vanderbiltian funds stopped
flowing their way. In May of 1871, just a few weeks prior to the final closing of Vanderbilt's doors, the Commodore had been em-
barrassed by having his name come up in an interfamily lawsuit
involving the Claflins. "I am a clairvoyant; I am a spiritualist; I have
power and I know my power," Tennie had informed a crowded
New York courtroom. "Many of the best men in the street know
my power. Commodore Vanderbilt knows my power. I have hum-
bugged people, I know. But if I did it, it was to make money."[11] Not
long after, in February of 1872, candidate Woodhull delivered and
published a speech in which she criticized Vanderbilt and other
railroad magnates as betrayers of the public trust.

Nevertheless, three years later, the by-then financially desperate
Victoria and Tennie published an open appeal to Vanderbilt in the
pages of the *Weekly*. "We want our hands supported," they wrote.
"We want our Paper endowed beyond the fear of disaster . . . we
want the cause of Her emancipation assisted that it may become an
active moving power. To do all this, would require a paltry sum only
when compared with your many millions—a sum whose absence
neither you nor your heirs would scarcely feel; but which for what
we ask it, would be salvation indeed."[12] Within a few weeks, when
there was no response from Vanderbilt, the sisters decided to try to
find a new market for their struggling paper. Nearly instantly, they
dropped the themes of free love and spiritualism, and adopted
Catholicism. Their hoped-for new constituency of readers did not
miraculously materialize, however. In the absence of Divine intervention, the *Weekly* folded in short order. Neither of the sisters ever
saw their old benefactor again after 1871.[13]

∞

Vanderbilt's withdrawal of support for Woodhull and Claflin ran in span with two charitable efforts in which Frank was concerned, and with which her elderly husband indulged her. One was a church in Manhattan; the other a college in the South.

One of Frank's closest friends in New York was a Methodist minister and educator by the names of Charles Force Deems. Born in Maryland in 1820, Deems had graduated from Dickinson College in 1839. After that, he pursued appointments as a minister in New Jersey and North Carolina, and as general agent for the American Bible Society.[14] Deems also served as professor of logic and rhetoric at the University of North Carolina, and professor of natural sciences at Randolph Macon College in Virginia before being appointed president of Greensboro Female College, where he served from 1850 through 1854. Thereafter, through to the end of the Civil War, Deems held various pastorates in North Carolina, and was associated with several schools in North Carolina's Randolph and Iredell counties, while also doing missionary work as far south as Mobile. "When Mrs. Vanderbilt resided in Mobile," reported the *New York Times,* "and was in humble circumstances, she became acquainted with Dr. Deems, and received kindness at his hands."[15]

One of Deems's three sons, the eldest boy named Theodore, died at Gettysburg while fighting for the Confederacy. Deems relocated to Manhattan (his wife's hometown) in the summer of 1865, there to start a religious newspaper called *The Watchman* and found the nondenominational Church of the Strangers. Frank and her mother followed on his heels. The church initially held meetings in the rented chapel of the University of the City of New York (later to be renamed New York University), at Washington Square just a few steps away from Vanderbilt's Washington Place home. From the day of their own first arrival in New York City, Frank and her mother counted themselves among the most devoted members of

Deems's flock: the majority of his "strangers" being, like them, Southerners displaced by the upheaval of the war.

Along with being a minister and educator, Deems was also an editor and author. His books included *The Life of Dr. Adam Clark* (1840), *The Triumph of Peace and Other Poems* (1840), and *The Home Altar* (1850). Erudite, temperate (to the point of being a prohibitionist), and bookish, Deems possessed the precise type of thoroughgoing piety and devotion to good works that the Commodore could barely tolerate. Back in the day of the voyage of the *North Star*, Vanderbilt had put up with Reverend Choules (and Choules with Vanderbilt) for the sake of the family. Now Vanderbilt, who still could not be lured to church, put up with Deems, as Frank's frequent houseguest, in the same spirit. In a rare candid utterance made years after Vanderbilt was dead, Deems recalled one of their first meetings and his early impression of the Commodore. "I met Daniel Drew at the house," wrote Deems. "It was shortly after one of the great financial battles between Commodore Vanderbilt and Mr. Drew. The lion and the tiger were lying down a little together. Mr. Drew had repeatedly attended the service I was holding in the university chapel, and echoed Mrs. Vanderbilt's earnest phrases of the usefulness of our little congregation." Vanderbilt, however, seemed unimpressed, as was Deems. "My impressions of his character at that time," Deems noted, "were, at least, not favorable. I regarded him as an unscrupulous gatherer of money, a man who aimed at accumulating an immense fortune and had no very pious concern as to the means."[16]

During the late summer of 1870, Vanderbilt acceded to a request made by his wife, and purchased an abandoned church that Deems had made it known he coveted, wanting to make it a permanent home for his congregation. That September, Vanderbilt acquired the former Mercer Street Presbyterian Church for $50,000. According to Deems's own autobiography, and every Vanderbilt biography published to date, Vanderbilt deeded the property to Deems outright. But this was not in fact the case. The prudent Vanderbilt simply gave Deeds a life interest in the real estate and building, which the preacher was not free to dispose of. According to the terms of the limited gift, control of the property would revert to Vanderbilt or his heirs/assignees following Deems's death. The deed on the property, which Vanderbilt knew would appreciate greatly in value through the years, remained in the name of Cornelius Vanderbilt, and eventually in the name of the Commodore's major heir, Billy.[17]

We have no record of Vanderbilt ever personally visiting the church save for when he was carried there for his funeral in 1877. Delivering a long and eloquent eulogy, Deems would use the occasion to refute scathing obituaries in the press, as well as numerous criticisms of the dead man that had recently been voiced from many New York pulpits. In singing his benefactor's high praises as a father, grandfather, husband, and Christian, Deems cited not only Vanderbilt's gift to the Church of the Strangers, but also his one other significant act of charity: a substantial endowment for what had by then come to be called Vanderbilt University, in Nashville.

This second gift had its roots in March of 1873, when Frank Vanderbilt's cousin-in-law, Methodist Bishop Holland McTyeire of Nashville, came to New York City for surgery and spent several weeks during his recovery as a guest of the Vanderbilts. When McTyeire finally went home in May, he carried with him a check in the amount of $500,000 for the endowment of the already planned Methodist "Central University." Soon the school's trustees voted to rename the institution after their benefactor. As a stipulation of his gift, Vanderbilt insisted that McTyeire be named life-chairman of the university's board of trustees. After two years of construction, the first classes commenced in the autumn of 1875. Vanderbilt was never to lay eyes on the school. On October 4, 1875, the dedicatory services featured not Vanderbilt but Deems dispatched from New York to read a brief message. There was also a telegram, signed by Vanderbilt but composed by Frank: "We send greeting to you all. May your institution be ever blessed by the great Governor of all things."[18] Vanderbilt had already, by this time, advanced about $250,000 more on top of his original gift for the completion of the campus. Other donations would follow. By the time of his death, the Commodore's total gift to Vanderbilt University would come to $1 million.

Even in its original installment of a mere $500,000, Vanderbilt's donation was hailed as the largest single act of philanthropy in American history to that time. Attention to the fine print, however, would have revealed that a substantial percentage of all the Commodore's various donations to the university were earmarked for an endowment fund which, by Vanderbiltian order, was to be kept in first mortgage bonds of the New York Central and Hudson River Railroad. Thus, as with the church on Mercer Street, Vanderbilt's charity was not entirely outright, although it did enable the work of men embarked upon noble missions.

While the Commodore distracted himself, in turn, with the sinners Woodhull and Claflin and the saints Deems and McTyeire, his son Billy (surrounded by a small group of capable lieutenants) focused his attention on running and expanding the Vanderbilt railroad empire. Anchoring Billy's inner circle now was the influential lawyer and politico Chauncey Mitchell Depew, hired in 1866 as general counsel for the Harlem and again in 1869 as general counsel for the Central. Depew later went onto the board of Central, and in 1875 was made counsel for all the properties of the Vanderbilt System.

Through the 1870s, Billy grabbed ever tightly onto the reins of power, increasing the value of the family's holdings at a rate that put even old Cornelius's prodigious money-making to shame. Through the rigors of the rough economic seas of 1869, including Black Friday that September, Billy masterfully supported the price of Vanderbiltian stocks while also using the ensuing panic as an opportunity to take control of the Lake Shore & Michigan Railway, thus extending the reach of the Central all the way to Chicago and St. Louis. (By 1876, the Vanderbilts would be running a fast train connecting Chicago and New York in what seemed like a supersonic twenty-six hours.) Possession of other small feeder roads was secured either by purchasing control of stock or negotiating long-term leases. Two years after the acquisition of the Lake Shore, Billy spent $3 million to build the Harlem-owned Grand Central Depot—at Fourth (today's Park) Avenue and Forty-second Street. An elaborate palace of railroading with a glass-domed roof covering more than five acres, the depot was dedicated in October of 1871. Across the broader landscape, old iron rails on antiquated lines were ripped up and replaced with modern steel. At the same time, most rail beds under the control of the Vanderbilts were now double-tracked, allowing for two-way traffic and thus effectively doubling the value of each route. Yield was further maximized when Billy ordered freight cars redesigned to handle twenty tons of material instead of the traditional eight.

For the sake of publicity, all of these elaborations were trotted out as genius-strokes of the Commodore, who barely realized they were happening. When the affairs of the Lake Shore came under a cloud during the panic of 1873, Billy installed his father, rather than himself, in the presidency of that concern, knowing the steadying effect the idea of the Commodore being at the helm would have. But Billy, who went on the board at the same time as a simple director, called the shots in the executive and finance committees of the Lake

Shore, where he sat with Schell and James Banker. Concurrently, Billy directed profits from various concerns into strategic investments, staking positions in such forward-looking firms as Western Union and the Municipal Gas Company. When announcements were made concerning these or other initiatives, they always went out as public letters over the signature of the Commodore who was now, quite literally, a figurehead.

As Billy's personal power rose, key sons-in-law went their own way while still sometimes colluding in Vanderbilt endeavors. Many, such as Cross, had long ago taken their nest-eggs large and small and retired, after being eased out by Billy. Others were more active. In 1872 Clark (along with Augustus Schell) rather surprisingly organized a pool with Jay Gould to corner Chicago & Northwestern stock. That same year, Clark—who also sat with Schell on the board of the Toledo, Wabash & Western—came into the presidency of the Union Pacific, in which role he acted to swing power toward an investment group consisting of himself, Schell, and Banker as representatives for the interests of the Vanderbilts. In this way Clark worked to draw Union Pacific through-traffic away from the Pennsylvania Railroad and to the Vanderbilt roads. (When Clark died suddenly in the summer of 1873, his numerous highly leveraged and speculative business affairs were a mess that eventually left his wife, Vanderbilt's daughter, without a dime.) Daniel Torrance in turn sat on the board of the Ohio & Mississippi Railroad.

By 1876 (the same year his sunken tracks under the new Park Avenue, just north of the Grand Central Depot, went into operation), Billy had improved the family's net worth significantly. The fortune that stood at $20 million just before the Civil War now represented more than $100 million in value. The bulk of that growth had come from the railroading investments of the preceding decade. While his father had been responsible for the $20 million of seed money that now constituted less than 20 percent of the total fortune, Billy considered himself to be the author of the balance. In this spirit, as his father grew older, Billy took measures to make sure the Commodore left a will that not only reflected Billy's role in the late consolidation of the family wealth, but assured as well that Billy would remain in solid control of the empire after the founder's death.[19]

The Commodore's final will (the text of which would remain a closely guarded secret and the subject of much worried family gossip until after Vanderbilt's death) bequeathed the entirety of the old man's fortune, save for some $3,700,000, to Billy and/or Billy's children. Frank, per the terms of her post-nuptial agreement negotiated with Billy, was to receive the long-promised $500,000 in bonds plus life use of the house at Washington Place along with 2,000 shares of the Central. Cornelius's eight surviving daughters were to receive Central bonds ranging in value from $230,000 to $500,000, with some of these bequests being in the form of trusts. (The allocation was based on need. Sophia Torrance, whose husband Daniel had become independently wealthy working with the Commodore, received $230,000. Maria Louise, the widow whom Horace Clark had left destitute, received $500,000.)[20] Cornelius Jeremiah was to get life interest in the income from a $200,000 trust, the corpus of that trust to go to Billy or Billy's descendents upon Cornelius Jeremiah's death. Various friends were also to be given small tokens of remembrance: $20,000 for Deems, $10,000 for Linsly, and so forth, with similar amounts going to a few Staten Island relatives. Almost more important than the amounts of the bequests were their *form*. No one other than Billy and Billy's children received any voting stock outright. Billy's clear intention in crafting the document the Commodore put his signature to was to maintain for himself complete, unopposed power as the supreme admiral of Vanderbiltian enterprise.

∞

As old age rose in the Commodore, his days lapsed into a predictable round. An early riser, he'd eat a breakfast of steak or lamb chops, eggs, and black coffee before idling away a few fairly unproductive hours in his private office, between the Washington Place house and the stables. His sole companion there was usually his longtime personal clerk, Lambert Wardell, who would take dictation when required, and also took care of the Commodore's own relatively small stock market transactions: though these became few and far between as time progressed. By the mid-1870s, Vanderbilt had few appointments but would, depending on his mood, briefly see whatever curiosity seekers or beggars who might drop in. The most any of them ever left with was an autograph: the same scrawled gift the Commodore regularly awarded to the messengers Billy regularly dispatched from the uptown offices (as of 1871 housed in floors above the Grand Central Depot) with papers requiring signing.

Following lunch at Washington Place, provided the weather was conducive, he'd take a carriage and trotters from the stable and, accompanied by his brother-in-law Robert or some other minion, race through Central Park or up Harlem Lane, or sometimes go over to South Street, there to watch with amazement as the mighty Brooklyn Bridge took shape in the distance. After that, depending on the extent to which Vanderbilt had his wits about him on any given day, he might engage a few games of high-stakes whist or euchre at either the Manhattan Club or the Union Club. In summer, he'd spend long weeks at Saratoga, most often at the United States Hotel, tended by Linsly, Lambert Wardell, Frank, and Mrs. Crawford. One of those with whom he played cards in Manhattan was Daniel Drew, against whom he appeared to hold no grudge. Another was Cornelius K. Garrison. Business disagreements were just that, and the friendships of old age quite another matter. The old opponents reminisced about their wars.

Artists sought him out. Portraitists and sculptors asked him to pose, as did Matthew Brady and other photographers. In his final years, he was part man, part romantic hero of American folk memory. He was also, however, increasingly a stranger and enigma to most of his family. Through the early 1870s, he seems rather systematically to have either dropped or picked arguments with most of his daughters and their children, not seeing them for long periods of time even though Frank regularly intervened to try to reconcile the Commodore with his kin. Linsly ascribed this truculent behavior in part to the Commodore's syphilis, and in part to his normal habit of being. Over the course of the long years, he'd generally always been indifferent to the niceties of extended family bonding. Now, as he moved towards the exit, the Commodore might provide for them in some small way in his will. But that didn't mean he had to spend time with them. Of course, Cornelius Jeremiah had long been outside the family circle. That left Billy, Billy's wife, and Billy's children and their wives and children defining the elite set of the Commodore's approved, preferred family.

Soon enough, he'd bid them all farewell.

24

AGAINST THE WORLD

THE EIGHTY-ONE-YEAR-OLD VANDERBILT VISIBLY SLOWED IN his activities after Christmas of 1875. After April 1, 1876, he never again left Washington Place. From April through to his death the following January, he remained not only in the house, but confined to the upstairs—either laying in a bed or sitting in a wheelchair.[1] His dilemma was final-stage syphilis, which had now begun attacking every vital corner of his body. After his death, an autopsy report, though withholding the fact of the syphilis, would admit that at the end the Commodore had "scarce a sound organ in his body."[2] From his perspective, the disease added up to chronic fatigue matched with chronic pain sometimes blunted by ongoing bouts of dementia.

The seventy-three-year-old Jared Linsly was laid up himself from April 15, 1876, to mid-May after being trampled by a horse and carriage on the streets of New York. While Linsly recovered, Vanderbilt labored under the care of several assisting physicians

working for Linsly, one being a Dr. Max Bodenheimer. It was during Bodenheimer's watch that Vanderbilt (who absolutely refused
to be treated with opium or any other sedative, even though racked
with pain) evidently put his foot down with Frank, insisting that if
he could not have magnetic treatments from Tennie Claflin, then
he must at least have them from someone. He was certain that only
the medicine others thought quackery could ease his misery. Frank
acquiesced in this, but at the same time expressed her preference
that the Commodore be ministered to by a male practitioner. Thus
it was that "Dr." Frederick Weill, a self-proclaimed "magnetician,"
received a summons to Washington Place. Weill kept an office a bit
to the north at 226 East Twenty-first Street. Bodenheimer was in
attendance when Weill arrived at about 9:00 P.M. on the evening of
May 9.

"Mrs. Vanderbilt came in about 15 or 20 minutes after I went
in," Weill remembered. "She stayed until the Commodore retired
to his private apartment for manipulation. Then Mrs. Vanderbilt
went there with us and stayed through the whole proceedings." After just a few minutes of treatment, the Commodore announced an
easing of his chronic suffering, and "said to Mrs. Vanderbilt that he
had been deprived a long time of the only thing that did him any
good. Mrs. Vanderbilt . . . was standing by the side of the bed during the manipulation." Weill returned the next day at the same
hour to find the Commodore already in bed, alone save for Frank.
"I stayed about an hour and a half. On this occasion the Commodore talked a good part of the time. . . . [He] repeated himself
often . . . the same statements sometimes a dozen times. He was
speaking mostly about his physical condition and the physical troubles he had had during his life."

The repetitive conversation was much the same on the third
night, with Frank standing close by. On the fourth night, however,

Weill found himself largely alone with his patient, Frank being busily engaged tending to something in the next room. With Frank not hovering, and his own mind somehow more focused, Cornelius managed to express himself without redundancy. "He told me about his life and the moral storms he had gone through," Weill remembered. Then, perhaps referencing his true ailment, Vanderbilt admitted "he was very fond of the fair sex [and] said he might last a century if it had not been for early indiscretions carried into maturer [*sic*] years." On the following evening, once again with Frank lingering one wall away, Vanderbilt complained loudly to Weill about his "very unpleasant surroundings." The Commodore said he "could not have his own way, but was controlled by others, that he was 'chained down.'" According to Weill, Vanderbilt repeatedly shouted out to his wife with various complaints. "Why wasn't I under this treatment long ago?" he demanded at one point. "We do for you the best we can," she answered. "We can't do anymore." As Weill departed after the fifth session, Vanderbilt expressed his desire for the doctor to return. However, when Weill next showed up at Washington Place, he was denied entry by the servants acting under Mrs. Vanderbilt's instructions. "I never saw the Commodore again."[3] Frank had evidently decided there was something about Weill she did not like—perhaps his developing camaraderie with the Commodore.

Linsly returned to active duty at the Commodore's bedside on or about May 15. "From that time forward," the doctor later recalled, "I saw him [Vanderbilt] continuously every day to the time of his death. I always consulted the Commodore in regard to the selection of assistant physicians. I named them and he approved them. . . . I was with the Commodore almost the whole of every day, and frequently at night. I devoted pretty much my whole time to his case. When I did not remain all night I usually went home at 10:00 P.M. I generally came in the morning at 9."[4]

Linsly's home and office at 22 Lafayette Place were close walking distance from Washington Place. Speaking not long after Vanderbilt's death, Linsly appeared to take just pride in his long association with the Commodore. "In May, when I returned to the Commodore's bedside, he said to me that he wished me to remain with him as long as he lived, and mentioned that I had been with him three weeks in Jersey when he met with the accident in 1833." By Linsly's recollection, Vanderbilt went on to comment: "Had I died in 1833 or 1836, or even 1854, the world wouldn't know that I'd ever lived." In other moods, however, Vanderbilt continued to criticize Linsly and the balance of the traditional doctors, sometimes to their faces, at other times to his magneticians.

According to Linsly, Vanderbilt occupied several different upstairs rooms at various periods in the course of any day, being carried from one to another upon his whim. Two front rooms (one a sitting-room and the other a library) were used most heavily by daylight. Vanderbilt had a bed installed in the library, and here he spent most of his daytime hours. At night he would retreat, depending on his condition and the likelihood of him urgently needing the facilities, either to the water-closet itself which contained a small bed, to a middle-bedroom close by the water-closet, or to his large rear bedroom. As Linsly recalled, whenever visitors were admitted upstairs during the day, they "went into the sitting-room first, passing by the door of the library where he was. The door was generally open, so that as they passed from the head of the stairs they could look into his room. There was another door between the two rooms toward the front of the house, which was generally partly opened." Sometimes Vanderbilt had himself placed in a wheelchair near the front window in the library and had his favorite horses brought round out of the next door stable so that he could look at them on the street below.

Two weeks after the dismissal of Weill, in the face of increasingly shrill demands from Vanderbilt, Linsly and Frank allowed for another "magnetician" to be called. Lieutenant Colonel W. W. Bennett (Ret.) had embarked upon the practice of this form of medicine after a long career in the United States Army. Although he lived in Jersey City, Bennett maintained an office at 33 West Twenty-fourth Street.

An acquaintance of Vanderbilt's nephew John DeForest Jr., Bennett was dispatched by DeForest to Vanderbilt's Manhattan residence on the very day of the mogul's eighty-second birthday, May 27. Bennett arrived at Washington Place at around noon. He found Vanderbilt in his sickroom surrounded by his wife, his mother-in-law, and a somewhat petulant Dr. Linsly, who was probably not happy to have yet one more quack to contend with. The Commodore lay naked upon a rubber sheet, covered by a thick blanket. Vanderbilt, Bennett later recalled, was "howling like a wild beast with pain." Bennett remembered that the Commodore's shrieks "could be heard all over the house, and he was calling on God to relieve his sufferings, and wondering why God should persecute him so." According to Bennett's perhaps self-serving recollection rendered after Vanderbilt was dead, his treatment with the magnets completely relieved the millionaire of all pain. The skeptical Linsly himself, if we are to believe Bennett, expressed astonishment at how Bennett's "miraculous" ministrations spared Vanderbilt further suffering. The magnets cured more than pain—or so it seemed. Vanderbilt reportedly told Bennett that before the latter's treatments, his urine had had to be "drawn by instruments," but afterwards it "flowed naturally and easily." Perhaps, as had happened before, the magnets did indeed facilitate at least a psychosomatic easing of Vanderbilt's symptoms. One assumes that Vanderbilt, his physician, and his family must have recognized some form of genuine improvement, albeit minimal and brief, as Bennett appears to have been kept on for three weeks.[5]

During that time, Vanderbilt and Bennett chatted on several occasions, whenever the Commodore had the strength and the clarity. On one occasion, Vanderbilt reportedly told Bennett he believed that Linsly and all the other traditional doctors who loitered about were nothing but a bunch of "damned fools." On another occasion, he relayed an omen (part dream, part hallucination) that he apparently thought ominous:

The Commodore told me he had a vision, and that it occurred before I was called to attend him; he said he saw a roadway shaped like a horseshoe, stretching around his bed; at the further end of the roadway he saw a number of his friends; others were passing along the road; from time to time he saw one of his friends go to the edge of the road and fall off; and he saw himself pass along the road several times, advance to the edge, return safely, and once more go over the road; the last time he had the vision he saw himself at the edge, and unable to move back, being likely to fall; he said he was clairvoyant, and had always been able to see the end of any sickness from which he had suffered but the present; he could not see how that was going to end.

Like Weill before him, Bennett developed a bad impression of Frank, thinking her not properly attentive to the Commodore's needs. "The Commodore was very fond of a kind of cake which he called a *cookie*; he often called for cookies, but received them only three or four times during [my attendance] upon him." At the same time, however, Bennett's reminiscence points up Vanderbilt as a most petulant and demanding patient. Bennett recalled that on one occasion Frank brought Vanderbilt a bowl of warm soup which he took one sip of and then dashed against the far wall of the sickroom, crying "Who in hell salted the soup?" To this Frank replied calmly that she did not know who had salted the soup, but would find out. Vanderbilt also wanted ice in a bowl near him at all times, so that he could place it in his mouth and let it melt. When the bowl ran out of ice, he shouted and swore until it was replenished. When a daughter sent the Commodore flowers, Vanderbilt sneered and rejected them. And when Bennett asked whether the Commodore would consent to receive visits from his various children Vanderbilt yelled: "No. Damn them. They are all bastards, but Bill!" Linsly recalled one occasion in particular when, informed that Cornelius Jeremiah waited downstairs, the Commodore told Frank: "Go right downstairs and tell him to go right out of the house and never come in again while I am living, or after I am dead. Mrs. Crawford, you go down and see that she tells him."

Linsly also remembered numerous occasions when several of the daughters—including Sophia Torrance, Ethelinda Allen (who lived quite near to Washington Place at the New York Hotel), Eliza Osgood, and Mary La Bau—were denied entrée to the sickroom on Vanderbilt's own authority, this despite earnest requests from both Frank and Mrs. Crawford that he see them. Through nearly all his last sickness, virtually every one of the children except Billy had to be content with peeks at their father through the half-open door between the sitting-room and the library. Mary La Bau did nothing to help ease the tension when, in mid-July, she stormed into the library without permission and confronted her father with a demand that he reveal the language of his will, then still secret. Vanderbilt, annoyed at the intrusion just as he was annoyed by just about everything at the time, pointedly refused to answer with any specificity. Linsly, who overheard the conversation, said: "I think I heard him tell her he had done the best he could. I heard him use that expression to different members of his family. I heard him say that he had made the best will for all parties, and that if he should make 100 wills he would not be able to make a better one." The exchange reinforced Vanderbilt's attitude that all but Billy, who had made most of the money, were vultures waiting to see him in his grave so that they could divide up the spoils.

As always, the grim Commodore seemed intent on making others suffer just as much, if not more, than he. Soup bowls continued to fly; so too the curses and abuse. Even the charitable Linsly, always ready to take Vanderbilt's side and stick up for his reputation post-mortem, eventually commented as follows about the Commodore's last days: "His sufferings were very great at times, and he was very irritable . . . [but] when I first knew him he displayed irritability. It was constitutional with him." It is perhaps not too astonishing, given Vanderbilt's petulance as he approached eternity, that Bennett, on one occasion, overheard Frank say to her mother: "The old man must die. I cannot stand this hell any longer."

As has been indicated, Billy, alone among the children, was permitted extensive time with his father. He showed up daily. Billy Vanderbilt and Lambert Wardell were the two business lieutenants who consulted regularly with the Commodore, earnestly soliciting the dying man's advice on routine matters (more for his own good than theirs) then trotting off to transact more important Vanderbiltian business according to Billy's own lights, just as had been the case for years. According to Linsly, Billy spoke to his father only once about the estate, this in July, the conversation happening at the father's request. Linsly recalled standing by as the Commodore pointed a shaky finger at the son and said: "Billy, after I'm dead a great responsibility will fall on you. You will find a piece of paper left to direct you what to do. There are several pieces of paper attached to my will. I charge you to carry out faithfully what I have directed in my will." To this Billy, who knew full well the contents of the instructions, silently nodded his assent.

Bennett's run of three weeks as the Commodore's magnetician ended when he made a fatal error: one that earned him Frank's wrath, and probably Billy's as well. Neither Linsly nor any of the other genuine physicians attending Vanderbilt would consent to help with the magnet sessions. Nor, for that matter, did Vanderbilt want them there. Holding more than two magnets in place at the same time, however, was too much of a job for just one man without help. For a time, Bennett enjoyed the assistance of a young lady by the last name of Danforth who (being an attractive young thing who, according to Bennett, "pleased the Commodore") was soon let go because she "did not satisfy the Commodore's family." Shortly thereafter, the apparently unwitting Bennett found himself approached at his office by none other than Tennie Claflin who, anxious to get back into the dying Cornelius's circle, offered her services.

The next day, Bennett carried a letter from Tennie to the Commodore. Handing it to Vanderbilt, Bennett—by his own account—said: "You recollect Miss Claflin—the lady who cured you when you were so sick before. Here is a letter from her." Bennett said later that the somewhat foggy Vanderbilt took a moment to register the name. Then he asked hesitatingly whether Miss Claflin was Mrs. Woodhull's sister. When Bennett replied in the affirmative, Vanderbilt answered that he could not read the letter that evening, and requested that Bennett bring it to him again the next day. But before Bennett could return again to Washington Place, he received a written message from DeForest telling him his services were no longer required. Vanderbilt never saw Bennett again, though several other magneticians came and went.

Through the spring, summer, and autumn, Vanderbilt's decline was at times glacial, but nevertheless always certain. The syphilis attacked the kidneys and liver, causing the functions of those organs to begin to fail. The syphilis also attacked the heart, the action of which became increasingly irregular. At the same time, Vanderbilt's mind became all the more vague and confused, and his rages all the more tempestuous. Totally consumed by his maladies, the Commodore seemed utterly disconnected from and disinterested in the world at large. During May, news of the grand opening of Philadelphia's Great Centennial International Exhibition seemed not to impress him. Likewise, the devout worshiper of Washington took no notice, and could not be roused, on the centennial day itself—July 4, 1876—while all of New York celebrated with fireworks and parades. Concurrent word of the slaughter of Custer and his men at the Battle of the Little Big Horn barely caught the Commodore's momentary attention. The same went for the thunderous debate surrounding the disputed presidential election of that year between New York's Samuel Tilden and Ohio's Rutherford B. Hayes. During August, there was a crisis point at which the Commodore appeared to be dying, but after that he rallied a bit into the autumn before continuing his long-term decline.[6]

Oblivious to the outer world, Vanderbilt focused what little attention he had on himself, his doctors, and a small circle of family and friends. Frank Work, an old railroading ally, visited regularly, and was admitted to the inner sanctum far more frequently than most Vanderbilt children and grandchildren. Work, by his own account, called on Vanderbilt about once a week until approximately two weeks before the Commodore's death—by which point Vanderbilt's coherence appears to have left him completely, and visits became irrelevant. Early on, when Vanderbilt still had stray extended bouts of lucidity, he and Work talked much about their two great shared passions: Wall Street and the trotters. But Work's recollections of later conversations with Vanderbilt show a delusional man whose faculties were leaving him.

"The physicians were generally present when I went to see him," Work recalled. "In all these visits, from April till January, nine months, I never saw any other persons with the Commodore than those I have named. Sometimes I stayed only five minutes, and sometimes an hour. Sometimes he was in his bedroom, and sometimes in the library."[7] Work remembered that during one of his very last visits he and Vanderbilt conversed on the topic of Satan. The Commodore told Work excitedly that he and the Lord were fighting the Devil, and that together they were going to "whip" him. On another occasion, Vanderbilt insisted that once he was dead, he would join George Washington in God's innermost circle: Washington being the greatest American of the country's first generation, and himself being the greatest American of the country's second generation. Even in his last feeble-mindedness, the Commodore's gargantuan ego loomed large as ever.

Pastor Deems came as well. According to Deems, in his final months the Commodore became convinced that the spiritualism to which he'd been devoted for decades was bunk. Whether or not Vanderbilt actually said as much to Deems, or whether the preacher, after Vanderbilt's death, was simply trying to make a case for the Commodore's not being a heathen, we cannot know. Also unknown is whether or not Vanderbilt might have made such a statement under duress in the form of intense coercion from either the devout Frank, the devout Deems, or both. Each of these individuals forthrightly believed that spiritualism was a blasphemy against God, and that any adherents of that sham faith would certainly be doomed to hell. Thus it only stands to reason that Deems and Frank would likely tag-team the failing Vanderbilt, harping on the topic until he finally denounced séances and those who practiced them.

Deems later claimed that, as Vanderbilt approached the brink, he affectionately recalled how "his mother had got the maxims of the Bible implanted so firmly in his heart that nothing could eradicate them." Deems also insisted that Vanderbilt told him: "Doctor, when I am gone I leave you to do justice to my memory. I want it

known that I always believed the Bible, and on that subject you
have had no more influence over me than this fan which I hold in
my hand."[8] The statements seem completely out of keeping with
the truth of Vanderbilt's religious practice (or lack of it), and his
pronounced, demonstrated disinterest in the Commandments
throughout the years. Nevertheless, such was Deems's testimony.

By all accounts, Vanderbilt spent a quiet Christmas, oblivious to
the mountain of greetings that arrived downstairs, his mind mostly
gone. A week later, peritonitis set in. Now, suddenly, doctors (*real*
doctors) came and went with increased frequency and urgency.
Upon the New Year, a ripple of rumor—not the first, but somehow
more real and believable than any previous—circulated through financial markets: Vanderbilt's end was near. A pool of reporters
rented a room directly across the street from Washington Place.
There they maintained a death-watch. Leering faces stared out an
upstairs window. The journalists imported brandy, cigars, and
binoculars, and ran in a special telegraph line through which they
intended to beam just one key, final piece of news. Billy shook his
fist at the window as he came and went, damning them as gawkers,
tourists, sensationalists. He told Frank he hated them one and all.
Despised them.

The end came late on the morning of Thursday, January 4—just
as a blizzard raged outside, one that within hours of the Commodore's death would cause the collapse of the glass roof at the Grand
Central Depot. Deems and Frank subsequently gave the press a glorious account of the Commodore's last hours. In vivid detail, they
told of Vanderbilt's earnest and eloquent declarations of faith, and
his many requests for hymns as he breathed his last. But in truth,
Vanderbilt was unconscious throughout the morning of his passing,
and even if conscious would not have been lucid enough to pray,
quote verse, or name songs, his mind having by that time been com-

pletely eaten by the disease.[9] The fact of Vanderbilt's unconscious-
ness gives a ring of truth to at least one aspect of the death scene as
related by Deems and Frank. It is likely that Vanderbilt's accumulated children and grandchildren did indeed gather round him in
the death chamber—for he no longer had the power or cognizance
to curse and shout for them to leave. (Meanwhile, in Tompkinsville,
Staten Island, the Commodore's sister Charlotte DeForest, two
years his senior, breathed her last. Charlotte, who died just one day
after the Commodore expired, was buried in the cemetery at New
Dorp just twenty-four hours after her brother arrived there.)

As word of the Commodore's passing spread, flags at Grand Central, City Hall, and most Manhattan schools and clubs came to half-
mast. Across town, the directors of Vanderbilt's firms met in joint
session for the express purpose of drafting, approving, and releasing a
fittingly somber tribute. A small committee consisting of Chauncey
Depew, Samuel Barger, and several others put together the draft.
Vanderbilt's servants hailed him as "the foremost representative of
public enterprise and material progress." Speaking truth, they lauded
the Commodore as having been "the creator, and not the creature, of
the circumstances which he molded to his purposes. He was the architect of his own fortune." Then, speaking something other than
truth, they added that in all of Vanderbilt's enterprises the "rights
and the welfare of the smallest stockholder were as well guarded as
his own."[10]

Like most newspapers, the *Herald* chose to sing Vanderbilt's
praises rather than speak ill, or accurately, of the dead. Vanderbilt,
editorialized the *Herald*'s James Gordon Bennett Jr., "knew himself
better than his critics knew him. Roads which had been the play-
things of gamblers and the preserves of politicians prospered under
his hard, cold, daring management. . . . The lesson to be learned
from the life of Vanderbilt is simple and impressive. Courage in the

performance of duty enabled this man to become one of the kings of the earth. The hard, strong-limbed boy who guided his vessel from ferry to ferry nearly seventy years ago lived to be a ruler of men. He had no advantages in his battle, no political, social, educational aid. It was one honest, sturdy, fearless man against the world, and in the end the man won."[11]

Bennett was being generous—but both he and his father had always liked Vanderbilt personally. The father, who had gone to his grave in 1872, had frequently raced against the Commodore in good-natured trotter contests; and both the Commodore and Bennett Jr. despised the dwarfish genius who'd lately made a profession out of besting each of them: Jay Gould.

A few preachers and journalists spoke more bluntly and critically than Deems and Bennett. Before Vanderbilt was in the ground, Beecher (still smarting from his old scandal, and not unmindful of Vanderbilt's relation with Woodhull and Claflin) used the occasion of his regular Friday evening prayer-meeting at Plymouth Church to criticize the dead man. During his talk, Beecher relayed a conversation with Lyman Abbott during which Abbott praised Vanderbilt's devotion to old hymns, and his affinity for John Bunyan's pious *Pilgrim's Progress*. To this, Beecher responded: "Yes. I am glad he liked the old hymns, but if he had sung them thirty years ago it would have made a great difference. He did not sing hymns as long as he could get about. We don't want to give God the tag end of our lives."[12]

Writing in his weekly magazine *The Nation,* Edwin Lawrence Godkin was equally to-the-point. "In his business transactions," Godkin wrote, "[Vanderbilt] was over-reaching and exacting, often availing himself of questionable practices; his standard of honor was one which had little regard for his adversary, but it was nevertheless a real standard and one to which he adhered." Godkin added that

Vanderbilt's "great defect" was his "want of education, and his worst faults were the natural results of the circumstances which surrounded the first thirty years of his life. That he emerged from these circumstances to be the man he was, is the only fact from which we can judge what more liberal associations might have made of him."[13]

Meanwhile, to try to counter the Beechers and Godkins of the world, Deems released a sugarcoated tidbit published in numerous papers, including the *Times*:

THE COMMODORE's GIFT
TO A SUNDAY SCHOOL

About a week ago Commodore Vanderbilt sent $50 to the Sunday School of the Church of the Strangers as a subscription to the Christmas festival. Sufficient money had previously been collected to defray the expenses of the entertainment, and it was decided to invest the money in flowers. Each one of the Sunday School children will be presented with a flower-pot, and either a tuberose, a hyacinth, or lily bulb. The pupils are expected to cultivate the bulbs and present the same to the Sunday School next Easter Sunday. Prizes will be awarded to those having the best specimens. . . . The idea was conceived by Rev. Dr. Charles F. Deems, the Pastor of the Church of the Strangers, while the death of Cornelius Vanderbilt at this time adds special significance to the project.[14]

Frank, who had written the $50 check to Deems while the Commodore hovered comatose in a fog of mental collapse, had her husband outfitted in style for his final voyage. Frank, reported the *Brooklyn Daily Eagle*, purchased the Commodore a "metallic casket" with a plush interior featuring "pearl colored satin, handsomely upholstered, with a cushion of the same material for the head to rest on. The outside is covered with the finest black silk velvet, and ornamented with solid silver trimmings, plain in design and chasing, but exceedingly rich in appearance. The handles, which run the entire length of the casket, are . . . of silver, with the hand grasps covered with the same velvet used in covering the body of the receptacle. The plate, also of solid silver, in unique design, contains the following inscription: 'Cornelius Vanderbilt, Born May 27, 1794, Died January 4, 1877.'"[15]

Frank scheduled a viewing and prayer-service to be held at Washington Place on Saturday, January 6. Then on Sunday, Deems conducted the funeral at the Church of the Strangers. In his sermon, the good reverend made one final pitch to sell the world—and perhaps God himself—on the skinflint whoremonger's supposed devoutness.

That man lying there never owned a dime or a foot of ground; he had those things as a steward of God. Money can't buy love. You can't shed tears over a rich man's bier because he was rich. No. Money can't buy tears. Look at all these men in the galleries who have wrought with him during life and who are brought here by love for his memory. If one grain of love is worth ten thousand of admiration, then Cornelius Vanderbilt was rich indeed. I believe that this man had true repentance to God, had a singularly childlike faith in the Lord Jesus Christ as Savior, and that, having yielded Him such faith and trust during all his life, he is numbered now with the saints in glory everlasting.[16]

Following the rites in the church, the family and Deems escorted the casket down to the Battery. From there, via private steam ferry, they carried Vanderbilt across the harbor he'd known so well in his youth. All along the short route to Staten Island, tugs and steam-boats blew their whistles in salute, while sloops and schooners dipped their ensigns. (One wry observer later commented—proba-bly more sardonically than truthfully—that he'd seen a score of wa-terfront whores genuflect as Vanderbilt's funereal vessel slipped her moorings and eased off, carrying one of their most reliable cus-tomers away from Manhattan forever.) Once the Vanderbilt boat arrived at Vanderbilt Landing, near to his boyhood home, the mem-bers of the party boarded carriages (and the boxed Vanderbilt a hearse) for the short trek of four miles to New Dorp and the Mora-vian Cemetery.

Here the body was carried up into the "new" Moravian Church built in 1844. The church was still decorated with Christmas greens, and was packed with Staten Islanders, some of whom were cousins, and some friends who had known Vanderbilt for most of his life. Five rows up front were reserved for the family, who filed in behind the casket. The pastor of the church, the Reverend William Vogel, said a brief prayer after which Deems read the final part of the Episcopal burial service, including the committal. Following this, Deems announced that the closed casket would be opened one last time, so that the family and those assembled might bid the Commodore *adieu*. After the family had finished gawking, all oth-ers assembled formed a line looping down the center aisle, round the casket, and back up the same aisle. Once this was done, the im-mediate family once again gathered before the box, looking on as the undertaker clamped down the lid for good.

A reporter for the *New York Times* noted what happened next:

A procession was then formed, Rev. Dr. Deems and Rev. Mr. Vo-gel leading. The coffin was born behind them by six men, and the family followed immediately after the coffin, the simple procession passing across the porch, around the church to the right, and then back a few yards to the Vanderbilt vault. The entrance to the vault is through an iron door on the easterly front of the base of a granite monument 30 feet in height. The monument is a very plain one, a marble figure of a veiled female only relieving its severity. . . . The coffin having been deposited in an outer case, it was lowered into the entrance of the vault. With uncovered heads the spectators waited until it had been laid away, when Rev. Dr. Deems turned, and facing the attentive throng, pronounced the benediction. . . . Mrs. Vanderbilt, who had stood near the door of the vault, leaning upon the arm of W. H. Vanderbilt, stepped to the door of the tomb and looked in for a moment, several other ladies standing with her, after which they moved away toward the waiting carriages.[17]

Thus did Cornelius join his parents, first wife, and youngest son in the simple tomb he'd built so long before. After this, with God's mercy having been duly requested, the Commodore's survivors departed the cemetery. The mourners rolled back down the hill to the landing, boarded the boat, and returned to Manhattan—there to confront each other, and Cornelius's tangled legacy.

EPILOGUE: TOMBS

WHILE OTHERS SEEMED CONTENT ENOUGH, THREE OF CORNELIUS Vanderbilt's children thought to mount a vigorous court proceeding against the Commodore's will, which they viewed not only as unfair, but as the product of a deranged mind.

The first hint of the altercation came in a *New York Times* report published February 20, 1877. The *Times* said parties to whom Cornelius Jeremiah owed money were insisting that he procure representation to challenge the settlement of the Commodore's estate. "Mr. C. J. Vanderbilt," the *Times* continued, "of restless disposition, seldom long in one place, has not been at home [in New York City] for several days, and it is reported that in a conversation three days ago in Washington with his brother he did not allude to the subject, and his silence has been construed by that part of the family which is content with the Commodore's bestowal of riches, into submission."

However, said the *Times*, other persons "who assume to speak with authority say that, notwithstanding this apparent acquiescence, the dissatisfied brother has continued his preparations . . . to demand that a more equitable distribution of the Vanderbilt estate among the children shall be ordered."[1]

In proceedings just a few days later, lawyers for Cornelius were joined by counsel representing Ethelinda Allen and Mary Alicia La Bau in announcing their intention to fight the will. According to statements made in court on March 5, the attorneys for the aggrieved parties would endeavor to prove that the Commodore was not in control of his faculties at the time he signed the will. They would also endeavor to prove that Billy Vanderbilt had taken advantage of this situation in order to enable a will accruing almost entirely to the sole benefit of himself and his heirs. A report in the *Times* of March 9, 1877, summarized the anticipated argument:

That the will . . . was obtained by fraud and circumvention and undue influence brought to bear upon [the Commodore] by his son, William H. Vanderbilt, and others acting with him to that end; that Commodore Vanderbilt was laboring under a morbid and mental delusion and mania at the time the will was made, inducing an absence of natural affection, and that these disqualifications, taken in connection with his physical debility, and the weakness consequent upon old age, disqualified him from making any testamentary disposition of his estate, or from acting in any testamentary capacity. That mania, and a continued morbid and unnatural desire and fervent inclination on the part of the Commodore to perpetuate his name, wealth, and power by a concentration of his property in his son William H., and his progeny, had so perverted and distorted the normal condition of his mental faculties as to utterly incapacitate him from making any testamentary disposition of his vast estate, which equity demanded should be divided fairly amongst his next of kin.[2]

Although all three contestants showed signs of initially backing off these arguments, various arcane suits and countersuits nevertheless went on into the spring of 1879. Testimony, most of it embarrassing, ranged from discussions of the Commodore's mental condition and womanizing habits to Cornelius Jeremiah's own womanizing, gambling, and wanton indebtedness. An out of court settlement was reached only after New York Supreme Court judge Charles A. Rapallo, attorney for the estate, managed to track down the Commodore's many previous wills and use them to demonstrate that Cornelius Jeremiah and his two sisters were far better treated in the final will, which they were contesting, than any will made in the years before. Following this revelation, the Surrogate Court ruled in favor of the final will, and ordered that it be proved. After this, anxious to wrap up the proceedings and avoid the threat of annoying and embarrassing appeals, Billy Vanderbilt cut a deal. He provided not only the two contesting sisters, but the balance of his surviving sisters as well, with half a million dollars apiece out of his share of the estate. He also significantly increased the size of the trust fund upon which Cornelius would earn income. At the same time, the daughters of the late Horace Greeley, who'd died in 1872 with Cornelius Jeremiah owing him tens of thousands of dollars, received $61,000 directly from Billy in settlement of that obligation.

Later on, Cornelius Jeremiah, acting alone, briefly tried to bring suit to seize full possession of his trust—but the Surrogate Court refused to even entertain the motion. Following this, Cornelius Jeremiah went on a round-the-world tour with his companion, a hanger-on by the name of "Dr." George Terry from Toledo who, though he failed miserably in the treatment of epilepsy and depression, worked wonders when it came to facilitating Cornelius Jeremiah's gambling and enabling his abuse of alcohol. Before he went abroad, Cornelius Jeremiah ordered the construction of a fine new home in West Hartford: a mansion in which he would never spend a night.[3] On April Fools' Day of 1882, shortly after his return from his grand tour and a side journey to Hot Springs, Arkansas, Cornelius Jeremiah committed suicide in a room at New York's Glenham Hotel, putting a bullet in his brain. Alone with Cornelius Jeremiah, sitting in an adjoining room at the time he did the deed, was Terry, whom some whisperers accused of murdering the man the *New York Times* now referred to as the "discarded son" of the Commodore.[4] By the terms of Cornelius Jeremiah's will, Terry as executor was to receive $120,000. (Attorney Samuel Colt, another executor, was to receive $50,000.) After Cornelius Jeremiah's death, however, he was found to be bankrupt, with claims on his estate far exceeding the dead man's assets. (Bear in mind, the corpus trust upon which Cornelius Jeremiah had relied for income in recent years reverted to Billy upon Cornelius Jeremiah's death.)[5]

Billy Vanderbilt arranged for the Commodore's discarded son to be buried at a cemetery in his adopted home city of Hartford, with Billy paying for the headstone. Not long after, he began planning an elaborate resting place for himself, his parents, his brother George Washington Vanderbilt, and his own male children and grandchildren to the exclusion of his sisters, daughters, and their offspring. Towards this end, during 1884, Billy Vanderbilt acquired fourteen acres embracing a substantial part of Lighthouse Hill, Ocean Terrace—not just the highest point of Staten Island, but the highest point on the entire Atlantic seaboard south of Maine. (The acres, laying immediately adjacent to and just behind the lands of the Moravian Cemetery, itself elevated high on Todt Hill, overlook not only the cemetery, but the lands at the end of New Dorp Lane [now the National Gateway Recreation Area] where Billy once farmed, and the ocean beyond.) Here, he planned an imposing mausoleum. With landscaping by Frederick Law Olmstead, the structure was to be designed by Richard Morris Hunt, whose first sketches proved too elaborate for Billy's taste. "We are plain, quiet, unostentatious people, and we don't want to be buried in anything . . . *showy*," Billy told Hunt. "The cost of it is a secondary matter, and does not concern me. I want it roomy and solid and rich. I don't object to appropriate carvings, or even statuary, but it mustn't have any unnecessary fancy-work on it."[6] But showy is in the eye of the beholder, and ostentation is a relative concept. Hunt himself would go on to build several magnificent homes for various of Billy's children. Given the grandiosity of the subsequent commissions, Hunt was probably wise in discounting Billy's disingenuous plea for simplicity.

In the end, Hunt designed the front of the Vanderbilt tomb (built at a cost of $235,000) to mimic the mausoleum attached to the twelfth-century Abbey Church of Saint-Gilles-du-Gard near Arles, in France. Work began in early 1885. Having approved Hunt's design, on March 18 Billy commissioned the Quincy, Massachusetts, firm of McKenzie & Patterson to do the building. "The tomb . . . ," reported the *New York Times*, "will be of the Romanesque style, 100 by 115 on the ground and 63 feet from the surface to the apex of the domes, of which there will be two." The *Times* added that the exposed portions of the structure would be of Quincy granite, while the vestibule and catacombs would be built "of marble and the arches and piers of limestone. . . . It will require about 8,000,000 pounds of granite, marble and limestone combined to complete it. . . . The firm will have to add over 100 men to their working force in order to prosecute the work."[7] Just as the work began, the Commodore's widow Frank passed away suddenly, of pneumonia, on May 4. For the time being, Frank was installed beside her husband

and his first wife in the original Vanderbilt crypt. Seven months later, on December 8, Billy dropped dead of an apoplectic stroke.

Five days earlier, the sixty-four-year-old had visited his old farm at New Dorp, there to tell the caretaker that he'd shortly be giving the land to his youngest son, George.[8] On his way back, he stopped at the Moravian Cemetery, paid his respects at the old crypt, and then went up Lighthouse Hill to see the progress being made on the new mausoleum. The project was at that point half complete, with some twenty tons of bronze gratings being installed. Walking about the place with the superintendent of the work, Billy marveled at the project: the largest private tomb in the United States, including thirty-six niches above ground, and room for plenty more caskets under the floor. Three arched doorways opened to a vestibule running the width of the mausoleum. A few steps across the vestibule, two wide doors made of five-inch-thick Indiana limestone opened to the tomb proper as set into the hillside: thirty feet wide, sixty feet deep, with a forty-foot ceiling.

Opposite the limestone door was an apse containing an altar and a chapel capable of holding about 150 people attending commitment services. Spreading out from the apse, each side of the tomb held four bays. In turn, each bay—protected by its own cast-bronze gate—incorporated nine individual vaults.[9] As Billy walked about the expansive space, he clapped his hands together and grinned at the echo. Above the various gates hovered carved lunettes featuring themes from the Bible. To the left: creation, expulsion from Eden, Moses receiving the Ten Commandments, and David praising the Lord. To the right: the wise Solomon rendering judgment, the Virgin Mary holding the Christ child, Jesus on the cross, and—of course—Jesus ascending. Not by accident, the plan was for the progenitor of the Vanderbilt millions, Cornelius, to lie in the first niche of the first bay, directly beneath the carving of the creation.

As Billy departed New Dorp that day, he could not possibly have imagined how quickly he'd be returning to the cemetery, though not the tomb. On Friday, December 11, Billy's body was carried to the Moravian Cemetery from Manhattan, after a funeral service at St. Bartholomew's, on Madison Avenue near Forty-fourth Street, where Billy had been a member of the vestry. Upon arrival at the cemetery, Billy's casket was placed in a receiving vault: the new Vanderbilt mausoleum not being finished, and the old crypt being filled to capacity with a party of six: the Commodore, his two wives, his parents, and George Washington Vanderbilt. One year later, on December 3, 1886, Billy's body became the first installed in the new mausoleum during a late-night transfer under the watchful gaze of three of his sons, William, Cornelius II, and Frederick.[10] A few days later, the bodies of the Commodore and the Commodore's two wives, as well as that of George Washington Vanderbilt, were carried up the hill.[11]

Among those present at the re-internment was old Captain Jacob Vanderbilt, who lived not far away in the Clove Hill section of Clifton, just above Stapleton. Captain Jake would live on until 1893, dying in his eighty-sixth year.[12] Although he lies in the Moravian Cemetery, he is not interred in the mausoleum.[13]

For reasons unexplained, the Moravian Cemetery seems to be a favorite of mobsters. One strolls by monuments to "Big" Paul Castellano and Frank DeCicco—along with the obelisk under which the Commodore spent the first few of his post mortem years, and where his parents still linger—before arriving at a formidable gated stone arch delineating the closed Vanderbilt plot. From here, behind a gate, a circuitous drive-way proceeds uphill. The wide path runs one-fifth of a mile through a ruinous, overgrown woodland that was once a masterpiece of landscape design. Graded for horse-drawn carriages, this driveway was originally designed by Frederick Law Olmstead to permit only glimpses of its destination as one approached. But these days, with the woods having gone wild, Olmstead's carefully planned peeks are all obscured. The only remaining open section of the landscape is a wide lawn fronting the mausoleum itself. The massive temple, meanwhile, is sporadically decorated with graffiti, and just as sporadically cleaned. Lately, after a generation or so of neglect, a few family members have taken a renewed interest in the place. Thoroughbred racing aficionado and investor Alfred Gwynne Vanderbilt Jr., who died in 1999, constituted the first internment the mausoleum had seen in decades. His son, another Alfred, has since been active in doing what he can to restore, stabilize, and protect Hunt's edifice.

Within the mausoleum, dozens of descendents of Cornelius and William H. Vanderbilt sleep, unaware of how their excesses diminished the fortune through succeeding generations. Of the hundreds of Vanderbilt descendents alive today, virtually none control significant wealth inherited from the Commodore's original pile. When a gaggle of some 120 heirs assembled at Vanderbilt University for a reunion in 1973, there was nary a millionaire among them. This is remarkable, when one considers that by the time of his death in 1885, Billy Vanderbilt had nearly doubled the family fortune. In the eight years since the Commodore's death, Billy had brought the total value from approximately $105 million to just above $200 million: an amount exceeding the contents of the U.S. Treasury at the time. (In 2005, to control the same percentage of Gross Domestic Product that Billy controlled in 1885, one would have needed to be worth nearly $218 billion dollars. As has been previously mentioned, the average 2005 net worth of Bill Gates was estimated by *Forbes* Magazine to be $51 billion.)[14]

But 1885 represented the high water mark in the family's finances. Billy was the last great Vanderbilt earner. His children, grandchildren, and great-grandchildren would be the great Vanderbilt spenders: the builders of elaborate homes, the masters of great pleasure yachts, the squanderers of inheritance. Billy divided his estate somewhat more equitably than had his father, giving each child (every one of them already made rich from outright gifts made through the years) $5 million absolutely, and additionally the incomes from individual $5 million trusts. But the bulk of Billy's estate went to his two eldest sons, with roughly half of the total value earmarked for Cornelius II and William K. Vanderbilt. Today, such palaces as Cornelius Vanderbilt II's "Breakers" in Newport, William K. Vanderbilt's "Marble House" in the same town, George Washington Vanderbilt II's "Biltmore" in North Carolina (all of them designed by Hunt), not to mention Frederick Vanderbilt's Italianate mansion on the banks of the Hudson River at Hyde Park (designed by McKim, Mead & White), stand as stunning reminders of Vanderbiltian excess as practiced in its heyday by the Commodore's grandchildren.[15]

Among all these stately relics, the grim old founder—who knew not one of these magnificent homes—has long seemed nothing more than an odd, obstinate, and forbidding asterisk. In this book, I've endeavored to put a face on the single-minded enterprise, and the self-centered cynicism, which formed the genesis of something now vanished: the greatest private fortune the world has ever known.

ACKNOWLEDGMENTS

My two chief partners in crime are my literary agent Chris Calhoun and my editor Bill Frucht. Every writer should have accomplices such as these. Thanks as well to Kay Mariea, the Perseus Group's director of editorial services, for invaluable support.

I'm grateful to the descendents of Wheaton J. Lane, Jared Linsly, and Webster Wagner, who made vital papers available. I'm also grateful to the staffs at the New York Historical Society, the Bentley Historical Library of the University of Michigan, the Staten Island Historical Society, the New York University Library, the Library of Congress, the Drew University Library, the New Jersey Historical Society, the University of Rhode Island Library, the Architects Information Center (Washington, D.C.), the Detroit Public Library, the Reference Library of the Museum of the City of Mobile, the New York Genealogical Society, the New York Public Library, and the Staten Island Institute of Arts and Sciences.

Friends are the fruit of life. Leading those who cheered me on and told me this book was worth writing were: Debbie Allen, John P.

Avlon, Ashleigh Banfield, John Perry Barlow, Chris Breiseth, Douglas Brinkley, Eileen Charbonneau, Ben Cheever, Karen Daly, Arthur Goldwag, Howard Gould, Kingdon and Mary Gould, Ed Gullo, Bob Hoch, Jonathan Hoffman, Rich Kelley, Jack Lane, Brian Madden, Edmund and Sylvia Morris, Dan Payne, Anne Rice, Cordelia Roosevelt, Frank Roosevelt, Phil Roosevelt, Richard Snow, H. R. Stoneback, Jim Strock, Shawn Thomas, Robert Titus, Artie and Beverly Traum, Jeff Walker, Geoffrey C. Ward, and Jim and Julianne Warren. Chris Bentley read every chapter and offered valuable criticism; a few other readers took smaller bites.

Three friends in particular helped me navigate a uniquely stressful period during the writing of the book. Marie Kutch, Nikki Natale, and John Staudt gave me the backup I needed to suffer fools confidently, if not gladly. For that, and for their continued friendship, I shall always be grateful.

As always, my wife Christa and our son and daughter—Bill and Katherine—have tolerated my immersion in a century and a family other than our own. They are the best parts of my life, and they know it.

Edward J. Renehan Jr.
Wickford, North Kingstown, RI
19 April 2007

NOTES

1. Both the Hudson River Railroad Freight House (a.k.a. St. John's Park Freight House) and the pediment met the wrecking ball in the early 1930s. Just a few years before that, in 1929, executives of the New York Central ordered the removal of the Vanderbilt Statue to the front of Grand Central.

2. The diary of George Templeton Strong, 16 December 1869, Strong Papers, New York Historical Society (hereafter Strong). Strong liked to use the term *bestial*. He employed it frequently to describe things he abhorred. On November 6, 1838, the WASP nativist diarized about Irish and Italian immigrants: "It was enough to turn a man's stomach—to make a man adjure republicanism forever—to see the way they were naturalizing this morning at the *Hall*. Wretched, filthy, bestial-looking Italians and Irish, and creations that looked as if they had risen from the lazarettos of Naples for this especial object; in short, the very scum and dregs of human nature filled the clerk of C[ommon] P[leas] office so completely that I was almost afraid of being poisoned by going in. A dirty Irishman is bad enough, but he's nothing comparable to a nasty French or Italian loafer."

3. *Packard's Monthly* (23 March 1872).

4. George Templeton Strong to Madison Schuyler, 9 March 1871, Strong Papers, New York Historical Society.

5. New York *Daily Tribune,* 23 March 1878.

6. *New York Times,* 12 October 1876.

7. Ibid., 15 January 1854.

8. To derive this number I am using the calculator to be found at the Web site measuringworth.com. The precise figure, calculated to the year 2005, is $158,144,981,862.15 vs. $105 million in 1877 value as share of GDP. In other words, to purchase the same percentage share of GDP that $105 million bought in 1877, one would have needed $158,144,981,862.15 in 2005.

9. New York *World,* 16 November 1877.

10. Arthur D. Howden Smith lived from 1887 to 1945. He was manically productive, penning biographies, business studies, short stories, and numerous popular pulp novels. Although largely forgotten today, in Smith's own time his pulp-novel fame rivaled that of his contemporary Edgar Rice Burroughs, the author of the Tarzan stories. Some of Smith's more popular novels included *Porto Bello Gold* (a prequel to Robert Louis Stevenson's *Treasure Island*), *The Dead Go Overside, The Doom Trail,* and *Swain's Saga.*

11. Arthur D. Howden Smith, *Commodore Vanderbilt: An Epic of American Achievement* (New York: Cosimo Classics, 2005), 308. (First published 1927 by Robert R. McBride & Co., New York.)

12. This book was *From Indian Trail to Iron Horse: Travel and Transportation in New Jersey, 1620–1860* (Princeton, NJ: Princeton University Press, 1939). Wheaton Joshua Lane was a scion of one of the founding families of Hampton, New Hampshire. He graduated from Phillips Exeter Academy in 1921 and Princeton University in 1925, thereafter earning a masters degree from Yale (1926) and a doctorate from Princeton (1935). Lane spent most of his career teaching in the history department at Princeton. In 1966, he and Richard M. Huber coedited the *New Jersey Historical Series* commemorating the state's tercentenary. Lane died in

1983 at the age of eighty-one. He is buried in Hampton, not far from the town library which bears the family name.

13. For a complete report of the accident see "Fatal Disaster on the Hudson River Railroad" in *Frank Leslie's Illustrated Newspaper,* New York, for the week ending January 21, 1882. Wagner's former mansion in the Montgomery County town of Palatine Bridge, New York (in the Mohawk Valley) is one of New York's greatest and most criminally neglected historical and architectural gems.

CHAPTER 1

1. Both Arthur D. Howden Smith and Wheaton J. Lane (see below) provide a different date for Aris's birth. My data is based on the latest genealogical research conducted by descendents, and on personal inspection of relevant documentation in private collections. Generally, the best resources for Vanderbilt genealogical data are the *New York Genealogical and Biographical Record* XVII, 61–77, and the records of the Moravian Church at New Dorp, Staten Island.

2. A section of the original Vanderbilt farm was later used by the U.S. Army as Miller Air Field, and in the 1970s became part of Gateway National Recreational Area.

3. Archie Robertson, "The Island in the Bay," *American Heritage* 17, no. 5 (August 1966).

4. Aris's and Hilletje's children were Jan Van Derbilt, b 1678; Annetje Van Derbilt, b 1681; Jannetje Van Derbilt, b 1682; Femmetje Van Derbilt, b 1684; Rem Van Derbilt, b 1686; Hendrick Van Derbilt, b ca 1690; Jacob Van Derbilt, b 24 January 1692; Aert Van Derbilt, b 1693; Jeremyas Van Derbilt, b 19 October 1695; and Cornelius Van Derbilt, b 1697.

5. Wheaton J. Lane, *Commodore Vanderbilt: An Epic of the Steam Age* (New York: Alfred A. Knopf, 1942), 6.

6. Charlotte Megill Hix, *Wills and Letters of Administration, Richmond Co., N.Y. 1670–1800* (Baltimore: Heritage Books, 1983), 170–171.

7. See "The Huguenots of Staten Island," *Continental Monthly, Devoted to Literature and National Policy* 1, no. 6 (June 1862).

8. For complete information on the *Irene,* see "Moravian Immigration to Pennsylvania 1734–1767," in *Transactions of the Moravian Historical Society,* vol. 5, pt. 2, compiled by John N. Jordan and printed 1896.

9. Biographers Lane, Smith, and Croffut (see below) say that Sophia was the daughter of one Eleanor who was the elder sister to the Commodore's father—but they are missing a generation. See *Abstracts of Wills on File in the Surrogates Office, City of New York* (New York: Collections of the New York Historical Society, 1901), 180.

10. Astonishingly, Wheaton Lane—usually so good on essential and key facts—joins Smith in making no mention of the early orphaning and subsequent disinheritment of the Commodore's father, that Cornelius Van Derbilt born in 1764. See *Abstracts of Wills,* 180.

11. Smith, *Commodore Vanderbilt: An Epic of American Achievement,* 6–7.

12. Robertson, "The Island in the Bay."

13. Anonymous, *Illustrated Sketch Book of Staten Island, NY: Its Industries and Commerce* (New York: Page & Tyler, 1886), 144.

14. Smith suggests that the Commodore's father at this time operated the periauger out of Stapleton, on the northeastern coast of Staten Island nearly in the middle of the treacherous Narrows. However, there is no contemporary documentation for this. It seems unlikely that he would live right on the Kill van Kull in Port Richmond and needlessly journey several miles overland to reach the water at Stapleton. Unlike the Narrows, the Kill van Kull offered the type of protected access to New York Harbor that one in a small periauger would find more than appealing. Later, after a move to Stapleton, both Cornelius and his son, the future Commodore, would embark and return from that port—but not before.

15. Anna Root, "Lines Written on the Death of Mrs. Phebe Vanderbilt by Her Granddaughter Anna V. P. Root of Staten Island." Original in the files of the New York Genealogical Society and Biographical Library.

CHAPTER 2

1. Cornelius Vanderbilt's May birth was recorded in the registry of the Moravian Church on December 16, 1794.

2. The Shore Road (a.k.a. Bay Street) home stood until 1922, at which point it was razed to make way for a theater, the *Paramount*, now a sporting goods store. The only original Vanderbilt house still standing on Staten Island is the now decrepit home of John King Vanderbilt, a cousin of the Commodore's, located at 1197 Clove Road in the Sunnyside neighborhood, built circa 1836. Designated a New York City Landmark in 1987, this Greek Revival house is now empty, abandoned, and covered with graffiti.

3. Lane, *Commodore Vanderbilt: An Epic of the Steam Age*, 10.

4. Smith, *Commodore Vanderbilt: An Epic of American Achievement*, 9.

5. Louis D. Johnston and Samuel H. Williamson, "The Annual Real and Nominal GDP for the United States, 1790–Present," Economic History Services, October 2005, http://www.eh.net/hmit/gdp/.

6. Robert E. Wright, *Banking and Politics in New York, 1784–1829* (Ann Arbor: University Microfilms, 1997).

7. New York *Daily Tribune*, 23 March 1878.

CHAPTER 3

1. Wheaton J. Lane says it was eight acres, but extant tax records show that Cornelius Vanderbilt Sr. held only one acre at Port Richmond at the time. Lane, together with Smith and William Crofutt (see below), also says the work was done as a prerequisite for a loan of $100, to be repaid, but does not source that data. Neither do either Lane or Smith source data asserting Vanderbilt's subsequent payment of several large cash overrides to his parents. Thus, since I've not been able to document the payments, they are not included in the narrative.

2. William A. Croffut, *The Vanderbilts and the Story of Their Fortune* (Chicago: Belford, Clarke and Company, 1886).

3. Lane, *Commodore Vanderbilt: An Epic of the Steam Age*, 15.

4. Ibid., 16.

5. From Linsly's testimony in the 1877–78 court case related to Vanderbilt's will, this reported in the *New York Times* of November 15, 1877.

6. William E. Verplanck and Moses W. Collyer, *Sloops of the Hudson* (New York: G. P. Putnam's Sons, 1908), 7.

7. Lane and Smith have the *Swiftsure* as a periauger, but this appears to have been an assumption on their part. Harbor records from the time show the *Swiftsure* as a sixty-five-foot sloop. Vanderbilt would later reuse the same name for one of his steamboats. Lane and Smith also assert Vanderbilt's investment at about this time in several other periaugers— but once again, the records show otherwise.

8. Edwin G. Burrows and Mike Wallace, *Gotham: A History of New York City to 1898* (New York: Oxford University Press, 1999), 411.

9. For general data on the history of the New York port see Robert G. Albion, *The Rise of New York Port, 1800–1840* (New York: Charles Scribner's Sons, 1939).

10. Lane, *Commodore Vanderbilt: An Epic of the Steam Age*, 18.

11. Smith, *Commodore Vanderbilt: An Epic of American Achievement*, 42–43.

12. *New York Times*, 9 October 1882.

13. Burrows and Wallace, *Gotham*, 419.

14. Washington Irving, *History, Tales and Sketches* (New York: Library of America, 1983), 37.

CHAPTER 4

1. For details see: Charlotte Magill Hix, *Descendants of Nathaniel Johnson of Staten Island, New York* (Garden City, NY: C. M. Hix, 1977). Copy in the genealogical research library of the New York Public Library.

2. Lane, *Commodore Vanderbilt: An Epic of the Steam Age*, 21.

3. Phebe Hand Vanderbilt also knew something that Croffut, Smith, and Lane did not. The three biographers labored and wrote under the false assumption that Cornelius and Sophia were first cousins rather than first cousins once-removed. Phebe knew better.

4. Croffut, *The Vanderbilts and the Story of Their Fortune*, 24.

5. Lane, *Commodore Vanderbilt, An Epic of the Steam Age*, 21.

6. Ibid., 22.

7. In Arthur G. Adams's *The Hudson Through the Years* (New York: Fordham University Press, 1997) he refers to the *Dread*, the *Governor Wolcott*, and the *General Armstrong* as periaugers all, but these centerboard vessels were in fact sloops and schooners as described.

8. Croffut, *The Vanderbilts and the Story of Their Fortune*, 25.

9. Brooklyn *Daily Eagle*, 5 January 1877.

10. Lane, *Commodore Vanderbilt: An Epic of the Steam Age*, 22.

11. Robert H. Boyle, *The Hudson: A Natural and Unnatural History* (New York: W. W. Norton & Co., 1969), 50–51.

12. Verplanck and Collyer, *Sloops of the Hudson*, 120.

CHAPTER 5

1. New York *Daily Advertiser*, 12 June 1817.

2. Burrows & Wallace, *Gotham: A History of New York City to 1898*, 494.

3. New York *Daily Advertiser*, 15 December 1817.

4. Lane, *Commodore Vanderbilt: An Epic of the Steam Age*, 27.

5. *New York Times*, 10 January 1877.

CHAPTER 6

1. George Dangerfield, "The Steamboat's Charter of Freedom," *American Heritage*, October, 1963.

2. The lion's share of Aaron Ogden's papers are in the Ogden Family Collection of the New Jersey Historical Society.

3. Lane, *Commodore Vanderbilt: An Epic of the Steam Age*, 28.

4. Most of the Thomas Gibbons Papers are in two Gibbons Family Collections, one housed by the New Jersey Historical Society, the other in the Special Collections of Drew University.

5. Much of what was Whitehall is now the Savannah Municipal Airport. The Argyle Island slice of the plantation was later renamed *Gowrie*.

The Gibbons family kept control of the mainland portion of Whitehall until well after the Civil War.

6. George R. Lamplugh, *Politics on the Periphery: Factions and Parties in Georgia, 1783–1806* (Newark, NJ: University of Delaware Press, 1986), 94.

7. Details of Thomas Gibbons's holdings come from his will of 1826 in the Gibbons Family Papers, Drew University Special Collections (hereafter Gibbons/Drew).

CHAPTER 7

1. New York *Evening Post,* 12 February 1818.

2. Ibid., 17 February 1818.

3. *New York Times,* 9 April 1867.

4. Original contract between Thomas Gibbons and Cornelius Vanderbilt, 26 June 1818, Gibbons/Drew.

5. Smith, *Commodore Vanderbilt: An Epic of American Achievement,* 80.

6. Peter Baida, "Mangerial Babble," *American Heritage* 36, no. 3 (April/May 1985).

7. Lane, *Commodore Vanderbilt: An Epic of the Steam Age,* 33.

8. Cornelius Vanderbilt to Thomas Gibbons. December 1818, Gibbons/Drew.

CHAPTER 8

1. Smith, *Commodore Vanderbilt: An Epic of American Achievement,* 84.

2. Thomas Gibbons to Daniel Webster, 13 December 1819, Gibbons/Drew.

3. For more on Marshall, see Jean Edward Smith's superb biography: *John Marshall: Definer of a Nation* (New York: Henry Holt & Company, 1996).

4. Lane, *Commodore Vanderbilt: An Epic of the Steam Age,* 35.

5. New York *Evening Post,* 13 October 1819.

6. Lane, *Commodore Vanderbilt: An Epic of the Steam Age,* 42.

7. Ibid., 39.

CHAPTER 9

1. New York *Daily Advertiser,* 9 April 1820.

2. *New York Times,* 9 October 1849.

3. Undated letters from Cornelius Vanderbilt to Thomas Gibbons, Gibbons/Drew.

4. Roy Finch, *The Story of the New York State Canals: Governor De-Witt Clinton's Dream* (Albany, NY: New York State Engineer and Surveyor Bureau, 1925), 3.

5. Maurice G. Baxter, *The Steamboat Monopoly: Gibbons v. Ogden, 1824* (New York: Knopf, 1972), 27.

6. Ibid., 312.

CHAPTER 10

1. Lane, *Commodore Vanderbilt: An Epic of the Steam Age,* 38.

2. In 1832 William Gibbons purchased an estate at Madison, New Jersey, that he named "The Forest" and where he built a mansion. He died there on December 10, 1852. The estate was later acquired by Daniel Drew, who made it into a seminary for Methodist ministers that now is Drew University. Mead Hall on the campus is the former William Gibbons mansion.

3. Will of Thomas Gibbons, Gibbons/Drew.

4. John Quincy Adams, *Memoirs of John Quincy Adams: Comprising Portions of His Diary from 1795 to 1848,* ed. Charles Francis Adams (Philadelphia: J. B. Lippincott, 1875), 127.

5. Lane, *Commodore Vanderbilt: An Epic of the Steam Age,* 46.

6. "The Journal of William R. Gorgas," *Hudson River Valley Review* 18, no. 2.

CHAPTER 11

1. Smith, *Commodore Vanderbilt: An Epic of American Achievement,* 102.

2. Ibid., 103.

3. Both Smith and Lane place the family initially on Manhattan's Stone Street, but this is incorrect. Vanderbilt had previously maintained business addresses on Stone Street (1816–1819), with a brief interlude on Beaver Street. In 1836, he removed his family from Madison Street to 173 East Broadway. See the relevant annual editions of the *New York Directory* for details.

4. New York *Evening Post*, 11 July 1829.

5. Samuel Orcutt, *Old Town of Stratford and the City of Bridgeport, Connecticut* (Fairfield: Fairfield County Historical Society, 1886), 650.

6. "Steamboat Explosions," *New York Review*, April, 1839.

7. Edgar Mayhew Bacon, *The Hudson River from Ocean to Source* (New York: G. P. Putnam's Sons, 1902), 134.

8. New York *Evening Post*, 7 August 1831.

9. Adams, *Diary of John Quincy Adams*, 443–444.

10. Jared Linsly (1803–1887) is buried in Northford Cemetery, North Branford, Connecticut. Linsly Hall at Yale University is named for him.

11. New York *Herald*, 3 May 1839.

CHAPTER 12

1. Benjamin Perley Poore, *Perley's Reminiscences of Sixty Years in the National Metropolis* (Boston: W. A. Houghton & Co., 1886), 39.

2. Mary Caroline Crawford, *Romantic Days in Old Boston* (Boston: Little, Brown, 1910), 326–328.

3. New York *Evening Post*, 2 June 1835.

4. Ibid., 15 February 1837.

5. A model of the hull of this vessel is in the collection of the Rhode Island Historical Society.

6. Lane, *Commodore Vanderbilt: An Epic of the Steam Age*, 69.

CHAPTER 13

1. Moses Y. Beach, *Wealth and Biography of the Wealthy Citizens of New York City, 1845* (New York: New York Sun Publishing Co., 1845), 74.

2. Henry Brewster Stanton, *Random Recollections* (Johnstown, NY: Blunck & Leaning, 1885), 144.

3. Samuel Ward Stanton, *American Steam Vessels* (New York: Smith & Stanton, 1895), 47.

CHAPTER 14

1. The precise addresses were 134 Madison Street and 178 East Broadway.

2. The Staten Island mansion remained in the Vanderbilt family until 1881, when Billy sold it to a Manhattan businessman named George Daly. Shortly thereafter the place was largely destroyed by fire. Daly rebuilt, and he and his family remained there into the early twentieth century. The precise location was what is now 487 Bay Street, home to Harbor Isle Chevrolet. For details on the fire, and a description of the house, see the *New York Times*, 4 January 1882.

3. Brooklyn *Daily Eagle*, 26 January 1890. Vanderbilt's heirs sold 10 Washington Place in 1890, five years after Frank Crawford Vanderbilt's death. The house was torn down in 1891.

4. Jared Linsly medical diaries (hereafter *Linsly Diaries*), in the possession of the author.

5. Many books identify Kissam as a Presbyterian minister from Brooklyn, but this is incorrect. See his listing in Edward Tanjore Corwin's *A Manual of the Reformed Protestant Dutch Church in North America* (New York: Board of Publication of the Reformed Protestant Dutch Church, 1859), 36. The *Manual* shows that Kissam was ordained in 1817, and that at the time of his daughter's marriage he was a minister in Bethlehem, New York, near Albany, a place also known in Kissam's time as Cedar Hill. Kissam's three sons eventually became prominent financiers in Brooklyn, and he spent his dotage in that district.

6. In the twentieth century, the farm became Miller Field, now a part of the Gateway National Recreation Area.

7. Elliott Gorn and Warren Goldstein, *A Brief History of American Sports* (Urbana: University of Illinois Press, 2004), 75.

8. New York *Herald,* 9 June 1858.

9. Bonner's papers are in the Manuscripts Division of the New York Public Library. He lived 1824–1899.

10. Matthew Hale Smith, *Sunshine and Shadow in New York* (New York: J. D. Burr, 1869), 617.

11. Junius Henri Browne, *The Great Metropolis* (New York: H. H. Bancroft & Co., 1869), 572.

12. James Dabney McCabe, *Great Fortunes and How They Were Made* (New York: Hannaford Press, 1872), 78.

13. James L. Ford, *Forty Odd Years in the Literary Shop* (New York: Dutton, 1921), 54.

14. McCabe, *Great Fortunes,* 79.

15. New York *Ledger,* 1 April 1848.

CHAPTER 15

1. George Henry Tinkham, *California Men and Events* (San Francisco: Record Publishing Co., 1919), 67–68.

2. New York *Herald,* 2 February 1851.

3. *New York Times,* 14 August 1861.

4. Ibid., 25 July 1853.

5. Croffut, *The Vanderbilts and the Story of Their Fortune,* 45.

6. *New York Times,* 5 March 1852.

7. New York *Herald,* 14 September 1852.

8. Lane says 2.5 percent, but this is incorrect.

9. *Daily Alta California,* 2 April 1853.

CHAPTER 16

1. Croffut, *The Vanderbilts and the Story of Their Fortune,* 46.

2. Lane, *Commodore Vanderbilt: An Epic of the Steam Age,* 104.

3. New York *Herald,* 1 June 1853.

4. Croffut, *The Vanderbilts and the Story of Their Fortune,* 47.

5. *New York Times,* 20 May 1853.

6. Brooklyn *Daily Eagle,* 26 January 1890. Note: The *North Star* had first endeavored to set off on May 19, but ran aground on rocks at Corlaers Hook, in the East River, soon after starting from her dock at the foot of what was then Corlaers Street, near the Allaire Works. Thereafter, she was briefly laid up in dry dock for refurbishing before her second departure on May 21. The original location of Corlaers Hook was obscured years ago by landfill. The hook was near the east end of the pedestrian bridge that today runs over the FDR Drive near Cherry Street.

7. John Overton Choules, *A Sermon: Upon the Death of the Hon. Daniel Webster* (New York: Evans & Brittan), 1852.

8. John Overton Choules, *The Cruise of the Steam Yacht North Star* (New York: Evans & Dickerson; Boston: Gould & Lincoln, 1854), 18.

9. Ibid., 56.

10. *Daily News* (London), 4 June 1853.

11. Choules, *The Cruise,* 82.

12. Ibid., 116.

13. Ibid., 164.

14. *Linsly Diaries,* 5 July 1853.

15. Flint's cenotaph still stands at Brooklyn's Greenwood Cemetery.

16. Choules, *The Cruise,* 207.

17. Richard P. Wunder, *Hiram Powers: Vermont Sculptor, 1805–1873,* vol. 2 (Newark, NJ: University of Delaware Press 1991), 100.

18. Powers made one plaster mold of the Vanderbilt bust (since destroyed), and two marble twenty-four-and-one-half-inch copies. One is today at Vanderbilt University, the other at "The Breakers" mansion in Newport, Rhode Island, the palatial residence built by Cornelius Vanderbilt's grandson of the same name.

19. Margaret Fuller, *At Home and Abroad, Or, Things and Thoughts in America and Europe* (Boston: Ticknor & Fields, 1856), 212.

20. Powers also executed a portrait bust of Calhoun, today in the collection of the North Carolina Museum of Art.

21. Choules, *The Cruise,* 224.

22. Ibid., 245.

23. *New York Times,* 24 September 1853.

24. Choules, *The Cruise,* 349.

25. *New York Times,* 24 September 1853.

CHAPTER 17

1. This chapter has been generally informed throughout by later research conducted by Wheaton J. Lane following the publication of his Vanderbilt biography in 1942. These papers are in private hands.

2. For complete details on Morgan's career see James P. Baughman, *Charles Morgan and the Development of Southern Transportation* (Nashville, TN: Vanderbilt University Press, 1968).

3. New York *Herald,* 7 August 1853.

4. Lane, *Commodore Vanderbilt: An Epic of the Steam Age,* 109.

5. James Dabney McCabe, *Great Fortunes and How They Were Made* (Cincinnati & Chicago: E. Hannaford & Co., 1872), 198. This original Vanderbilt family tomb still stands near the front of the Moravian Cemetery. However, the Commodore and his descendents are interred in the larger, later, and more palatial tomb, built after the Commodore's death, to be found on private grounds abutting the rear of the cemetery. Only the Commodore's parents are interred in the old vault.

6. *New York Times,* 4 January 1882.

7. New York *Herald,* 27 July 1854.

8. Ibid., 17 March 1856.

9. *New York Times,* 22 November and 27 November 1856.

CHAPTER 18

1. Ralph Whitney, "The Unlucky Collins Line," *American Heritage* 8, no. 2 (February 1957).

2. *Congressional Globe,* 33rd Cong., 2d sess., 252–256.

3. Lane, *Commodore Vanderbilt: An Epic of the Steam Age,* 146.

4. New York *Tribune,* 8 March 1855.

5. New York *Herald*, 4 April 1855.

6. New York *Tribune*, 30 November 1857.

7. New York *Herald*, 24 October 1859.

CHAPTER 19

1. New York *Herald*, 25 March 1855.

2. Ibid., 17 April 1855.

3. *New York Times*, 18 April 1855.

4. *The War of Rebellion: Official Records*, 1st Series, vol. VIII, 643.

5. *New York Times*, 24 November 1870.

6. A copy of Vanderbilt's Congressional Gold Medal is in the Library of Congress, but Vanderbilt's own original remained in the family and was lost, probably pilfered, when the Commodore's Staten Island mansion burned in the 1880s.

7. Lane and Smith also claim that in 1863 Vanderbilt was one of several wealthy New Yorkers who each subscribed $1,000 for a secret fund totaling $15,000, solicited by Lincoln through Thurlow Weed for some secret purpose. No proof of the story exists outside the testimony of the journalist and politician Weed, who referenced the event in his autobiography. Weed was a notorious fabricator of tales designed to highlight his own importance to history. Weed's papers at the New York Historical Society contain no documentary evidence of the event, nor do the scattered papers of other supposed contributors.

8. Cornelius Vanderbilt to Cornelius Vanderbilt Jr., author's collection.

9. Ellen Williams Vanderbilt was born in 1820 and died in 1872. The couple had no children. The Commodore reportedly liked Cornelius Jeremiah's long-suffering wife, though reports that she astonished him by paying back money he'd advanced seem to be spurious.

10. Folklore—repeated by a host of writers including Lane and Smith—speaks of a watershed moment when Billy bested his father in a small transaction concerning the purchase of loads of manure as signaling the point of Vanderbilt's revelation that his son was an astute man of business. Things are never that simple; in fact, Billy proved himself slowly over many years.

CHAPTER 20

1. *New York Times*, 23 September, 25 September, 4 October, and 18 October 1854; also 3 July 1855.

2. George Lee Schuyler was both a nephew and a twice grandson-in-law to Alexander Hamilton, two of whose granddaughters (sisters, the daughters of George Schuyler's first cousin) he married. In addition to being Hamilton's nephews, Robert and George Schuyler were grandsons of Major General Philip Schuyler, a hero of the American Revolution, as well as Livingston descendents. Many of George Lee Schuyler's papers are in the Hamilton/Schuyler Family Collection of the William L. Clements Library, University of Michigan. George was born in 1811 in Rhinebeck, New York, and died in 1890 while a guest on a yacht moored at Newport, Rhode Island. He was one of the original organizers of the New York Yacht Club. Robert Livingston Schuyler was born in 1798 in Rhinebeck. He received a bachelor of arts degree from Harvard, where he presumably did not study ethics, in 1817, graduating in a class that included Caleb Cushing, George Bancroft, and George R. Noyes.

3. For more on Addison Jerome see William Worthington, *Ten Years on Wall Street* (Hartford, CT: Worthington, Dustin & Co., 1870), 160–162.

4. Bouck White, *The Book of Daniel Drew* (Garden City, NY: Doubleday, Page & Co., 1913), 180.

5. *New York Herald*, 15 October 1863.

6. For a bit more on Morrissey, see John Knowles Medberry, *Men and Mysteries of Wall Street* (Boston: Fields, Osgood & Co., 1870), 163–164.

7. Accounts in Lane, Smith, and Croffut regarding the second Harlem corner are unreliable. For accurate details, see reports in the New York *Herald* for March 10, March 17, March 24, April 7, April 30, and May 18, 1864.

8. See Baylis's obituary in the *Brooklyn Daily Eagle*, 15 July 1882.

9. Through the next four years, Jerome, Tobin, and Baylis gradually decreased their holdings in the Harlem, selling only to Cornelius or Billy

Vanderbilt. By 1867, Cornelius would hold 74,316 shares in his own name, and Billy 11,024.

CHAPTER 21

1. New York *Tribune,* 25 November 1867.

2. New York *Herald,* 15 July 1863.

3. Ibid., 14 January 1867.

4. New York State Assembly, 90th sess., 1867, II, Doc. 19.

5. Albany *Argus,* 4 July 1867.

6. New York *Herald,* 12 November 1867.

7. *New York Times,* 12 December 1867.

8. Joy's extensive papers are in the Bentley Historical Library of the University of Michigan.

9. The papers of Webster Wagner (hereafter, *Wagner*), who partnered with Vanderbilt in the New York Sleeping Car Company 1866 through 1876, have been made available to the author by Wagner's descendents. They reveal the Commodore as having an active role in business affairs through the 1860s but then significantly diminishing in his business profile from about 1870 onward. Copy in collection of the author.

CHAPTER 22

1. *New York Times,* 26 May 1872.

2. For complete details on the Erie War, see Edward Renehan, *Dark Genius of Wall Street* (New York: Basic Books, 2005): 115–137.

3. *Linsly Diaries,* 2–16 August 1868.

4. New York *Tribune,* 20 August 1868.

5. Mary Gabriel, *Notorious Victoria* (Chapel Hill, NC: Algonquin Books, 1998), 31.

6. Ibid., 34.

7. Johanna Johnston, *Mrs. Satan: The Incredible Saga of Victoria C. Woodhull* (New York: G. P. Putnam's Sons, 1967), 39–40.

8. *Linsly Diaries,* 10 November 1868.

9. Lane says the De Groot involved in the pediment was the son of the De Groot who'd captained Vanderbilt's steamers, but here he is wrong. The Albert De Groot in question is the one who lived 1813 through 1884, was made rich by his association with the Commmodore, and in 1868–69 wanted to orchestrate a very large "thank you." De Groot's first letter to the public, proposing the project, appeared in the *New York Times* on 17 February 1868. Also see the article and portrait of De Groot in *Frank Leslie's Illustrated Newspaper,* 27 November 1869, as well as the *New York Times,* 2 September 1869. In 1872, De Groot funded a statue of Benjamin Franklin by Plassmann which today stands in downtown Manhattan at Nassau Street and Park Row, on the east side of the street (in front of Pace University, just south of the Brooklyn Bridge entrance ramp).

10. *New York Times,* 17 March 1868.

11. *Frank Leslie's Illustrated Newspaper,* 27 November 1869.

12. Wagner, *Diaries.*

13. *New York Times,* 2 September 1869.

14. *Frank Leslie's Illustrated Newspaper,* 27 November 1869.

15. *New York Times,* 11 November 1869.

16. Croffut, *The Vanderbilts and the Story of Their Fortune,* 100.

CHAPTER 23

1. *New York Times,* 22 August 1869.

2. Ibid., 5 May 1885.

3. The Frank Crawford Vanderbilt papers are part of the Burton Historical Collection of the Detroit Public Library. Additional papers of Frank Crawford Vanderbilt are housed in the Reference Library of the Museum of the City of Mobile, Alabama.

4. McTyeire lived 1824–1889. His papers are in the McTyeire-Baskervill Papers housed in the Vanderbilt University Special Collections and University Archives.

5. For details of the Crawford genealogy, see John Crawford and Frank Armstrong Vanderbilt, *Laurus Crawfurdiana: Memorials of That*

Branch of the Crawford Family Which Comprises the Descendants of John Crawford of Virginia, 1660–1883 (New York: privately printed, 1883). Copy in the files of the New York Genealogical Society and Biographical Library.

6. Arthur T. Vanderbilt, *Fortune's Children* (New York: William Morrow, 1989), 45.

7. *New York Times*, 5 May 1885.

8. Ibid., 2 March 1878.

9. Ibid., 6 February 1870.

10. New York *Herald*, 6 February 1870.

11. Emenie Nahm Sachs, *The Terrible Siren: Victoria Woodhull, 1838–1927* (New York: Harper & Bros., 1928), 91.

12. *Woodhull & Claflin's Weekly*, 7 April 1875.

13. Tennie and Victoria both eventually built new and successful lives in England.

14. Deems lived until 1893.

15. *New York Times*, 2 September 1870.

16. Charles F. Deems, *Autobiography of Charles Force Deems and Memoir* (New York: Fleming H. Revell, 1897), 250.

17. *New York Times*, 2 September 1870.

18. Lane, *Commodore Vanderbilt: An Epic of the Steam Age*, 317. Deems's several self-serving accounts of the Vanderbilt University contribution not only put Deems himself in the middle of the effort to seduce the Commodore but also minimize McTyeire's role by failing to mention Frank Vanderbilt's close family connection to McTyeire.

19. *Linsly Diaries*, undated entry.

20. See Sophia Johnson Vanderbilt Torrances's obituary in the *New York Times*, 26 February 1912. Sophia was the Commodore's last surviving child.

CHAPTER 24

1. A story recounted in every Vanderbilt biography to date telling how the Commodore roused himself in the spring of 1876 and shouted

down a reporter who called at Washington Place to inquire whether reports of Vanderbilt's death were true appears to be spurious and therefore is not included in this narrative.

2. Lane, *Commodore Vanderbilt: An Epic of the Steam Age*, 319.

3. All facts and quotes concerning Weill's treatment of Vanderbilt come from Weill's testimony in the 1877–78 court case related to Vanderbilt's will, this reported in the *New York Times*, 6 March 1878.

4. This and all subsequent Linsly quotes come from Linsly's testimony in the 1877–78 court case related to Vanderbilt's will, this reported in the *New York Times*, 15 November 1877.

5. All facts and quotes concerning Bennett's treatment of Vanderbilt come from Bennett's testimony in the 1877–78 court case related to Vanderbilt's will, this reported in the *New York Times*, 8 March 1878.

6. Brooklyn *Daily Eagle*, 4 August 1876.

7. This and all subsequent Work quotes come from Work's testimony in the 1877–78 court case related to Vanderbilt's will, this reported in the *New York Times*, 7 March 1878.

8. Deems, *Autobiography*, 268–271.

9. Linsly medical record, notes, 4 January 1877.

10. *New York Times*, 6 January 1877.

11. New York *Herald*, 5 January 1877.

12. *New York Times*, 6 January 1877.

13. *Nation*, 11 January 1877.

14. *New York Times*, 6 January 1877.

15. Brooklyn *Daily Eagle*, 7 January 1877.

16. Deems, *Autobiography*, 280.

17. *New York Times*, 8 January 1877. To get to the original Vanderbilt tomb in the Moravian Cemetery, proceed down the paved path that runs along the left side of the New Dorp Moravian Church until you come to the first paved pathway that intersects from the left. Turn left on this path and proceed straight ahead to the imposing obelisk that rises before you. This is the original Vanderbilt tomb, with the name VAN DER-BILT inscribed, where the Commodore's parents still lie.

EPILOGUE

1. *New York Times,* 20 February 1877.

2. Ibid., 9 March 1877.

3. Cornelius Jeremiah's home was on a hill that came to be known as Vanderbilt Hill, now West Hill. His former estate comprises the development on and about West Hartford's West Hill Drive, off Farmington Avenue. The house was razed in the early years of the twentieth century. See the *New York Times,* 24 June 1881, for a detailed description of the mansion.

4. *New York Times,* 2 April 1882.

5. See the extensive files relating to Cornelius Jeremiah's several suits against his brother Billy, and also those files related to the settlement of his estate, in the Samuel P. Colt Papers, Special Collections, University of Rhode Island. See also the *New York Times,* 29 June 1883, for details on the auction of Cornelius Jeremiah's Hartford mansion and possessions to partially satisfy debts.

6. William Henry Vanderbilt to Richard Morris Hunt, copy in Frank Crawford Vanderbilt Papers, New York Historical Society.

7. *New York Times,* 19 March 1885.

8. Ibid., 10 December 1885.

9. For more details on the Vanderbilt mausoleum, see Percy Preston Jr., "The Vanderbilt Mausoleum on Staten Island, New York City," *Magazine Antiques* (September 2005). Also see Croffut, *The Vanderbilts and the Story of Their Fortune,* 213–218. Note that neither the Vanderbilt grounds at the Moravian Cemetery nor the mausoleum itself are open to the public.

10. *New York Times,* 4 December 1886.

11. Ibid., 6 December 1886.

12. Ibid., 20 and 23 March 1893.

13. All other descendents of Billy Vanderbilt, such as daughters and granddaughters and their families, have been relegated to burial in the grounds surrounding the mausoleum. Meanwhile, Vanderbiltian descendents not coming down through Billy's line are completely on their own.

14. To derive this number, I am using the calculator to be found at the Web site measuringworth.com. The precise figure, calculated to the year 2005, is $217,949,256,342.96 vs. $200 million in 1885 value as share of GDP. In other words, to purchase the same percentage share of GDP that $200 million bought in 1885, one would have needed nearly $218 billion in 2005.

15. Another of William Kissam Vanderbilt's homes, "Idle Hour" in Oakdale on Long Island, is now the Max and Clara Fortunoff Hall of Dowling College. Of course, many of the Commodore's other grandchildren and great-grandchildren built equally grandiose residences down through the years.

INDEX